Y0-ABC-443

Erasmus on Women
Edited by Erika Rummel

Erasmus on Women offers selections from Erasmus' manuals on marriage and widowhood, his rhetorical treatises, and the *Colloquies*. The texts deal with courtship, marriage, childrearing, and widowhood. Selections treating particular topics, such as prostitution, scholarship, and activism, are placed within the context in which they are discussed by Erasmus.

Erasmus' dialogues present a lively cast of virgins and mothers, housewives and harlots, shrews and activists. The fifteen texts and excerpts offered here represent a mixture of traditional and progressive thought. Along traditional lines, he commends women for their role as caregivers and for their service to God and society. In contrast, he holds progressive views (by the standards of his time) on the education of women and breaks with tradition by challenging the idea that celibacy is superior to the married state.

Erasmus' views were radical for his time and frequently involved him in controversy. Lavishly praised by some, his writings were bitterly denounced by others. Yet the wide dissemination of his writings makes him an important witness to the social thought of the sixteenth century.

ERIKA RUMMEL is an associate professor in the Department of History at Wilfrid Laurier University. She is editor of *The Erasmus Reader*, author of *The Humanist-Scholastic Debate in the Renaissance and Reformation*, and a member of the editorial board of the Collected Works of Erasmus.

Erasmus on Women

edited by Erika Rummel

B
785
. E62
E54x
1996
WEST

UNIVERSITY OF TORONTO PRESS
Toronto Buffalo London

© University of Toronto Press Incorporated 1996
Toronto / Buffalo / London
Printed in Canada

ISBN 0-8020-0816-x (cloth)
ISBN 0-8020-7808-7 (paper)

(∞)

Printed on acid-free paper

Canadian Cataloguing in Publication Data:

Erasmus, Desiderius, d. 1536
Erasmus on women

Includes index.
ISBN 0-8020-0816-x (bound) ISBN 0-8020-7808-7 (pbk.)

1. Erasmus, Desiderius, d. 1536 – Views on women.
I. Rummel, Erika, 1942– . II. Title

B785.E62E5 1996   305.4   C95-933373-8

This volume is based on the Collected Works of Erasmus (CWE).

University of Toronto Press acknowledges the financial assistance to its
publishing program of the Canada Council and the Ontario Arts Council.

Contents

Abbreviations

WORKS FREQUENTLY CITED

Allen   P.S. Allen *Opus Epistolarum Des. Erasmi Roterodami*
            (Oxford 1906–58)

CWE   The Collected Works of Erasmus (Toronto 1974–)

LB   J. Leclerc, ed. *Erasmi Opera Omnia* (Leiden 1703–6)

Thompson   C.R. Thompson, trans. *The Colloquies of Erasmus*
            (Chicago 1965)

ERASMUS ON WOMEN

Introduction

Although the texts in this collection are by a single author, they offer a kaleidoscope of views current in the Renaissance. Erasmus' comments on women range from ad hoc remarks in his letters to lengthy treatises on marriage and widowhood, from lively dialogues with a mixed cast of virgins and mothers, housewives and harlots, to a funeral oration for a matriarch. Because Erasmus appropriates a variety of voices, the texts offer a mixture of traditional and progressive thought. Among the traditional ideas is Erasmus' praise for women as care-givers, their validation through service to God and society, in prayer and charitable work, in the conscientious fulfilment of household duties, in the upbringing of children, especially daughters, and in providing physical comfort and companionship to husbands. By contrast, he holds progressive views – by the standards of his time – on the education of women and breaks with tradition by challenging the idea that celibacy is superior to the marital state.

Erasmus' writings offer a plethora of material for social historians, but frustrate specialists who are searching for his personal views. Two obstacles stand in their way: the rhetorical character of Erasmus' writings, which muffles and disguises the authorial voice; and scepticism, which prompts him to suspend judgment. It is particularly difficult to discern Erasmus' voice in the *Colloquies* since the genre allows the use of arguments on both sides of a question. As in natural conversation, speakers in Erasmus' dialogues present diverging points of view. In the colloquy *Marriage*, Xanthippe suggests violent solutions to marital conflicts; Eulalia counsels flexibility and submissiveness. In *The Abbot and the Learned Lady*, Antronius discourages learning in women; Magdalia praises it. In *The New Mother*, the protagonists argue vigorously for and against male superiority. A male character in *The Godly Feast* blames the shortcomings of women on their husbands: 'Often it's our own fault that our wives are bad.'[1] A female character in *Marriage* expresses the opposite view: 'Usually it's our fault that husbands are bad.'[2] Not surprisingly, one of Erasmus' critics observed: 'He says one thing sitting down, and another standing up.'[3]

In the case of manuals like *The Institution of Marriage* or *The Christian Widow*,[4] which do not suffer from the ambivalence inherent in the dialogue, the process of interpreting Erasmus' views is complicated by the conventions governing the genre. Well-established literary traditions tend to depersonalize individual treatises. In manuals offering advice on moral and social behaviour the author is not expected to be innovative. His merits are not gauged by the standard of originality. Providing an elegant summary of traditional thought and citing authoritative sources was more to the point. Such works therefore often represent cumulative wisdom and popular currents of thought rather than the views of an individual. In Erasmus' treatises on marriage and widowhood, the conception of women's role can be traced to biblical, classical, and patristic sources. It is questionable whether the appropriation and internalization of ideas found in these sources make them 'Erasmian.' They represent Erasmian views only in the sense that a Sunday sermon represents the views of the preacher, who believes in the scriptural message he delivers.

Similar problems of interpretation confront us in the case of set pieces such as *In Praise of Marriage* or the funeral oration for Berta Heyen.[5] The views expressed in them are dictated largely by the occasion. Such writings often have both an epideictic and a didactic purpose. This means they are designed to display the author's powers of invention, his craftsmanship and erudition and at the same time to edify readers and give them a supply of elegant phrases and useful arguments. It is indicative that *In Praise of Marriage* was eventually included as a sample in a letter-writing manual, where it was complemented by an epistle advocating the opposite point of view.[6] Clearly such pieces were meant to provide a collection of commonplaces rather than an expression of the author's views. The rhetorical nature of such works was pointed out by Erasmus himself. He noted that his *In Praise of Marriage* belonged to the genre of declamations, which 'deal with imaginary subjects for the purpose of exercizing one's ingenuity ...; the nature of these exercises is to treat the argument from both sides.' An author who labels his composition a declamation 'disclaims all responsibility for the opinions stated.'[7] Although the thrust of the argument may betray the author's sympathies, the rhetorical purpose of such texts prevents us from pinpointing his view with certainty. In many cases, it seems, Erasmus was more interested in arguing than in settling a case.

The problems of interpretation inherent in the rhetorical works of Erasmus are compounded by his epistemological position. The equivocation we find in his writings is more than a literary game or a technical expedient. It is the corollary of his scepticism. One can hardly expect unequivocal statements on complex issues such as the role of women in society from a man who holds that 'human affairs take so many shapes that definite answers cannot be provided for them all'; who says that circumstances vary so widely that 'more intelligent people do not say "You must not do this, you must not do that," but "this is in my view the safer course; this I regard as tolerable."'[8] It is not surprising, therefore, that Erasmus carefully qualifies his own statements and offers to 'yield to better counsel, and even expose [his own] to ridicule, if that is merited.'[9]

The difficulties of interpretation dogging the reader of the texts in this volume do not invalidate their use as sources of social history; they merely prevent us from ascribing the views expressed specifically to Erasmus. What emerges from the text is a composite picture of women's role in society, reflecting a spectrum of views held in Erasmus' time rather than a coherent set of views advocated by him personally.

With these qualifications in mind we turn to the texts in this volume. Both *The Institution of Marriage* and *The Christian Widow* are filled with clichés. Erasmus' summary of women's shortcomings in the *Institution* is a case in point. 'The female sex is afflicted by two vices,' he pontificates. 'They live to be pleasing in appearance. This desire has its origin in vainglory. Secondly, they cannot tolerate injury and are keen on revenge. This flaw arises from the weakness of their intellect and their ignorance of true nobility. For a truly noble mind overlooks injury ... Furthermore, because the female is led by emotions, she measures honour by external standards and cannot tolerate being outdone in such matters.'[10] This is also the message of *The Council of Women*,[11] a spoof in the tradition of Aristophanes' comedy *The Female Parliamentarians*. The dialogue opens with a group of women announcing that they will fight for their 'social position,' but it soon becomes clear that their notion of status extends only to matters of dress and etiquette.

Another area in which Erasmus expresses conventional views is his support for parental authority. He expects women to obey their elders and respect their choice of marriage partner. The seventeen-year-old protagonist in *The Girl with No Interest in Marriage* is admonished not to act against the wishes of her parents 'who have authority over us by God's will.'[12] In an anecdote relating exemplary behaviour, a father brings his authority to bear on his married daughter. When he took her to task for resisting the wishes of her husband, '[his] speech grew so heated that he seemed barely able to keep his hands off her.' As a result, 'moved partly by fear, partly by the truth, the girl promptly went down on her knees before the father' and promised to obey her husband in future.[13] Erasmus also supports traditional values in depicting women as spiritually superior to men ('The order of women offers more examples of religion and piety')[14] but inferior to them in the social hierarchy. In the colloquy *The New Mother* Fabulla maintains the general superiority of women, but her bantering exchange with Eutrapelus is a mock battle of wits and meant as a comic interlude. In real life women were not expected to argue. 'A wife who makes war on her husband is making war on God, who said "You shall be in your husband's power, and he shall be lord over you." Charity softens this rule, but it does not remove the husband's power.'[15] Elaborating on the patriarchal model of marriage, Erasmus depicts the ideal husband as an enlightened despot: 'A tyrant commands what is pleasing and advantageous to himself; a husband considers what is best also for the person to whom he gives orders.'[16]

At the personal level and in the interest of good relations, Erasmus stresses mutuality. 'Each partner must always show respect for the other' or as the suitor in *Courtship* says, 'I'll be your king; you'll be my queen.'[17] The husband should occasionally defer to his wife's wishes, especially in matters concerning her domain, 'cooking, shopping, looking after the small children and supervising the servants.' More generally 'the husband must not be reluctant to yield to his wife if she appears to be more knowledgeable.'[18] In the colloquy *Marriage*, the speakers offer contrasting views on marital relations. Xanthippe advocates a tit-for-tat approach ('If he won't treat me as a wife, I won't treat him as a husband'),[19] but her name suggests that her attitude is shrewish and therefore reprehensible. Her conversation partner, Eulalia ('well-spoken'), recommends a more conciliatory approach. Her recipe for a successful marriage is to remind the husband of his duty but leave the practical peacekeeping efforts to his wife: 'See that everything at home is neat and clean and there's no trouble that will drive him out of doors. Show yourself affable to him ... avoid gloominess and irritability.' A wife, moreover, 'must take every precaution to be pleasing to her husband in sexual relations, in order that married love may be rekindled and renewed and any annoyance or boredom driven out of mind.'[20] *The Institution of Marriage*, however, suggests that husbands must do their part to foster the relationship. Erasmus suggests that they use kisses, affectionate letters, love poems, and presents to retain their wives' goodwill.[21]

The strictures imposed on one party usually imply corresponding obligations for the other. Parents determine the choice of marriage partner, but have a responsibility to make an informed decision and act in their daughter's best interest. They are criticized for acting foolishly or in bad faith. This is the message of the colloquy *A Marriage in Name Only*, in which a sixteen-year-old shares the fate of her classical namesake Iphigeneia. She is sacrificed by her parents, who force her to marry a nobleman wasted by syphilis. Such an act is abominable. 'As private individuals, the [parents] are disloyal to their family; as citizens, to the state.'[22] The actions of husbands are governed by a similar balance of power and responsibility. Erasmus reflects ideas common in his time when he suggests that the husband rules the roost, but is responsible for the physical and moral well-being of his wife: 'He fosters and protects the weaker sex.'[23] Men's perceived superiority to women obliges them to give special consideration to them: 'Remember that your strength is a gift bestowed by God to enable you to help those weaker than you.' Accordingly, a good husband 'does not look down on his wife because in the marital union she plays a secondary role, being weaker in body and mind; on the contrary, he will give her greater consideration to compensate for the deficiencies of nature with a husband's love. Husband and wife are one body, but the weaker members are entitled to more consideration.'[24]

Erasmus' manual for widows is also largely traditional. We find there the usual commonplaces about women being prone to emotional excesses and in need of a firm hand governing their lives. For this reason Erasmus favours remarriage for young widows. Left to their own devices and 'freed from the jurisdiction of husbands, and corrupted with their chatter' they lead a useless life. 'For all these evils marriage is a remedy. The authority of a husband will bring the natural levity occasioned by his wife's youth and sex under control.'[25] Older widows, however, hold a place of honour in society. They are seen as spiritually close to God and beneficial to society through their charitable work and their wise counsel.

What Erasmus says about women is perhaps as telltale as what he refrains from saying. It is interesting, for example, that he generally steers clear of the concept of woman as temptress, the Tertullian image of the female as 'gateway of the Devil.'[26] It is also remarkable that in the panoply of characters found in his writings that popular figure, the witch, is conspicuously absent. In his letters he occasionally refers to witchcraft, and in one case declares that reports he heard are plausible, but in the end he labels them 'popular myth.'[27] He employs a jocular tone in relating another case. In a nearby village a 'witch' was burned at the stake. Among her confessed misdeeds was bringing to the village several sacks of fleas. Erasmus himself was plagued by fleas, he said, but unable to catch the pesky creatures. 'Is this power granted only to witches?' he asked ironically.[28]

Although the roles Erasmus assigns to women in *The Institution of Marriage* and *The Christian Widow* are conventional, he departs from traditional thought in the value he places on the matrimonial state. In his rejection of the medieval/Catholic hierarchy that placed celibacy above matrimony he anticipated Reformation thought. His position on celibacy aroused a great deal of controversy in 1518. He was sharply criticized by the vice-chancellor of the University of Louvain, who turned a graduation address into an attack on *In Praise of Marriage*.[29] Although Erasmus replied with an apology justifying his views, they remained a target for Catholic theologians. Some brought doctrinal points to bear; others made personal attacks. One called him a 'teacher of carnal knowledge' and wondered aloud how Erasmus, a cleric, had become so knowledgeable about marriage. He suggested that Erasmus had broken his vows and was 'in the category of adulterer, rapist or fornicator.'[30] Like the reformers, Erasmus praised marriage as significant for the well-being of individuals and society as a whole. 'Christians are married to safeguard their chastity, to increase their virtue through mutual association, to bring children into the world not only as a debt to nature but for God.' In *The Institution of Marriage* he insists that 'the well-being of society depends on it.'[31]

Erasmus' attitude toward celibacy was no doubt motivated by his own experience. Having been obliged by his guardians to enter the

Augustinian order at a young age and against his inclinations, he went through a series of complex psychological reactions. *On Disdaining the World*, written shortly after he took the vows, appears to be an attempt to convince himself of the wisdom of choosing a celibate, monastic life. While a literary exemplum in that text praises a certain Margarete for entering a convent in defiance of the wishes of her parents and friends, the concluding chapter, which was added at a later date, contains dire warnings to young people who embrace the celibate life for the wrong reasons or from a lack of self-knowledge.[32] The colloquies *The Girl with No Interest in Marriage* and *The Repentant Girl* use such a scenario. A sixteen-year-old rejects marriage and, over her parents' protests, enters a convent. She soon repents, however, and returns to the parental home. Her narrow escape from the convent is depicted by Erasmus as a happy ending to the story.

Erasmus' thought on women and learning is liberal, measured by the standards of his time. As a humanist he places a high value on education for both male and female children. However, occasional praise of learned women does not make Erasmus a 'feminist,' as suggested by some scholars.[33] He does not recognize women's intrinsic equality or advocate their autonomy from patriarchal control. He readily uses the derogatory phraseology of his time, likening gossips and slanderers to *mulierculae*, 'little women,' and he regularly lumps women together with other undesirable or marginalized segments of society, as in the phrases 'the uneducated mob, women, and superstitious people,' 'the class of servants and of women,' 'children, old people, and women whose tongue is less controlled because their mental powers are weak.'[34] Nor does he eulogize learned women as paragons of their sex. On the contrary, he praises them for acting out of character, that is, being unlike women.[35] These remarks are in the tradition of Gerson, who praised Christine de Pizan for being a 'manly female,' or Lauro Quirini, who lauded Isotta Nogarola for having sought out 'the whole and perfect virtue that men attain.'[36] Moreover, Erasmus advocates education for women, not as a means of self-improvement, but, as he says in a letter to fellow-humanist Guillaume Budé, to keep them out of trouble. Reading and studying are the 'occupations that best protect the mind from dangerous idleness ... the mind trained is attracted to virtue ... nothing is more intractable than ignorance.' In addition, educated women have entertainment value: 'One can really enjoy their society. I differ profoundly from those who keep a wife for no purpose except physical satisfaction, for which half-witted females are better fitted.'[37] In *The Abbot and the Learned Lady*, Magdalia expresses the wish to obtain learning for her own sake, but she does not serve as a role model. Rather, she is an example that the 'world's stage is topsy turvy.'[38] Her function in the dialogue is to shame men (and clerics in particular) into acquiring learning, for, as Erasmus says in *The Christian Widow*, 'men will be ashamed not to do what they see can be done by a woman.'[39]

By his own admission, Erasmus was a late convert to the idea that women should be given a liberal education. He used to think that they could not benefit from education. More's daughters convinced him of the contrary. 'Scarcely any mortal man was not under the conviction that, for the female sex, education had nothing to offer in the way of either virtue or reputation. Nor was I myself in the old days completely free of this opinion; but More has quite put it out of my head,' he reported.[40] Erasmus must be given credit for allowing experience to change his mind and for departing from preconceived ideas. It is notable, moreover, that he endowed the female characters in his dialogues with lively personalities and authentic-sounding voices. After all, his own exposure to women was limited. He was orphaned at an early age and did not grow up in a family but in an all-male institutional setting. His clerical status (which he took seriously) prevented him from intimate contact with women. He shared living space with (sometimes reluctant) hostesses and domestics, more particularly his elderly housekeeper, who inspired the acid-tongued servant in the colloquy *The Poetic Feast*, but most of his documented contact with women was through correspondence.[41] If some of the female characters in Erasmus' works are, by our standards at least, suffering insult and oppression at the hands of men, others in turn are allowed to take aim at them with barbed remarks. The glib servant Margaret in *The Poetic Feast* certainly holds her own against her master's male guests. In *The New Mother* Fabulla effectively refutes Eutrapelus' argument that the male is superior because God created him first: 'Artists usually surpass themselves in later works.' She agrees with Eutrapelus that men, not women, defend the country in times of war, but hints that women who die in childbirth have laid down their lives for society as well. 'There's not a single one of you who, if he once experienced childbirth, would not prefer standing in a battle line.' In another colloquy, *Shipwreck*, the male passengers do all the screaming and hand-wringing, while a young mother keeps her head, saving her own and her baby's life. Similarly in the funeral oration of Berta Heyen, the widow shows more dignity and self-control than male family members.[42] Erasmus' repertoire of exemplary figures is well stocked with heroines from classical and biblical sources.[43] In his correspondence, too, the image of women is balanced. He immortalizes bickering domestics and cheating innkeepers along with learned housewives and politically influential women, providing a representative cross-section.[44]

It is true that Erasmus was no feminist in the contemporary sense of the word, but neither was he a misogynist. Indeed there are indications that he was occasionally uncomfortable with the patronizing tone and authoritative role he was expected to assume as the author of manuals. His apologetic remarks in the preface to *The Institution of Marriage* may be applied to what he says about women in general: 'Perhaps my remarks may seem as inept ... as those of the philosopher whom Hannibal considered foolish for disputing about war when he had never taken part in one.'[45]

Erasmus' writings were controversial in his own time. They were lavishly praised by some readers, bitterly denounced by others. There can be no doubt, however, that the wide dissemination of his writings make him an important witness to the social thought of the sixteenth century. Whether Erasmus' comments have any validity today or show any sensitivity toward women by today's standards remains a matter of dispute. The final verdict rests with individual readers and will depend to some extent on their ideological position.

The texts in this volume are arranged under the headings 'Unmarried Women,' 'Wives,' and 'Widows.' This order, adopted here for structural purposes, reflects the conventions of Erasmus' age. The division is patristic in origin and was well established in medieval and Renaissance thought. It was customary to define women by sexual activity, which in turn determined their legal status and place in the social hierarchy.[46] At the same time these divisions reflect the natural sequence of events in a woman's life. The texts deal consecutively with upbringing, courtship (involving a choice between marriage and celibacy), marriage, childbearing, and widowhood. Selections dealing with special topics (prostitution, scholarship, activism) are categorized according to the context in which they were discussed by Erasmus.

The translations in this volume are texts published or forthcoming in the Collected Works of Erasmus (Toronto 1974–).

NOTES

1 For the text of these three colloquies see below 131, 156, 174.
2 Thompson 60, and below 140.
3 *De imitatione Ciceroniana* (Lyons 1535) 28 in the facsimile edition ed. E. Telle (Geneva 1974)
4 For selections from these two texts see below 79, 187.
5 For these two works see below 57, 230.
6 For the text cf CWE 25.
7 CWE 71:91–2
8 CWE Ep 858:228–35
9 LB V:643
10 LB V:704F–5A
11 See below 180.
12 Thompson 289
13 Thompson 312
14 CWE 66:193
15 See below 122.
16 LB 706C
17 See Heath 104, Thompson 264.
18 Below 124
19 Below 132
20 Below 141
21 LB 689D–F
22 Below 150
23 LB 620D
24 Heath 89–90. Rather ironically, a similar argument was used by Isotta Nogarola to excuse Eve: 'Where there is less intellect and less constancy there is less sin.' *Her Immaculate Hand*, ed. M. King and A. Rabil (New York 1983) 59
25 CWE 66:243–4
26 Cf Wiesner 12.
27 Allen, Ep 2846:152

28 Ibid 2880:36. In the Latin text the word *tantum* is ambivalent. It can mean 'only' or 'such great' [power].

29 See headnote to *In Praise of Marriage*, 57.

30 E. Rummel, *Erasmus and His Catholic Critics* (Nieuwkoop 1989) II, 133–4.

31 LB 615B–E

32 See below 23.

33 As claimed by Vanden Branden, *La Maison d'Erasme* (Brussels 1992) 110–11 and L.-E. Halkin, *Erasmus: A Critical Biography* (Oxford 1993) 192. A good discussion of the problematic use of the term can be found in B. Gottlieb, 'The Problem of Feminism in the Fifteenth Century,' *Women of the Medieval World: Essays in Honor of John H. Mundy*, ed. J. Kirshner and S. Wemple (Oxford 1985) 337–64.

34 CWE Ep 1167:491–2; CWE 29:376, 283

35 He praises Marguerite of Navarre for wisdom and piety, qualities that 'can hardly be found even in priests or monks' (Allen, Ep 1615:11–13); of Catherine of Aragon he says that she disdains 'womanish nonsense' and devotes her time to reading (ibid, 1381:40) and asserts that her learning was such that it was 'surprising in a woman' (Ep 855:35).

36 King and Rabil 191, nn179, 181

37 Ep 1233:115–31, 149–52. It should be noted, however, that Erasmus mentions similar motives also in his treatise on the education of boys: 'By being occupied with his studies, a child will avoid the common pitfalls of youth'; the purpose of education is, among other things, to make him 'a faithful protector of his family, a good husband to his wife, and a solid and useful citizen of his country' (CWE 25:297, 302).

38 Below 178

39 CWE 66:253

40 CWE Ep 1233:112–15

41 See P.G. Bietenholz and T.B. Deutscher eds. *Contemporaries of Erasmus: A Biographical Register of the Renaissance and Reformation* vol 1 (Toronto 1985), under 'Margarete Büsslin.'

42 Thompson 144 and below 238

43 Cf, for example, CWE 66:201 (classical examples), 204 (biblical examples).

44 Cf O'Donnell, especially 43–53.

45 Allen, Ep 1751:7–9

46 Cf Ian Maclean, *The Renaissance Notion of Women* (Cambridge 1987): 'All law recognizes puer (puella), virgo viripotens, marita, mater, gravida, lactans, vidua [girl, marriageable virgin, married woman, mother, pregnant,

breastfeeding woman, widow] as states in the life of a woman which require special dispensation in law. These states are made up of the marriage paradigm (maiden/wife/widow) and the physiological paradigm [virgin, wife, mother, etc].' See also the examples given by M. King, *Women of the Renaissance*, 23–4, which show that the three categories (virgin, wife, widow) were well established in the manuals of theologians and firmly lodged in social thought.

1. The World: A Corrupting Influence?

From *The Institution of Marriage*

This selection from *The Institution of Marriage* contains Erasmus' most coherent statement on the upbringing of daughters. He wrote a number of systematic works on education, but addressed himself primarily to the schooling of boys. Among the tracts dealing with this subject are *De pueris instituendis* (On education for boys), *De civilitate morum puerilium* (On good manners), and *De ratione studii* (On the method of study). Although the Latin word *pueri*, which appears in the titles of two of the treatises, can mean both 'boys' and 'children,' the contents clearly applies to boys, and the examples and anecdotal material mention boys only. This is characteristic of pedagogical tracts from the sixteenth century and not surprising, given the fact that young males were the principal beneficiaries of formal education at that time. Statistics gathered from the archives of Venice in 1587, for example, show that approximately twenty per cent of all boys attended formal schooling, as opposed to less than one per cent of girls (cf Paul Grendler, *Schooling in Renaissance Italy* [Baltimore 1989] 43).

Erasmus' comments on the upbringing of girls are made in the context of discussing their preparation for marriage. For the publication history of *The Institution of Marriage* see the headnote to the main entry, 79.

The translation is by Michael Heath.

This is how girls are brought up at court in certain countries: in the morning, they get busy with the curlers and the make-up, then off to mass to see and be seen; breakfast, followed by some gossip, followed by the midday meal. After that, take your places for some mindless chatter! The girls sink down here and there, and the men rush to put their heads in their laps. The girl who never refuses one is highly praised for her manners. Then it is time for some silly games, most of them rather coarse as well; so the afternoon is whiled away until it is time for supper. After supper, more of the same amusements as after the previous meal.

It is in such an atmosphere that the sons and little daughters of princes are brought up. But they are not much better brought up in the country. The sons and daughters of the gentry spend their days in the company of greasy, idle servants, who are often slovenly and immoral into the bargain. How else are they to pass the time? Well, they could pass the time a lot more profitably weaving tapestries. Aristotle wants high-born children kept away from the slaves because of their low character and lowbrow humour.[1] The Ancients had special rooms in which the men could meet, other rooms set aside for the women, and the parthenons, or maidens' chambers, where the girls could spend their time.

To learn how carefully a girl's chastity must be safeguarded, listen to that wise man Sirach: 'You have sons: train them and bend them to your will from their earliest years. You have daughters: protect their bodies and do not let them see you smile.'[2] What kind of advice is this? How can a father not love his daughters, especially if they are dutiful and God-fearing, and, if he loves them, how can he look upon them with an unsmiling face? But in fact, if you truly love your daughters, that is why you will hide your smiles when you see them. Where is the danger? It is important that girls of that age should always be constrained by feeling of respect, and too much cheerfulness in their father's face will detract from this not a little. If his daughters do something unbecoming, they are rebuked by a stern glance from their father; if they have done nothing wrong, their father's expression must still be serious (but not harsh) to remind them not to err.

What would Sirach say if he could see some of these modern fathers who, in the presence of their growing – and even fully grown – daughters, boast in their cups of their own youthful indiscretions, spotlighting the temptations of adolescence? Even worse, they blurt out the secrets of the marriage bed. And yet, if their sons go astray, these fathers will disinherit them; and if anything happens to their daughters, they will confound heaven and earth. Why rage at your children, you faithless father? It is yourself you should punish, since you put them up to it: can you be surprised if the young people do things of which they have heard you boast so often? 'What words will you find to upbraid your son?' as the woman in the play said.[3] It is worse to boast of your misdeeds than to commit them, but it is worst of all to do it in front of your children. Are you surprised that your offspring do not respect you, since you have no respect for them? What chance have your children of having decent moral standards, when they are undermined by you, who should be their most scrupulous guardian?

Some people use obscenities so often that they sometimes slip out unexpectedly. I witnessed a remarkable example of this in Brussels, at the church of St Gudula. The church was crowded with people when a certain married lady, of impeccable reputation and excellent family, came in. The floor was slippery with snow from people's shoes, and suddenly she slipped and fell; in her surprise, she uttered a loud cry, naming, as many women do out of habit, the male member. Everyone roared with laughter, and she blushed with shame. It just slipped out, but why do people get into such bad habits? Could they not learn, just as easily, to name Jesus or Mary when something unexpected happens to frighten them? Some people have a similar habit of cursing when something goes wrong, or of swearing when they tell a story; but when they say 'A hundred devils!' might they not just as well say: 'God be good to me'? Some people can scarcely utter four words without swearing; children take in such things from an early age.

Love stories, which are so influential with the young, very easily take hold of immature minds, and a good many of them contain an element of coarseness. Storytellers who corrupt innocent minds with their far from innocent tales must be kept away from young girls, for it is poison that they drip into those tender ears.

In some countries these days, as a sort of annual ritual, new songs are published for the girls to learn. They all have similar themes: a husband deceived by his wife, a girl escaping her parents' vigilance, a secret tryst arranged with a lover; these tricks are recounted with approval, and successful debauchery is applauded. The style in which these poisonous tales are told is so foul, so full of innuendo and suggestiveness, that pure filth could not be filthier. A lot of people, especially in Flanders, earn a living from such stuff; if the law were more vigilant, the authors of these lullabies would be flogged by the hangman, and made to sing dirges, not dirty ditties. And yet these brazen corrupters of youth make a living from their crimes, and there are even parents who think that learning such songs will count as a social grace in their daughters.

The Ancients considered that music belonged to the liberal arts; but since those rhythmic sounds have such power to affect the human spirit, some concluded that the soul itself was music, or at least contained musical harmony, since like attracts like. Thus they carefully distinguished between the different modes, among which the Dorian took the palm, and considered music so important that they thought it necessary to make laws prohibiting the import into the state of any music that might corrupt the citizens.[4] And is not our music, leaving aside the foul language and disgusting themes, full of frivolousness, not to say madness? There used to be a kind of performance in which, without using words, the actors could represent whatever they wished by no more than the movements of their bodies.[5] It is similar with these songs: even without words, you can guess the obscenity of the subject from the style of the music, not to mention the frantic shrilling of the pipes and the thumping rhythm of the drums, all adding to the frenzy – and we let girls dance to this music, get a taste for it, and think it can do them no harm.

In fact we have even brought this kind of music out of the dancehalls and taverns and into the churches; still more ridiculous, we pay people huge salaries to wreck the dignity of the services with their absurd warbling. I would not ban music from services, but I would insist on settings that are worthy of them. Nowadays the sacred texts are accompanied by the most unholy sounds; you might as well dress Cato in Thaïs's clothes.[6] These licentious singers even include obscene words. If the law will not take action, priests and bishops should be on the watch for this.

As Aristotle said: 'A foul mouth will not shrink from foul deeds.'[7] The question is: what is obscene? Some deeds, such as theft and murder, are foul, but the words describing them are not considered obscene. Similarly, some things are not offensive in themselves, but if you describe them in unvarnished language they become obscene: for example, to have one's wife, to discharge one's belly, to pass water. No part of the body is shameful, since God created them all good and beautiful; yet in some cases decency demands that they be concealed, and even that they should not be named directly, but indicated by some modest circumlocution. 'Vulva' is a blameless word, and so is 'womb,' and yet the ignorant consider them disgusting. You may say 'a woman's nature' without giving offence, when you mean her pudenda; there are similar euphemisms for the male pudenda. A similar reticence must be observed in describing the actions of these organs, which I discussed earlier. Thus the first definition of obscenity is to name directly things that, for decency's sake, should be described more guardedly.

The second definition is to describe indecent acts, though not in crude language, in such a way as to make indecency seem acceptable and laudable. For example, it is not obscene to use the word 'adultery,' but if someone describes in lurid detail the methods used by the wife to deceive her husband and receive her lover, that is obscene. If it is essential to describe indecent acts, it must be done with loathing, just as good deeds must be described with every sign of approval. However, other people's misdeeds should never be recounted unless some useful purpose is served by it. It is also obscene to put a vicious interpretation on some perfectly innocent act, but worse than obscene to adapt some blameless piece of writing to a filthy theme, as did Ausonius in his *Cento nuptialis*, a work utterly unworthy of a Christian.[8] Again, although it is not obscene to speak of theft or murder, there are nonetheless certain monstrous crimes, most of them the products of lust, that boys and girls ought not to hear mentioned unless it is absolutely necessary, and even then with great circumspection and detestation. Paul speaks of this in Ephesians 5[:12]: 'The things they do in secret it would be shameful even to mention.'

I have run through all these different kinds of filthy language to help you avoid any hint of obscenity. I said something earlier about obscene pictures: Aristotle believes that lewd pictures and sculptures are so detrimental to morality that the state should impose laws prohibiting the possession of any image containing a hint of lasciviousness.[9] The tongue speaks to the ears, a picture speaks to the eyes, but a picture is more graphic by far than words and generally makes a deeper impression on the mind. Aristotle also prescribed a severe penalty even for an indecent utterance. What was it? If the offender were free-born, but not yet old enough to join the men at table, he would be refused that honour; if he were older, he would be scourged, the treatment reserved for slaves, since he had committed a slave's offence.

An undisciplined tongue is indeed the kind of servile fault that should be unthinkable in any noble spirit, but even more in those whom Christ's blood released from enslavement to sin into the freedom of the children of God. You have heard the pagan philosopher's view: should not Christians be all the more ashamed to lionize, as witty and jolly fellows, the most foul-mouthed reprobates? Not to mention the licentiousness of our signs and paintings, which depict and set before our eyes things normally too disgusting even to name. These subjects are on public display in the taverns and market squares and meet our eyes whether we like it or not – images 'that would inflame even the desires, long extinguished by age, of a Priam or a Nestor.'[10] Alas, the indifference of our law and its officers!

It is all the more sinful when people introduce indecency into subjects that are by nature innocent. Firstly, why is it necessary to have certain stories depicted in church at all? Why a youth and a girl lying in the same bed? Why David watching Bathsheba from his window and summoning her to be defiled, or embracing the Shunammite who was sent to him?[11] Why the dance of Herodias's daughter? The subjects are indeed taken from the holy books, but why has so much artistic licence been used to depict the women? There are things surrounding the altars where the Eucharist is performed that would not be allowed into any decent home.

Thus you must keep out of your house all loose-living, idle, and pampered young people, together with drunken servants, gossiping women, dancing girls, mountebanks, actors, actresses, and indecent pictures: in short, anyone or anything that could poison the minds of the young through their eyes, ears, or in any other way. So far from such people and influences being brought into your home from outside, should you find that any of them has crept unnoticed into your household, it must be ignominiously expelled at once.

I feel compelled to ask why Christian law is so forbearing. Some people make a living from this trade: they obtain a good-looking girl from somewhere and teach her, young as she is, to perform erotic dances and mimes; they worm their way into the banquets of the nobility and even of bishops. As soon as she is old enough, she is made a whore, and one poor ruined girl earns enough to keep three strapping youths and a woman who claims to be her mother; these libertines get a gold piece or two from every satisfied client. If magistrates ever took any thought for morality, it would be here: they would ask the vagabonds where they found the girl (and perhaps discover that she has been spirited away from a respectable home) and why, despite being perfectly fit, they have chosen to lead this idle and vicious existence. To help them make a full confession, they would deserve at the very least the honour of a public thrashing and banishment from the city. This topic would provide abundant material for a tirade, but I must set a limit to my complaints and complete my task.

Idleness is, in fact, a danger to anyone, but it is most dangerous by far to impressionable youth. Children must therefore always be given something to keep them occupied, even a game, if you wish, so long as it is worthwhile. Idleness is still more dangerous if accompanied by wealth and isolation. The celebrated playwright's dictum is not far from the truth: 'The thoughts of a woman alone always turn to evil.'[12] There are few women who have achieved that masculine strength of mind that enables them to debate important matters with themselves, and never to be less alone than when they are alone. It is certainly true that solitude is unprofitable to boys and girls. The philosopher feared for the youth whom he saw standing alone, lost in thought, and asked him what he was doing. 'I am talking to myself,' he said. 'Are you sure that you are not talking to a rogue?' replied the philosopher.[13] But if a girl is intent on her prayers or on her book, she is neither idle nor alone; in prayer, she is talking to God, and in reading the sacred books she is listening to God's word. But there is no end to the advice I could give, much of it passed on by the Ancients, and as much by modern writers.

NOTES

1 Aristotle, *Politics*, 7.17.7
2 Eccl. 7:23–4
3 Terence, *Phormio*, 1042
4 See Plato, *Republic*, 3.398–401. The ancient Greeks considered the Dorian the only authentic mode; Lydian and Phrygian modes were considered barbarian or effeminate.
5 I.e., pantomime

6 Cato, the 'censor,' (234–149 B.C.) was considered the epitome of moral strength among the Romans; Thaïs was a Greek courtesan.

7 Aristotle, *Politics*, 7.17.8

8 Ausonius' *Cento* was written at the request of the Roman emperor Valentinian c 368 A.D. It is a patchwork of lines from Virgil's works and includes a graphic description of a wedding night.

9 Aristotle, *Politics*, 7.17.9–10

10 Juvenal, 6.325–6. The Homeric kings Nestor and Priam were proverbial for advanced old age.

11 The stories of David, Bathsheba, and Abishag the Shunammite are told in 2 Sam. 11 and 1 Kings 1.

12 Publilius Syrus, *Sentence*, 376

13 An anecdote told of the philosopher Crates by Seneca, *Epistulae morales*, 1.10.1

2. The Cloister: A Safe Haven?

a) *On Disdaining the World*

The tract from which this selection is taken appeared in 1521. Erasmus tells us that he published the work to oblige his friends and his Basel publisher, Johann Froben. He himself considered the piece immature, and in the preface informed the reader that it did not represent his own views but was written on commission. The first eleven chapters of the work are an endorsement of monasticism; the twelfth, which was added at a later date, is a volte-face. It is critical of monastic institutions and warns young people not to make vows rashly. In ancient times monasteries were solitary places, in which a community of saintly men lived a truly Christian life, Erasmus writes. 'Now most monasteries are in the midst of worldly affairs' (CWE 66:173).

Convents for women had undergone a similar deterioration. Places of religious devotion and cultural accomplishment during the Middle Ages, they had lost their spiritual and intellectual focus in Erasmus' time and had become convenient repositories for daughters of the nobility who could not find a suitable match or for the poor who lacked a dowry. Unlike Margarete, the heroine of the following selection, these women had no sense of vocation.

The text of the passage is taken from chapter 11 of Erasmus' treatise on monasticism, which is entitled 'The pleasures of a secluded life.' Margarete is not otherwise identified, although Erasmus' narrative appears to be autobiographical. This account should be read in conjunction with the next selection (25 below), which treats a similar topic but is written from a different point of view and may well reflect Erasmus' evolving consciousness of the problems of monastic life.

The translation is by Erika Rummel (cf CWE 66:168–9).

Here I must ask for your indulgence when I relate the story of that tearful last meal that the best of virgins, Margarete, whom I have always loved like a sister, had in the company of her parents. I myself was present, and with me many others whom the daughter had taken pains to invite as her advocates to join her in her entreaties; for she had been vainly pleading with her father for six years now to let her become a nun. She had already conquered her mother's heart, for neither parent objected out of meanness. Both easily surpass their peers as much in virtue (and that is rare in prosperous circumstances) as in position and appearance, so that no one fails to love and praise them: but they are so disposed toward their children that they love them deeply and fondly.

Well then, we began to belabour the father and, to keep the story short, he agreed, overcome partly by his own embarrassment, partly by compassion for his daughter, partly by our importuning him. Thereupon you could have seen a tragedy unfold: the father embraced his daughter and, kissing her, began to cry as if he must lay her into her grave at once. The mother, overcome with grief, fainted. Her only brother, a young boy, and an older sister, both lacking fortitude – one because of his youth, the other because of her sex – sobbed loudly and embraced their sister in turns. 'By these tears,' they said, 'and by a sister's and brother's love, if they count for anything, we beg you not to desert us in our misery, lest your single person be the undoing of us both!' Of her other friends some wept silently, others prayed, others again gave her advice or reproached her – but certainly no one's cheeks remained dry. At length even we who had come to plead the daughter's case were moved by the tears and lamentations of all the guests, and particularly by the sight of her father, an eminent man crying like a baby, tears welling from his eyes. Moved by this spectacle we ourselves began to cry, disgraceful though it is to tell. We were almost sorry to have caused such a commotion. What was a young woman to do in the midst of this? A young woman, fragile by reasons of her sex, age, and disposition, refined by her upbringing? Even St Paul reports that, when he was about to say farewell, he was moved by the tears of his brothers, though not moved to change his mind, and said: 'What are you doing, weeping and disturbing my heart?' [Acts 21:13]. But Margarete, notwithstanding her great love for her parents, was dry-eyed and composed, and gently assured her father that there was no reason to worry himself. By rights he should be joyful since it was not a loss but a gain to have a daughter to pray on his behalf before God. In like manner she tried earnestly to soothe the troubled minds of her mother and the remaining guests with kisses, prayers, and words of admonition. In vain: the banquet went on, prolonged into the night with sobbing, weeping, and lamenting, while Margarete alone kept her cheerful disposition.

Whenever those who, as I have said, have no other criterion but their palates, see such goings-on (for they sometimes do), they too burst into tears, wondering at the young people's fortitude and feeling shame for their own weakness. Now, what do they suppose is happening? Surely they do not believe that these young and beautiful people with such physical and mental accomplishments, can be led, or rather turned, away from the pleasures of this world so easily unless they have already found more intense pleasures? That they would hasten to undertake these labours with such high spirits unless they found them sweet? Yes, my dear Jodocus, this is obviously the answer. Our labour is sweet to those who know it, bitter and harsh to those who do not know it.

b) *The Girl with No Interest in Marriage*

In the preceding section Erasmus presents a scenario in which a young woman enters a convent against the wishes of her parents. Two years later he published the following dialogue, which presents a similar situation, but whereas 'Margarete' in *On Disdaining the World* was made out a heroine, young Catharine is depicted as a headstrong fool and soon repents of her rash deed. The original purpose of the *Colloquies*, in which the present dialogue appeared, was to teach boys correct Latin. A prototype, entitled *Familiarum colloquiorum formulae* (Formulae for familiar conversation) was published in Basel in 1518. The book was an instant success and reprinted within months in Paris, Antwerp, Vienna, and Cracow. Between 1522 and 1533 a dozen editions appeared, which contained significant new material. The added dialogues changed the nature of the book. It became a vehicle of social criticism. The characters introduced by Erasmus commented on current issues: moral problems, political questions, and religious reform. The book soon became the focus of controversy. Critics charged Erasmus with indecency and heterodoxy and protested the use of the book in schools. It was investigated by the powerful faculty of theology at Paris and condemned for its 'Lutheran' ideas. Even progressive thinkers like the authors of the *Counsel ... concerning Church Reform* (1538) considered the *Colloquies* morally corrupt and recommended that they be suppressed. In 1564 the Council of Trent condemned the *Colloquies*, and they were placed on the Index of Prohibited Books.

The present dialogue was first printed in the 1523 edition of the *Colloquies* and was criticized for deprecating monasticism and flying in the face of tradition by questioning the spiritual superiority of celibacy over matrimony. In *The*

Usefulness of the Colloquies (1526), an apologia defending his book, Erasmus explained his purpose in *The Girl with No Interest in Marriage*:

> I denounce those who, despite the opposition of parents, lure boys and girls into a monastery, playing upon their innocence or their superstitiousness, persuading them there is no hope of salvation outside a monastery. If the world is not full of such fishermen; if countless happy natures, which had been chosen vessels of the Lord had they sensibly taken up a career suited to their natural talents, are not most miserably buried alive by these creatures – then I have been wrong in my warning. But if ever I am compelled to speak my mind plainly on this topic, I will give such a description of those kidnappers, and the magnitude of their mischief, that all will agree I had plenty of reason to utter these warnings. I wrote politely, however, to avoid giving malevolent men an occasion for making trouble (Thompson 629).

The translation is by Craig Thompson.

EUBULUS, CATHARINE

Eubulus I'm glad dinner's finally over, so that we may enjoy this walk. There's nothing more pleasant.
Catharine I'm glad too. I was tired of sitting so long.
Eubulus How green and smiling the world is everywhere! This is its youthful season, surely.
Catharine So it is.
Eubulus But why isn't *your* springtime equally bright?
Catharine Why do you say that?
Eubulus Because you're rather sad.
Catharine Do I look different?
Eubulus Want me to show you how you look?
Catharine Very much.
Eubulus See this rose, with its petals partially drawn in at dusk?
Catharine I do. What of it?
Eubulus That's what you look like.
Catharine A fine comparison!
Eubulus If you doubt me, take a look at yourself in this little fountain – Just what was the meaning of so many sighs during dinner?
Catharine Stop asking about what doesn't concern you.

Eubulus Oh, but it very much concerns me. I can't be cheerful unless I see you're cheerful too. But there: another sigh! My, what a deep one!

Catharine Something torments me, but it's not safe to tell what.

Eubulus You won't tell me, when I love you more than my own sister? Don't be afraid, Catharine dear. Whatever's the trouble, you can trust it safely to these ears.

Catharine I'm safe in saying that I fear there's no use telling it to one who can't help.

Eubulus How do you know? If I can't help in the business itself, maybe I can give comfort and advice.

Catharine I can't talk about it.

Eubulus What *is* the matter? Do you hate me?

Catharine Hate you? Less than I do my own brother. And yet my heart won't let me speak.

Eubulus Then will you admit it if I guess? Why are you evasive? Promise, or I won't stop urging you.

Catharine All right – I promise.

Eubulus I simply don't see what you lack to make you perfectly happy.

Catharine If only what you say were true!

Eubulus In the first place, you're in the bloom of youth, for if I'm not mistaken you're now in your seventeenth year.

Catharine That's correct.

Eubulus So I suppose fear of old age doesn't torture you as yet.

Catharine Nothing troubles me less.

Eubulus You're blessed by beauty in every respect, and that's a special gift of God.

Catharine Of my beauty, such as it is, I neither boast nor complain.

Eubulus Then, your complexion and figure suggest you enjoy good health, unless you've some latent disease.

Catharine Nothing of that sort, thank God.

Eubulus Your reputation is unstained.

Catharine I trust it is.

Eubulus You're blessed with a wit worthy of your beauty. I wish I had your aptitude for the liberal arts.

Catharine If I have any, it's the gift of God.

Eubulus And you've charming manners, which are often hard to find even in the most favoured beauties.

Catharine Certainly I hope my conduct does me credit.

Eubulus Many persons are ashamed of an unfortunate family tree. Your parents are well-born, highly respectable, prosperous, and devoted to you.

Catharine I've no complaint on that score.

Eubulus Why beat about the bush? Of all the girls in this neighbourhood, there's none I'd rather marry if my lucky star would shine.

Catharine And I'd choose no other husband if marriage had any attraction for me.

Eubulus And yet it must be something very important that makes you so unhappy.

Catharine It's nothing trivial.

Eubulus You won't be angry if I guess it?

Catharine I've already promised.

Eubulus I know by experience how awful a torment love is – Come, now, confess. You promised.

Catharine There's love involved, but not the kind you suspect.

Eubulus What kind are you talking about?

Catharine Guess.

Eubulus Well, I've used up all my guessing. But I won't let go of this hand until I've wrung an answer from you.

Catharine How insistent you are!

Eubulus Whatever this trouble is, confide it to me.

Catharine Since you urge me so, I'll tell you. From earliest childhood I've had a marvellous longing.

Eubulus What is it, I ask you?

Catharine To join a community of holy virgins.

Eubulus To become a nun?

Catharine Yes.

Eubulus Huh! Coals instead of treasure![1]

Catharine What's that you say, Eubulus?

Eubulus Nothing, darling, I was clearing my throat. But go on.

Catharine My parents always resisted this longing of mine with the utmost firmness.

Eubulus I'm listening.

Catharine On the other hand, I opposed their parental sense of duty with entreaties, coaxings, and tears.

Eubulus A pretty state of affairs!

Catharine At last, when I wouldn't stop begging, swearing, vowing, and weeping, they promised that when I reached my seventeenth year they would give in to my wish if my mind were still set on it. That year has come, my resolution remains the same, but my parents back out of the agreement and won't consent. It's this that breaks my heart.

I've shown you my hurt; now heal it if you can.

Eubulus First, my sweet, I'll give you this advice: control your desires, and if you don't get what you want, want what you can get.[2]

Catharine I'd rather die than not have my wish.

Eubulus And precisely where did you get this fatal desire?

Catharine Once when I was still a little girl I was taken to a certain convent. We made a tour of the place and saw everything. The nuns delighted me with their shining faces: they seemed angels. Everything in the church was beautiful and fragrant too; the well-trimmed gardens were in full bloom. What more need I say? Wherever I looked, everything I saw attracted me. The perfectly charming conversation of the nuns added to these impressions. I found there one or two whom I used to play with as a child. From that hour my heart began to burn with longing for this life.

Eubulus I'm not going to say a word against the order of nuns – though not all modes of life are equally suitable to all persons[3] – but considering your particular temperament, which I think I've inferred from your looks and behaviour, I'd urge you to marry a husband of similar tastes and establish a new community at home. Your husband would be the father of it, you the mother.

Catharine I'd rather die than give up my resolution of virginity.

Eubulus Virginity's an excellent thing if pure and undefiled, but there's no need on this account to hand yourself over to an order that you can't get out of afterwards. You may preserve your virginity at home with your parents.

Catharine Yes, but not so safely.

Eubulus On the contrary, sometimes more safely, in my judgment, than among those gross monks who are always puffy from overeating. They're not geldings, for your information. 'Fathers' they're called, and this name they often take care to deserve. In the old days, virgins lived nowhere more chastely than with their parents, and had no other 'father' than the bishop. But do please tell me: of all the orders, which one have you chosen to sentence yourself to?

Catharine The Chrysercian.[4]

Eubulus I'm acquainted with it – near your home.

Catharine That's right.

Eubulus I know the whole lot of them very well – a fine set indeed to renounce father and mother and a decent family circle for! The prior has been out of his head this long while, what with old age, drink, and his own natural character. Wine's the only subject *he* knows. He has two brethren worthy of him, John and Jodocus. Of these, John, though perhaps not a bad man, has no manhood about him except his beard; not a single shred of learning, and not much more common sense. Jodocus is so stupid that if he weren't protected by his sacred habit he'd walk about in public in a fool's hood with flapping ears and tinkling bells.

Catharine They seem highly respectable men to me.

Eubulus I know them better than you do, my dear Catharine. Maybe they patronize you in the presence of your parents in order to convert you.

Catharine Jodocus is especially cordial.

Eubulus That flatterer! But even supposing they're good and learned men now, they'll be ignorant and vicious tomorrow; and whatever they turn out to be, you'll have to put up with them.

Catharine At home I'm embarrassed by the numerous dinner parties. The married folks' talk there isn't always fit for girls' ears, either. And it happens sometimes that I can't refuse a kiss.

Eubulus The person who tries to avoid any embarrassment whatever had better quit this life. You must accustom yourself to hearing everything but admitting only the good into your mind. Your parents allow you a room of your own, I imagine?

Catharine Of course.

Eubulus You can retire to that if a dinner party becomes too boisterous. And while they're drinking and joking, do you converse with your bridegroom, Christ; pray, sing psalms, give thanks. Your parental home won't stain you, but you'll make it more pure.

Catharine Yet to be in a community of virgins is safer.

Eubulus I've nothing to say against a chaste community, but I wouldn't want you to be deceived by vain fancies. When you've spent some time there and have seen it at closer range, perhaps everything won't dazzle in quite the same fashion it seemed to do earlier. All the veiled aren't virgins, believe me.

Catharine Say something good, please.

Eubulus True words are good words, assuredly – unless, perhaps, the praise hitherto deemed appropriate to the Virgin Mother has passed to many others, so that they too may be termed virgins after childbearing.

Catharine God forbid!

Eubulus What's more, not everything's virginal among those virgins in other respects, either.

Catharine No? Why not, if you please?

Eubulus Because there are more who copy Sappho's behaviour than share her talent.[5]

Catharine I don't quite understand what you mean.

Eubulus And I say these things in order that the time may not come when you do understand, my dear Catharine.

Catharine But my mind's made up, and from the fact that this disposition has continued so many years and grown more ardent from day to day I conclude it comes from God.

Eubulus On the contrary, the very fact that your worthy parents oppose it so strongly makes me dubious about this disposition of yours. If what you're attempting were right, God would have inspired their minds too. But this inspiration you imbibed from the elegance you saw when still a little girl, from the flattering addresses of the nuns, from affection for old friends, from the sacred rites, from the only too ostentatious ceremonies, from the shameless urgings of fatuous monks, who are after you in order to drink deeper. They know your father is kind and generous. They'll entertain him – but on condition he bring enough wine with him to satisfy ten nimble sots, or else they'll drink at his house. Hence I'd advise you not to embark on any new course against the wishes of parents, who have authority over us by God's will.[6]

Catharine In this case it's right to disregard father and mother.

Eubulus In some situations it's right to disregard father and mother for the sake of Christ. For a Christian to abandon his pagan father who is solely dependent on him for support, and allow him to starve, would not be right. If you had not yet professed Christ in baptism and your parents forbade you to be baptized, you would do right to prefer Christ to unrighteous parents. Or if your parents were now driving you to wrongdoing and infamy, their authority ought to be spurned.

But what has this to do with a convent? You have Christ at home as well. Natures teaches, God commands, Paul admonishes, human

ordinances decree that children obey their parents.[7] And will you steal
away from the authority of excellent parents for the purpose of giving
yourself over to a spurious instead of a true father, and adopting
another mother in place of your real one? Or rather, adopt masters and
mistresses in place of parents? You're subject to parents, true, but all the
same they want you to be free. And that's why sons of a household are
called *liberi*[8] – because their condition is different from that of slaves.

Now you intend to surrender your freedom voluntarily and become
a slave. Christian compassion has, for the most part, abolished all of
the slavery characteristic of the ancient world save for a few remnants
here and there. But under pretence of religion a new kind of servitude
has been devised, such as now undoubtedly exists in most monasteries.
Nothing is to be permitted there except by rule; whatever comes *your*
way will be added unto *them*; if you stir a foot you'll be dragged back
from flight as though you had poisoned a parent. To make the servitude
more evident they change the dress given to you by parents[9] and – like
ancient slave dealers – change the name bestowed on you in baptism,
and instead of Peter or John they call one Francis or Dominic or Thomas.
Peter pledged his name to Christ; now, on becoming a Dominican,
he's called Thomas. If a man under military discipline throws off the
uniform given by his commander, he appears to have rejected that
commander. Yet we applaud the person who accepts a garment that
Christ, the Lord of all men, did not confer, and who, if this garment
is changed, is punished more severely than if he discarded a hundred
times the garb of his Lord and Master – that is, purity of heart.

Catharine But if one enters into this servitude of his own free will, his
action is said to be exceptionally meritorious.

Eubulus That's a truly pharisaical doctrine.[10] Paul teaches the contrary:
that he who is called free should not wish to become a slave but rather
endeavour to be free. Besides, your slavery is the more unfortunate
because you must serve many masters, because a great many of them
are foolish and vicious, because they are unsettled and there are often
new ones. Answer me this: do the laws release you from the jurisdiction
of your parents?

Catharine Not at all.

Eubulus May you buy or sell property without the consent of your
parents?

Catharine Of course not.

Eubulus What right have you, then, to give yourself away to I know not whom without parental consent? Aren't you their very nearest and dearest possession?

Catharine In a matter of religion natural laws lose their force.

Eubulus The question of religion is most urgent in baptism. Here the question is merely one of changing dress, of a way of life that in itself is neither good nor bad. Consider how many advantages you lose along with your freedom. Now you're free to read, pray, sing God's praises in your own room as much as you like and whenever you like. If you become tired of your room you may listen to church music, attend divine service, hear sermons. And if you see some lady or unmarried woman of outstanding moral excellence, you can improve yourself by her conversation; if some man endowed with unusual virtue, you can learn from him what might improve you. You're free also to select the preacher who teaches the purest Christian doctrine. All these things, which do most to draw you to true godliness, you lose once for all when you enter a convent.

Catharine But then I shan't be a nun.

Eubulus Names still move you? Ponder this matter carefully. These people brag about obedience. Will that praise be lacking to you if you obey your parents, whom God bids you obey? If you obey your bishop and your pastor? Or praise for poverty, when all you have is in your parents' hands? Though in ancient times the generosity of nuns to the poor was especially praised by holy men, they couldn't have practised that generosity had they been penniless. Your chastity, moreover, is not impaired even if you do live with your parents. So what remains? The veil, linen clothing inside and out,[11] certain rites that by themselves contribute nothing to religion and do not commend anyone in the sight of Christ, who regards only purity of heart.

Catharine A strange gospel you preach!

Eubulus But an absolutely true one. Since you're not emancipated from the authority of your parents, since you've no legal right to sell clothes or field, how do you contrive the right to give yourself into bondage under somebody else?

Catharine They say the authority of parents is no impediment to entering religion.

Eubulus Didn't you profess religion when you were baptized?

Catharine I did.

Eubulus Whoever follow the teachings of Christ are religious, aren't they?

Catharine Of course.

Eubulus Then what's this new religion that abrogates what the law of nature sanctioned, the old law taught, the law of the gospel approved, and apostolic teaching confirmed? This decree was not made known by God but devised in a council of monks. Thus some determine also that marriage between a boy and girl, without the parents' knowledge and even contrary to their wishes, is valid if contracted through 'words in the present tense'[12] (for so they call them). But this edict is ratified neither by common sense, ancient laws, Mosaic law, nor evangelical or apostolic teaching.

Catharine Then you think it's not right for me to become the bride of Christ except with parental approval?

Eubulus You've already 'married' Christ, I tell you, and so have we all. Who marries the same husband twice? This is only a question of place, dress, and rites. I don't believe the authority of parents ought to be slighted on account of these things. And you must take care lest, while intending to marry Christ, you marry others.

Catharine But these men declare nothing is more holy than to disregard parents in this matter.

Eubulus Ask those doctors to show you some passage in sacred Scripture that teaches this. If they can't do so, tell them to go drink a cup of Beaune wine; that they *can* do. To flee from unrighteous parents to Christ is a sacred duty. But what sacred duty is it, pray, to flee from good parents to the monastic life, which often means from good to bad? And yet even in ancient times a man converted from paganism to Christ owed respect to his idolatrous parents so far as this was possible without damage to his religion.

Catharine Do you condemn the whole monastic life, then?

Eubulus By no means. But just as I wouldn't want to argue that a girl who entered this kind of life should try to get out of it, so I wouldn't hesitate to warn all girls, particularly the talented ones, against throwing themselves rashly into something there's no escape from afterwards; especially since in those very communities virginity is often in considerable danger, and since you could accomplish at home whatever is accomplished there.

Catharine Well, you ply me with many and mighty arguments, but on this subject my mind can't be changed.

Eubulus If I can't persuade you – as I'd like to do, though – remember this at least: that Eubulus warned you. Meanwhile, I pray by all my love for you that this longing of yours may prove luckier than my advice.

NOTES

1 A proverbial expression denoting disappointed hopes (cf Erasmus' *Adages*, 1.9.30).
2 Terence, *Andria*, 305
3 Cf 1 Cor. 6:12; 10:22–3.
4 A name coined by Erasmus
5 Sappho, a Greek poetess, is associated with lesbianism.
6 A reference to the fourth commandment: 'Honour thy father and mother.'
7 Eph. 6:1; Col. 3:20
8 In Latin the same word, *liberi*, means both 'children' and 'free.'
9 I.e., after taking the religious vows she wears the nuns' habit.
10 The Pharisees are associated with knowledge and strict adherence to the Old Testament laws. Paul represents New Testament law. The reference is to 1 Cor. 7:23.
11 According to the regulation of some orders. The Augustinian order, to which Erasmus himself belonged, wore wool on the inside, linen on the outside.
12 A reference to clandestine marriages. In a betrothal the words were in the future tense.

c) *The Repentant Girl*

This sequel to *The Girl with No Interest in Marriage* was first published in 1523. The setting of the dialogue is unclear. The presence of the drunken prior of the community (below 36) suggests that Catharine is still in the convent, the concluding lines indicate that she has returned to her home. In *The Usefulness of the Colloquies* Erasmus emphasizes that Catharine was 'not a girl who has abandoned the monastic life after taking vows, but one who has returned to her beloved parents before taking vows' (Thompson 629).

The translation is by Craig Thompson.

EUBULUS, CATHARINE

Eubulus Hope I'm always greeted by such door-keepers!

Catharine And I always by such callers.

Eubulus But farewell, Catharine.

Catharine What do I hear? Am I bid farewell before I am greeted?

Eubulus I didn't come here to see you cry. What's the meaning of this? Your eyes are filled with tears the instant they catch sight of me.

Catharine Why run off? Do stay here, I say; I'll put on another look and we'll be gay enough.

Eubulus What birds are these I see here?

Catharine He's prior of the community. Don't steal away, they've been boozing a long time already. Sit down for a little while. After he's gone we'll have a chat as we used to do.

Eubulus Well, I'll obey you – who wouldn't listen to me. Now we're by ourselves. Tell me the whole story, for I'd like to learn it from *you*.

Catharine Of the many friends I thought so very wise, there was none, I see now, who gave me more sensible, mature advice than you, the youngest of them all.

Eubulus Tell me, how did you overcome the opposition of your parents?

Catharine First, by the shameless insistence of the monks and nuns; next, my mother's resolution was undermined by my pleas and coaxings. My father absolutely refused to be budged. He didn't surrender, but finally, when all the siege guns were brought against him, he too was worn down and subdued. This was done over the wine. They threatened him with a bad end if he refused Christ his promised bride.

Eubulus The shamelessness of the brutes! Then what?

Catharine For three days I'm kept at home by myself. During that time some women from this convent – lay sisters, they're called – were always on hand, encouraging my resolve to stick to my holy purpose and taking good care I should not be visited by any friend or relative who seemed likely to change my mind. Meanwhile, clothes were being fitted and all preparations made for the feast.

Eubulus What frame of mind were you in while all this was going on? Weren't you wavering?

Catharine No, but something so awful happened to me that I'd rather die ten times than suffer it again.

Eubulus What was it, I beseech you?

Catharine I can't utter it.

Eubulus To tell me is to tell your friend.

Catharine Promise you'll keep quiet about it?

Eubulus I was going to see to that even if you hadn't made it a condition. As if you don't really know me yet!

Catharine A horrible-looking spectre appeared to me.

Eubulus Your evil genius, no doubt, who put you up to this.

Catharine In fact, I think it was a devil.

Eubulus Tell me, what did it look like? As they do in pictures – hooked beak, long horns, harpy's claws, very long tail?

Çatharine You're joking. But I'd rather have the earth swallow me up than see such a spectre again!

Eubulus Were those female inciters present at the time?

Catharine No, and I never let them know about it, though they inquired most persistently about the trouble when they found me in a dead faint.

Eubulus Do you want *me* to tell you what it was?

Catharine Yes, if you can.

Eubulus Those women had put a spell on you, or rather had charmed your wits away. But you stuck to your decision all the while?

Catharine Certainly, for they said this happens to many who vow themselves to Christ; but if the tempter is vanquished in that first encounter, all will be peaceful thereafter.

Eubulus What was the fanfare like when you were led forth?

Catharine They dress me in all my finery and let down my hair, exactly as though I'm about to be married –

Eubulus To a fat monk! (Damn this cough!)

Catharine I'm escorted in broad daylight from my home to the convent. Crowds of people rush up to see the show.

Eubulus Smart actors! They know how to put on their plays before the simple-minded rabble. How many days did you spend in this sacred society?

Catharine Nearly twelve.

Eubulus But what changed that stubborn mind of yours?

Catharine I won't say what, but something very important. Six days after my arrival I send for my mother, vowing and swearing that if she wants me to survive she must get me out of the convent. She refuses and urges me to be steadfast. After that I summon my father. He even scolds me, adding that he had with much difficulty mastered his feelings, that I in turn must now master my pride and not bring on him the disgrace of having backed out of the bargain. At last, when I see I'm making no progress, I reply to my parents that if they so command me, I'll die to please them, for that's bound to happen if I don't escape. After hearing this they took me home.

Eubulus It's well for you to back out quickly before committing yourself to perpetual servitude. But I've still to hear what changed your mind so suddenly.

Catharine Nobody has yet learned that from me, nor will you.

Eubulus What if I guess it?

Catharine You won't, I'm sure of that. And if you should, I wouldn't say so.

Eubulus All the same, I do guess it – but meantime a lot of money's been lost.

Catharine Over forty crowns.

Eubulus Those gluttonous wedding guests! But I'm glad you're safe and sound even if the money's gone. Next time listen to good advice.

Catharine So I will, and like the fisherman I'll know by sad experience.

3. Marriage: The Solution?

a) *Courtship*

This dialogue was added to the *Colloquies* in 1523. (On the publication history of the *Colloquies* see above 25.) Like *The Girl with No Interest in Marriage* it questions the superiority of celibacy to marriage and was criticized by Erasmus' detractors, not only for its recommendation of marriage but also for the suitor's perceived freedom of language. Erasmus denies that there is anything indecent in the young man's words. 'Would that all suitors were such as I picture here, and marriages contracted with no other conversations!' He notes that the young woman refuses the suitor a kiss. 'But what don't girls commonly grant suitors nowadays?' According to Erasmus, the colloquy deals with such issues as 'not rushing into marriage, the selection not only of bodies but much more of minds, the stability of marriage, not contracting a marriage without parental consent, keeping marriage pure, rearing children in a godly way ... Aren't these matters proper for young people to know?' (Thompson 628–9).

The translation is by Craig Thompson.

PAMPHILUS, MARIA

Pamphilus Hello, hello, and hello, you cruel, hard-hearted, unyielding creature!

Maria Hello yourself, Pamphilus, as often and as much as you like, and by whatever name you please. But sometimes I think you've forgotten my name. It's Maria.

Pamphilus Well, you should have been named Martia.

Maria Why so? What have I to do with Mars?

Pamphilus You slay men for sport, as the god does. Except that you're more pitiless than Mars: you kill even a lover.

Maria Mind what you're saying. Where's this heap of men I've slain? Where's the blood of the slaughtered?

Pamphilus You've only to look at me to see one lifeless corpse.

Maria What do I hear? You talk and walk when you're dead? I hope I never meet more fearsome ghosts!

Pamphilus You're joking, but all the same you're the death of poor me, and you kill more cruelly than if you pierced with a spear. Now, alas, I'm just skin and bones from long torture.

Maria Well, well! Tell me, how many pregnant women have miscarried at the sight of you?

Pamphilus But my pallor shows I've less blood than any ghost.

Maria Yet this pallor is streaked with lavender. You're as pale as a ripening cherry or a purple grape.

Pamphilus Shame on you for making fun of a miserable wretch!

Maria But if you don't believe me, bring a mirror.

Pamphilus I want no other mirror, nor do I think any could be brighter, than the one in which I'm looking at myself now.

Maria What mirror are you talking about?

Pamphilus Your eyes.

Maria Quibbler! Just like you. But how do you prove you're lifeless? Do ghosts eat?

Pamphilus Yes, but they eat insipid stuff, as I do.

Maria What do they eat, then?

Pamphilus Mallows, leeks, and lupins.

Maria But you don't abstain from capons and partridges.

Pamphilus True, but they taste no better to my palate than if I were eating mallows, or beets without pepper, wine, and vinegar.

Maria Poor you! Yet all the time you're putting on weight. And do dead men talk too?

Pamphilus Like me, in a very thin, squeaky voice.

Maria When I heard you wrangling with your rival not long ago, though, your voice wasn't so thin and squeaky. But I ask you, do ghosts even walk? Wear clothes? Sleep?

Pamphilus They even sleep together – though after their own fashion.

Maria Well! Witty fellow, aren't you?

Pamphilus But what will you say if I demonstrate with Achillean[1] proofs that I'm dead and you're a murderer?

Maria Perish the thought, Pamphilus! But proceed to your argument.

Pamphilus In the first place, you'll grant, I suppose, that death is nothing but the removal of soul from body?

Maria Granted.

Pamphilus But grant it so that you won't want to take back what you've given.

Maria I won't want to.

Pamphilus Then you won't deny that whoever robs another of his soul is a murderer.

Maria I allow it.

Pamphilus You'll concede also what's affirmed by the most respected authors and endorsed by the assent of so many ages: that man's soul is not where it animates but where it loves?

Maria Explain this more simply. I don't follow your meaning well enough.

Pamphilus And the worse for me that you don't see this as clearly as I do.

Maria Try to make me see it.

Pamphilus As well try to make adamant see!

Maria Well, I'm a girl, not a stone.

Pamphilus True, but harder than adamant.

Maria But get on with your argument.

Pamphilus Men seized by a divine inspiration neither hear nor see nor smell nor feel, even if you kill them.

Maria Yes, I've heard that.

Pamphilus What do you suppose is the reason?

Maria You tell me, professor.

Pamphilus Obviously because their spirit is in heaven, where it possesses what it ardently loves, and is absent from the body.

Maria What of it?

Pamphilus What of it, you unfeeling girl? It follows both that I'm dead and that you're the murderer.

Maria Where's your soul, then?

Pamphilus Where it loves.

Maria But who robbed you of your soul? – Why do you sigh? Speak freely; I won't hold it against you.

Pamphilus Cruellest of girls, whom nevertheless I can't hate even if I'm dead!

Maria Naturally. But why don't you in turn deprive her of *her* soul – tit for tat, as they say?

Pamphilus I'd like nothing better if the exchange could be such that her spirit migrated to my breast, as my spirit has gone over completely to her body.

Maria But may I, in turn, play the sophist with you?

Pamphilus The sophistress.

Maria It isn't possible for the same body to be living and lifeless, is it?

Pamphilus No, not at the same time.

Maria When the soul's gone, then the body's dead?

Pamphilus Yes.

Maria It doesn't animate except when it's present?

Pamphilus Exactly.

Maria Then how does it happen that although the soul's there where it loves, it nevertheless animates the body left behind? If it animates that body even when it loves elsewhere, how can the animated body be called lifeless?

Pamphilus You dispute cunningly enough, but you won't catch me with such snares. The soul that somehow or other governs the body of [a lover] is incorrectly called soul, since actually it consists of certain slight remnants of soul – just as the scent of roses remains in your hand even if the rose is taken away.

Maria Hard to catch a fox with a noose, I see. But answer me this: doesn't one who kills perform an act?

Pamphilus Of course.

Maria And the one who's killed suffers?

Pamphilus Yes indeed.

Maria Then how is it that although the lover is active and the beloved passive, the beloved is said to kill – when the lover, rather, kills himself?

Pamphilus On the contrary, it's the lover who suffers; the beloved does the deed.

Maria You'll never win this case before the supreme court of grammarians.

Pamphilus But I'll win it before the congress of logicians.

Maria Now don't begrudge an answer to this, too: do you love willingly or unwillingly?

Pamphilus Willingly.

Maria Then since one is free not to love, whoever loves seems to be a self-murderer. To blame the girl is unjust.

Pamphilus Yet the girl doesn't kill by being loved but by failing to return the love. Whoever can save someone and refrains from doing so is guilty of murder.

Maria Suppose a young man loves what is forbidden, for example, another man's wife or a vestal virgin? She won't return his love in order to save the lover, will she?

Pamphilus But *this* young man loves what it's lawful and right, and reasonable and honourable, to love; and yet he's slain. If this crime of murder is trivial, I'll bring a charge of poisoning too.

Maria Heaven forbid! Will you make a Circe[2] of me?

Pamphilus Something more pitiless than that. For I'd rather be a hog or a bear than what I am now, a lifeless thing.

Maria Well, just what sort of poison do I kill men with?

Pamphilus You charm them.

Maria Then you want me to keep my poisonous eyes off you hereafter?

Pamphilus Don't say such things. No, turn them on me more and more.

Maria If my eyes are charmers, why don't the other men I look at languish too? So I suspect this witchcraft is in your own eyes, not in mine.

Pamphilus Wasn't it enough to slay Pamphilus without mocking him besides?

Maria A handsome corpse! But when's the funeral?

Pamphilus Sooner than you think – unless you rescue me.

Maria Have I so much power?

Pamphilus You can bring a dead man back to life, and that with little trouble.

Maria If someone gave me a cure-all.

Pamphilus No need of medicines; just return his love. What could be easier or fairer? In no other way will you be acquitted of the crime of homicide.

Maria Before which court shall I be tried? That of the Areopagites?[3]

Pamphilus No, the court of Venus.

Maria She's an easygoing goddess, they say.

Pamphilus Oh, no, her wrath's the most terrible of all.

Maria Has she a thunderbolt?

Pamphilus No.

Maria A trident?

Pamphilus By no means.

Maria Has she a spear?

Pamphilus Not at all, but she's goddess of the sea.[4]

Maria I don't go sailing.

Pamphilus But she has a boy.[5]

Maria Not old enough to scare me.

Pamphilus He's vengeful and wilful.

Maria What will he do to me?

Pamphilus What will he do? Heaven avert it! I wouldn't want to predict calamity to one whose welfare I have at heart.

Maria Tell me anyway. I'm not superstitious.

Pamphilus Then I'll tell you. If you reject this lover – who, unless I'm mistaken, is not altogether unworthy of having his love returned – the boy may, at his mother's bidding, shoot you with a dreadfully poisonous dart. As a result you'd fall desperately in love with some low creature who wouldn't return your love.

Maria You tell me of a horrible punishment. For my part, I'd rather die than be madly in love with a man who's ugly or wouldn't return love for love.

Pamphilus Yet there was recently a much publicized example of this misfortune, involving a certain girl.

Maria Where?

Pamphilus At Orleans.

Maria How many years ago was this?

Pamphilus How many years? Scarcely ten months ago.

Maria What was the girl's name? Why do you hesitate?

Pamphilus Never mind. I know her as well as I do you.

Maria Why don't you tell me her name, then?

Pamphilus Because I don't like the omen. I only wish she'd had some other name! Hers was the very same as yours.

Maria Who was her father?

Pamphilus He's still living. Eminent lawyer and well-to-do.

Maria Give me his name.

Pamphilus Maurice.

Maria Family name?

Pamphilus Bright.[6]

Maria Is the mother living?

Pamphilus Died recently.

Maria What illness did she die of?

Pamphilus What illness, you ask? Grief. And the father, though one of the hardiest of men, was in mortal danger.

Maria May one know the mother's name too?

Pamphilus Of course. Everybody knew Sophronia. But why this questioning? Do you think I'm spinning some yarn?

Maria Would I suspect that of *you*? More commonly this suspicion is directed against our sex. But tell me what happened to the girl.

Pamphilus She was a girl of respectable, wealthy background, as I said, and extremely beautiful; in short, worthy to marry a prince. She was courted by a certain young man whose social standing was similar to hers.

Maria What was his name?

Pamphilus Alas, a bad omen for me! Pamphilus was his name too. He tried everything, but she obstinately turned him down. The young man wasted away with sorrow. Not long afterwards she fell desperately in love with one who was more like an ape than a man.

Maria What's that you say?

Pamphilus So madly in love it's inexpressible.

Maria So attractive a girl in love with so hideous a man?

Pamphilus He had a peaked head, thin hair – and that torn and unkempt, full of scurf and lice. The mange had laid bare most of his scalp; he was cross-eyed, had flat, wide-open nostrils like an ape's, thin mouth, rotten teeth, a stuttering tongue, pocky chin; he was hunchbacked, potbellied, and had crooked shanks.

Maria You describe some Thersites[7] to me.

Pamphilus What's more, they said he had only one ear.

Maria Perhaps he lost the other in war.

Pamphilus Oh, no, in peace.

Maria Who dared do that to him?

Pamphilus Denis the hangman.[8]

Maria Maybe a large family fortune made up for his ugliness.

Pamphilus Not at all; he was bankrupt and head over heels in debt. With this husband, so exceptional a girl now spends her life and is often beaten.

Maria A wretched tale you tell.

Pamphilus But a true one. Thus it pleased Nemesis to avenge the injury to the youth who was spurned.

Maria I'd rather be destroyed by a thunderbolt than put up with such a husband.

Pamphilus Then don't provoke Nemesis: return your lover's love.

Maria If that's enough. I do return it.

Pamphilus But I'd want this love to be lasting and to be mine alone. I'm courting a wife, not a mistress.

Maria I know that, but I must deliberate a long time over what can't be revoked once it's begun.

Pamphilus *I've* thought it over a very long time.

Maria See that love, who's not the best adviser, doesn't trick you. For they say he's blind.

Pamphilus But one who proceeds with caution is keen-sighted. You don't appear to me as you do because I love you; I love you because I've observed what you're like.

Maria But you may not know me well enough. If you wore the shoe, you'd feel then where it pinched.

Pamphilus I'll have to take the chance; though I infer from many signs that the match will succeed.

Maria You're a soothsayer too?

Pamphilus I am.

Maria Then by what auguries do you infer this? Has the night owl flown?[9]

Pamphilus That flies for fools.

Maria Has a pair of doves flown from the right?[10]

Pamphilus Nothing of the sort. But the integrity of your parents has been known to me for years now. In the first place, good birth is far from a bad sign. Nor am I unaware of the wholesome instruction and godly examples by which you've been reared; and good education is better than good birth. That's another sign. In addition, between my family – not an altogether contemptible one, I believe – and yours there has long been intimate friendship. In fact, you and I have known each other from our cradle days, as they say, and our temperaments are pretty much the same. We're nearly equal in age; our parents, in wealth, reputation, and rank. Finally – and this is the special mark of friendship, since excellence by itself is no guarantee of compatibility – your tastes seem to fit my temperament not at all badly. How mine agree with yours, I don't know.

Obviously, darling, these omens assure me that we shall have a blessed, lasting, happy marriage, provided you don't intend to sing a song of woe for our prospects.

Maria What song do you want?

Pamphilus I'll play 'I am yours'; you chime in with 'I am yours.'

Maria A short song, all right, but it has a long finale.

Pamphilus What matter how long, if only it be joyful?

Maria I'm so prejudiced about you that I wouldn't want you to do something you might be sorry for afterwards.

Pamphilus Stop looking on the dark side.

Maria Maybe I'll seem different to you when illness or old age has changed this beauty.

Pamphilus Neither will I always be as handsome as I am now, my dear. But I don't consider only this dwelling place, which is blooming and charming in every respect. I love the guest more.

Maria What guest?

Pamphilus Your mind, whose beauty will forever increase with age.

Maria Truly you're more than a Lynceus[11] if you see through so much make-up!

Pamphilus I see your thought through mine. Besides, we'll renew our youth repeatedly in our children.

Maria But meantime my virginity is gone.

Pamphilus True, but see here: if you had a fine orchard, would you want it never to bear anything but blossoms or would you prefer, after the blossoms have fallen, to see the trees heavy with ripe fruit?

Maria How he prattles!

Pamphilus Answer this at least: which is the prettier sight, a vine rotting on the ground or encircling some post or elm tree and weighing it down with purple grapes?

Maria *You* answer *me* in turn: which is the more pleasing sight, a rose gleaming white on its bush or plucked and gradually withering?

Pamphilus In my opinion the rose that withers in a man's hand, delighting his eyes and nostrils the while, is luckier than one that grows old on a bush. For that one too would wither sooner or later. In the same way, wine is better if drunk before it sours. But a girl's flower doesn't fade the instant she marries. On the contrary, I see many girls who before marriage were pale, run-down, and as good as gone. The sexual side of marriage brightened them so much that they began to bloom at last.

Maria Yet virginity wins universal approval and applause.

Pamphilus A maiden is something charming, but what's more unnatural than an old maid? Unless your mother had been deflowered, we wouldn't have this blossom here. But if, as I hope, our marriage will not be barren, we'll pay for one virgin with many.

Maria But they say chastity is a thing most pleasing to God.

Pamphilus And therefore I want to marry a chaste girl, to live chastely with her. It will be more a marriage of minds than of bodies. We'll reproduce for the state; we'll reproduce for Christ. By how little will this marriage fall short of virginity! And perhaps some day we'll live as

Joseph and Mary did. But meantime we'll learn virginity; for one does not reach the summit all at once.

Maria What's this I hear? Virginity to be violated in order to be learned?

Pamphilus Why not? As by gradually drinking less and less wine we learn temperance. Which seems more temperate to you, the person who, sitting down in the midst of dainties, abstains from them or the one secluded from those things that invite intemperance?

Maria I think the man abundance cannot corrupt is more steadfastly temperate.

Pamphilus Which more truly deserves praise for chastity, the man who castrates himself or the one who, while sexually unimpaired, nevertheless abstains from sexual love?

Maria My vote would go to the latter. The first I'd regard as mad.

Pamphilus But don't those who renounce marriage by a strict vow castrate themselves, in a sense?

Maria Apparently.

Pamphilus Now to abstain from sexual intercourse isn't a virtue.

Maria Isn't it?

Pamphilus Look at it this way. If it were a virtue *per se* not to have intercourse, intercourse would be a vice. Now it happens that it is a vice not to have intercourse, a virtue to have it.

Maria When does this 'happen'?

Pamphilus Whenever the husband seeks his due from his wife, especially if he seeks her embrace from a desire for children.

Maria What if from lust? Isn't it right for him to be denied?

Pamphilus It's right to reprove him, or rather to ask him politely to refrain. It's not right to refuse him flatly – though in this respect I hear few husbands complain of their wives.

Maria But liberty is sweet.

Pamphilus Virginity, on the other hand, is a heavy burden. I'll be your king, you'll be my queen; we'll rule a family at our pleasure. Or does this seem servitude to you?

Maria The public calls marriage a halter.

Pamphilus But those who call it that really deserve a halter themselves. Tell me, I beg you, isn't your soul bound to your body?

Maria Evidently.

Pamphilus Like a little bird in a cage. And yet ask him if he desires to be free. He'll say no, I think. Why? Because he's willingly confined.

Maria Our fortune is modest.

Pamphilus So much the safer. You'll increase it at home by thrift, which is not unreasonably called a large source of income; I'll increase it away from home by my industry.

Maria Children bring countless cares with them.

Pamphilus But they bring countless delights and often repay the parents' devotion with interest many times over.

Maria Loss of children is a miserable experience.

Pamphilus Aren't you childless now? But why expect the worst in every uncertainty? Tell me, which would you prefer, never to be born or to be born to die?

Maria I'd rather be born to die, of course.

Pamphilus As those who have lived are more fortunate than those who never were born and never will be born, so is childlessness the more miserable in never having had and never expecting to have offspring.

Maria Who are these who are not and will not be?

Pamphilus Though one who refuses to run the risk of human life – to which all of us, kings and commoners alike, are equally liable – ought to give up life, still, whatever happens, you'll bear only half. I'll take over the larger share, so that if we have good luck the pleasure will be double; if bad, companionship will take away half the pain. As for me, if heaven summons, it will be sweet to die in your arms.

Maria Men bear more readily what nature's universal laws decree. But I observe how much more distressed some parents are by their children's conduct than by their death.

Pamphilus Preventing that is mostly up to us.

Maria How so?

Pamphilus Because, with respect to character, good children are usually born of good parents. Kites don't come from doves. We'll try, therefore, to be good ourselves. Next, we'll see that our children are imbued from birth with sacred teachings and beliefs. What the jar is filled with when new matters most. In addition, we'll see that at home we provide an example of life for them to imitate.

Maria What you describe is difficult.

Pamphilus No wonder, because it's lovely.[13] (And you're difficult too, for the same reason!) But we'll labour so much the harder to this end.

Maria You'll have tractable material to work with. See that you form and fashion me.

Pamphilus But meanwhile say just three words.[13]

Maria Nothing easier, but once words have flown out they don't fly back. I'll give better advice for us both: confer with your parents and mine, to get the consent of both sides.

Pamphilus You bid me woo, but in three words you can make success certain.

Maria I don't know whether I could. I'm not a free agent. In former times marriages were arranged only by the authority of elders. But however that may be, I think our marriage will have more chance of success if it's arranged by our parents' authority. And it's your part to woo; that isn't appropriate to our sex. We girls like to be swept off our feet, even if sometimes we're deeply in love.

Pamphilus I won't be backward in wooing. Only don't let your decision alone defeat me.

Maria It won't. Cheer up, Pamphilus dear!

Pamphilus You're more strait-laced towards me in this business than I should like.

Maria But first ponder your own private decision. Judge by your reason, not your feeling. What emotion decides is temporary; rational choice generally pleases forever.

Pamphilus Indeed you philosophize very well, so I'm resolved to take your advice.

Maria You won't regret it. But see here: a disturbing difficulty has turned up.

Pamphilus Away with these difficulties!

Maria You wouldn't want me to marry a dead man?

Pamphilus By no means; but I'll revive.

Maria You've removed the difficulty. Farewell, Pamphilus darling.

Pamphilus That's up to you.

Maria I bid you good night. Why do you sigh?

Pamphilus 'Good night,' you say? If only you'd grant what you bid!

Maria Don't be in too great a hurry. You're counting chickens before they're hatched.

Pamphilus Shan't I have anything from you to take with me?

Maria This sachet, to gladden your heart.

Pamphilus Add a kiss at least.

Maria I want to deliver to you a virginity whole and unblemished.

Pamphilus Does a kiss rob you of your virginity?

Maria Then do you want me to bestow my kisses on others too?

Pamphilus Of course not. I want your kisses kept for me.

Maria I'll keep them for you. Though there's another reason why I wouldn't dare give away kisses just now.

Pamphilus What's that?

Maria You say your soul has passed almost entirely into my body and that there's only the slightest particle left in yours. Consequently, I'm afraid this particle in you would skip over to me in a kiss and you'd then become quite lifeless. So shake hands, a symbol of our mutual love; and farewell. Persevere in your efforts. Meanwhile I'll pray Christ to bless and prosper us both in what we do.

NOTES

1 I.e., cogent proofs. The expression is proverbial; see Erasmus' *Adages*, 1.7.41.
2 The Homeric sorceress
3 A court in ancient Greece that dealt with murder cases. The severity of the judges was proverbial.
4 In ancient mythology Venus is said to have been born of the sea. The thunderbolt, the trident, and the spear are attributes of the ancient gods Jupiter, Neptune, and Athene.
5 Cupid
6 The name in the original is *Aglaius*, which means 'bright.' We do not know who is hiding behind this pseudonym.
7 A Homeric character, proverbial for his ugliness
8 Perhaps a reference to the ancient tyrant Dionysius
9 Considered a good omen by the ancient Athenians
10 Doves are the proverbial love birds.
11 A mythological figure, proverbial for his keen sight
12 According to an ancient proverb, 'what is beautiful is difficult' (see Plato, *Hipp. Maior*, 304 E).
13 'I am yours.'

b) *The Young Man and the Harlot*

This dialogue was first published in the 1523 edition of the *Colloquies* (for the publication history of the work see 25). The plot line used here is familiar from a narrative in the medieval *Lives of the Fathers*, which tells of the conversion of the Greek courtesan Thaïs by the hermit Paphnutius. The story also appears in the medieval *Golden Legend* and was adapted in the tenth century by the nun Hrotsvitha of Gandersheim. Erasmus was probably familiar with all of these sources.

The translation is by Craig Thompson.

LUCRETIA, SOPHRONIUS

Lucretia Welcome, Sophronius darling! Back to us at last? Seems to me you've been gone an age. I scarcely knew you at first.

Sophronius Why so, my dear Lucretia?

Lucretia Because you've come back with a bit of beard you didn't use to have. What's the matter, sweetheart? You look gloomier than usual.

Sophronius I want to have a talk with you – in private.

Lucretia Oh, aren't we alone, my cocky?[1]

Sophronius Let's withdraw to a more secret place.

Lucretia All right, let's go into the inner bedroom if you like.

Sophronius This place doesn't yet seem secret enough for me.

Lucretia How come you're so bashful all of a sudden? Here's my private dressing room; it's so dark we'll hardly be able to see each other.

Sophronius Examine every crack.

Lucretia There's not a single crack.

Sophronius Nobody close by who might overhear us?

Lucretia Not even a fly, dearie. What are you waiting for?

Sophronius Shall we escape God's notice here?

Lucretia Of course not: he sees through everything.

Sophronius And the angels' notice?

Lucretia Impossible to keep out of their sight.

Sophronius Then how is it that men aren't ashamed to do in the sight of God and in the presence of the holy angels what they would be ashamed to do before men?

Lucretia What's got into you? Have you come here to preach to me? Put on a Franciscan cowl, get up into a pulpit, and let's hear you, my bearded lad.

Sophronius I wouldn't object to doing just that if I could reclaim you from this sort of life. It's not only the most shameful but the most miserable kind as well.

Lucretia Why so, love? I must have some source of income. Everybody lives by his profession. This is my work, my livelihood.

Sophronius I'd like to have a talk with you on this very subject, my Lucretia, after you've calmed down a little.

Lucretia Save your sermon for another occasion. Let's enjoy ourselves now, Sophronius dear.

Sophronius Whatever you do, you do for money.

Lucretia You're not far wrong!

Sophronius You won't lose money: I'll pay you four times the usual sum if you'll only listen to me.

Lucretia Say what you please.

Sophronius First answer me this: have you any enemies?

Lucretia Not one.

Sophronius And are there, on the other hand, any women *you* hate?

Lucretia In so far as they deserve it.

Sophronius Then if you could do them a favour, would you do it?

Lucretia I'd rather mix poison for them!

Sophronius But think now whether you could do anything that would give them greater pleasure than to see you living this most disgraceful and wretched life. And what could you have done more grievous to those who wish you well?

Lucretia It was my fate.

Sophronius What is, as a rule, the hardest thing of all for persons deported to islands or banished to the wildest frontiers of the earth, you've chosen of your own free will.

Lucretia What's that?

Sophronius Haven't you voluntarily renounced all ties – father, mother, brothers, sisters, paternal and maternal aunts, and others to whom nature has bound you? For they're ashamed of you, and you can't bear to come within sight of them.

Lucretia Oh, no, I've exchanged my loved ones, to my profit, for instead of a few I now have many – of whom you're one. I've always looked upon you as a brother.

Sophronius Quit joking and treat the subject seriously, as it deserves. A girl with so many friends has no friend at all, Lucretia, believe me. Those who resort to you treat you not as a friend but rather as an object of contempt. See how low you've fallen, you wretched creature! Christ held you so dear that he redeemed you with his own blood, so dear that

he wanted you to share the heavenly inheritance; and you make yourself
a public sewer that every Tom, Dick, and Harry – the dirty, the vile, the
diseased – resorts to and empties his filth into. If you haven't yet caught
the new contagion called the Spanish pox,[2] you can't long escape it. If
you do get it, you'll be the most miserable creature alive, even if you
prosper in every other respect, even if you have fame and fortune. What
will you be but a living corpse? You used to think obeying your mother
burdensome; now you're at the beck and call of an utterly repulsive
bawd. You were fed up with parental reproofs; here you must often
endure beatings by drunken, maddened whoremongers. To do some of
the housework at home in return for bed and board disgusted you; here
what commotions, what late hours you put up with!

Lucretia Where has this new preacher come from?

Sophronius Now think it over. This bloom of beauty that draws lovers
to you will soon fade. What a pitiable sight you'll be then! What dung
heap will be more contemptible than you? You'll change from whore to
bawd, a distinction that doesn't fall to everyone. And if it does come,
what is there more wicked or more closely tied to devilish spitefulness?

Lucretia Almost everything you say is true, my Sophronius. But where
did you pick up this newfangled holiness? Generally you're the wildest
playboy of them all. Nobody used to come here oftener or at more
inconvenient times than you did. You've been in Rome, I hear.

Sophronius I have.

Lucretia But ordinarily people return from there worse than they
went.[3] How come it happened otherwise for you?

Sophronius I'll tell you: because I didn't go to Rome for the same
reason or in the same fashion. Others commonly go to Rome intending
to return worse – and abundant opportunities for that purpose are at
hand there. I set out with an honest man by whose urging I took a book
along instead of a flask: the New Testament, translated by Erasmus.[4]

Lucretia Erasmus? He's more than heretic they say.

Sophronius You don't mean that man's reputation has reached even
this place?

Lucretia No name is better known to us.

Sophronius Have you seen him?

Lucretia Never, but I'd like very much to see the person I've heard so
many bad reports of.

Sophronius From bad men, perhaps.

Lucretia Oh, no: from reverend gentlemen.

Sophronius Which ones?

Lucretia I'm not free to tell.

Sophronius Why?

Lucretia Because if you blabbed about it and the news reached their ears, a sizable share of my income would be gone.

Sophronius Have no fear: You are telling it to a stone.

Lucretia Let me whisper it.

Sophronius Silly, why do you have to whisper when we're alone? So God won't overhear? – Good heavens, you're a pious whore, I see; you give alms to the mendicants!

Lucretia But I make more profit from these mendicants than from you rich men.

Sophronius They rob honest matrons in order to throw their money on villainous whores.

Lucretia But go on about the book.

Sophronius I will; and so much the better. In it Paul, who doesn't know how to lie, taught me that neither whores nor whoremongers shall inherit the kingdom of heaven.[5] After reading this I began to reflect: 'The estate I expect to inherit from my father is a modest one, yet I'd rather renounce all whores than be disinherited by him. How much more care should I take lest my heavenly Father disinherit me! Against a father who disinherits or disowns, human laws offer some protection; against the God who disinherits, there is no remedy.' So straightway I made it a rule to have nothing to do with whores.

Lucretia If you could contain, that is.

Sophronius A large part of continence is the will to be continent. As a last resort one can marry. At Rome I poured out the whole Augean stable[6] of my sins into the bosom of a confessor. He exhorted me, wisely and with many words, to purity of mind and body, the reading of Scripture, frequent prayers, sobriety of life. The only penance he imposed was that I should kneel at the high altar and recite the psalm *Miserere mei, Deus;*[7] and, if I had the money, give a florin to some needy person. When I expressed surprise that he inflicted so light a penance for so much whoring, he replied good-humouredly, 'Son, if you truly repent and change your way of life, I don't care much about penance. But if you persist, lust itself will, in the end, exact more than enough penance from you, even if a priest does

not impose it. Look at me: blear-eyed, palsied, stooped. Yet I was
once such as you say you've been up to now, so I've had a taste
of it.'

Lucretia Then I've lost my Sophronius, I see.

Sophronius No, on the contrary, you've gained him. Before, he was
ruined; he was neither his own friend nor yours. Now he truly loves
you and longs for your salvation.

Lucretia Then what do you advise, Sophronius dear?

Sophronius First of all, that you abandon this life. You're still a girl:
your stain can be washed away. Or get married. I'll contribute something
towards the dowry. Or enter some religious house for fallen women,
or move to a different place and put yourself into the family of some
respectable housewife. I offer you my help for whichever of these you
choose.

Lucretia I'll love you for it, Sophronius. Look out for me; I'll follow
your advice.

Sophronius But meantime get away from here.

Lucretia What, so quickly?

Sophronius Why not today rather than tomorrow, if postponement
means loss, and delay danger?

Lucretia Where am I to go?

Sophronius Collect all your belongings and give them to me this
evening. A servant will take them secretly to some reliable woman.
Sometime later I'll take you out, as though for a walk. You'll hide at the
woman's place at my expense until I make arrangements for you, as I
soon will.

Lucretia Well, Sophronius, I trust myself entirely to you.

Sophronius Some day you'll be glad you did.

NOTES

1 The harlot uses the Latin word for penis.
2 Syphilis
3 Luther described Rome as the 'Babylonian whore.'
4 I.e., his edition of the New Testament (Basel 1516), which aroused a great
   deal of controversy. A number of passages from Erasmus' annotations on
   the text were declared heretical by the Faculty of Theology at Paris. All of his
   works were placed in the Index of Prohibited Books in 1559.

5 Eph. 5:5
6 Proverbial, one of the Herculean labours
7 Ps. 50:1

c) A Letter of Persuasion: *In Praise of Marriage*

This text, which served as a sample of a persuasive letter in a letter-writing manual, was first published as a declamation under the title *In Praise of Marriage* (1518). At the time Erasmus claimed that he had written the piece some twenty years earlier for the amusement of his English pupil and later patron Lord Mountjoy. The work was sharply criticized by theologians as a veiled attack on celibacy. Erasmus responded with an *Apologia for the Declamation on Marriage* (1519), in which he declared that the work did not represent the opinions of the author since it was a rhetorical exercise. In the letter-writing manual it was accordingly counterbalanced by a dissuasive letter arguing the opposite point of view. In any case, Erasmus said, 'the marriage I praise is very similar to virginity, a marriage in which one has a wife for the production of offspring, not the satisfaction of lust' (CWE 71:93). He furthermore argued that preferring marriage to celibacy might be regarded an error by some people, but it certainly was not heresy. In spite of his protestations, however, the controversy continued. The work was formally condemned by the theologians of Paris. Louis de Berquin, who translated it into French in 1525, was likewise condemned and executed for heresy in 1529.

The translation is by Charles Fantazzi.

47 / An example of a letter of persuasion

Although in your exceptional wisdom, my beloved kinsman, you are wise enough of yourself and need no counsel from others, yet I thought I owed it to our long friendship, which, beginning almost from the cradle, has grown though the years, and to your great kindness to me, and lastly to our very close relationship, that I should give you willing and frank advice in matters that I judged to be of great importance for the honour and welfare of you and your family, if indeed I wished to be the grateful and appreciative friend you have always considered me to be. There are times when we perceive others' interests better than our own. I have very often followed your advice in my affairs and have found out that it was as fruitful as it was friendly. Now if you in turn are willing to follow mine in your own affairs, I think that in the outcome I shall not be sorry for having given the advice nor you for having followed it.

On 8 April, when I was at my house in the mountains, Antonius Baldus, who as you know has your interests very much at heart and who has from the first been intimately connected with your family, had dinner with me. It was a joyless and tearful repast. He told me to our great mutual sorrow that your mother, a woman of great virtue, had departed this life; that your sister, overcome with grief and loneliness, had joined a group of women vowed to virginity, and that consequently the hope of prolonging your line had fallen upon you alone. He also informed me that your friends were of one accord in recommending to you, with the offer of a large dowry, a girl of noble birth, exceptional beauty, and excellent character, and who was very much in love with you, but that you, whether from inability to master your grief or from religious scruples, were so set on remaining celibate that neither devotion to your family, nor desire for offspring, nor the advice, prayers, and tears of your friends could induce you to abandon your resolve.

Nevertheless, perhaps on my advice you will change your mind and renounce the single state, a barren way of life hardly becoming to a man, and surrender yourself to holy wedlock. I do not wish in this exhortation to use to my advantage the dearness of your family, which for that matter should have prevailed over your feelings, or my own influence, but I shall show by the clearest of proofs that this alternative would be far more honourable, profitable, and pleasant for you, and, one might add, necessary even in this day and age.

First of all, if you are moved by considerations of honour, which should be a matter of primary importance among men of upright life, what is more honourable than marriage, which was honoured by Christ himself, who not only thought it fit to be present at a wedding together with his mother, but also sanctified the wedding feast with the first fruits of his miracles? What could be holier than that which the father of all creation founded, enjoined, and sanctified, and which nature herself consecrated? What is more worthy of praise, when those who find fault with it are condemned for heresy? Marriage is as honourable as the name of heretic is infamous. What is more just than to return to posterity what we ourselves have received from our forebears? What is more ill-advised than in the pursuit of sanctity to shun as unholy what God himself, the source and father of all holiness, wished to be held most holy? What is more inhuman than to shrink from the laws of the human condition? What is more ungrateful than to deny to one's descendants that which you would not be able to deny if you had not received it from your ancestors?

If we seek the author of marriage, we discover that it was founded and instituted not by Lycurgus, or Moses, or Solon,[1] but by the sovereign maker of all things, and from the same it received praise, and by the same it was made honourable and holy. In the beginning, when he created man out of clay, God realized that man's life would be thoroughly unhappy and unpleasant unless he joined Eve to him as a companion. Therefore he did not bring man's wife out of the clay from which he had brought man, but out of Adam's ribs, so that we might clearly understand that nothing should be dearer to us, nothing more closely joined, nothing more tightly glued to us than a wife.

After the flood, when God was reconciled to the race of mortals, he proclaimed, as we read, as his first law, not that they should embrace celibacy, but that they should 'increase and multiply and replenish the earth.' But how could they, unless they gave thought to wedlock? And without adducing the freedom of the Mosaic law or the necessity of those times as a reason, what other meaning can be attributed to the approval of Christ repeated and confirmed in the gospel writings? 'For this cause,' he says, 'shall a man leave father and mother and cleave to his wife.' What is more holy than loyalty to one's parents? Yet conjugal fidelity is preferred to this. On whose authority? On God's authority, to be sure. At what time? Not only in the time of Judaism but also during the Christian era.

Father and mother must be abandoned, and one must cleave to one's wife. A son set free begins to be his own master. A son disowned ceases to be a son. But death alone dissolves wedlock, if indeed it does dissolve it. It is only dissolved in the case of those who seek another marriage. As long as wedded love persists, the marriage is not considered to be dissolved.

Now if the other sacraments, which are the chief support of the church of Christ, are observed with scrupulous respect, who cannot see that much reverence is due this one, which was instituted by God before all the others? The rest were instituted upon earth, but this in paradise; the rest for a remedy, this for partnership in happiness. The rest were provided for fallen nature, this alone was granted for its preservation. If we hold as sacrosanct laws passed by mortals, will not the law of wedlock have the most sanctity of all, because we have received it from the giver of life, and because it alone came into existence almost simultaneously with the human race itself?

Finally, to strengthen the law by example, when Christ was invited as a young man to a marriage feast (as was mentioned above), he attended willingly with his mother; and not only did he attend, but he honoured it by an extraordinary favour, choosing no other occasion to inaugurate his miracles. 'Why then,' you will say, 'did Christ himself abstain from wedlock?' As if indeed there were not very many aspects of Christ's life that should excite our wonder rather than our imitation. He was born without a father, was given birth without pain to his mother, and came forth from a sealed sepulchre.

What is there in him that is not above nature? Such attributes belong to him alone. Let us who live under the law of nature look up to those things that are above nature, but emulate what is within our capacity.

'But he chose to be born of a virgin.' Yes, of a virgin, but a married virgin. A virgin mother befitted God; the fact that she was married signified the path we should follow. The state of virginity befitted the woman who by the inspiration of the heavenly spirit was to bear, herself immaculate, an immaculate child. Yet Joseph, her spouse, commends to us the laws of chaste wedlock. How could Christ have better commended the union of wedlock than through the mystery of that joining, stupendous even to angelic minds, of divine nature with a human body and soul; or in declaring his amazing and undying love for his church, what greater commendation than to call himself its husband and the church his bride? 'Marriage is a great sacrament,'[3] says Paul, 'in Christ and the church.' If there had been any holier bond in the universe, any stricter compact than wedlock, he would certainly have taken his illustration from that. What do we read like this concerning celibacy anywhere in the sacred writings? Wedlock is called honourable, and the marriage bed undefiled by the apostle Paul,[4] but celibacy is never even named there. Nor is it excused except by the compensation of a greater good. In all other respects one who follows the law of nature and procreates children is to be preferred to one who perseveres in the single state simply in order to have a more independent life. We read that men who are truly chaste and virgins are praised, but celibacy in itself receives no praise. Now the law of Moses curses barren wedlock,[5] and we read that some were excluded from the public altars on this account. For what reason then? Simply because like useless drones living for themselves they increased the race by no offspring. In Deuteronomy it is set forth as the greatest proof of God's blessing for the Israelites that no one among them would be barren, neither male nor female. Leah[6] is said to have been despised by her lord for not bearing children. Moreover in the Psalms[7] a wife's fruitfulness is included among the principal portions of blessedness. 'Your wife,' says the psalmist, 'is like a fruitful vine, your sons are like olive shoots round your table.' But if the law condemns and stigmatizes a barren marriage, it has condemned the unmarried much more severely. If nature is not exempt from penalty, still less will personal inclination escape it. If those whose goodwill has been thwarted by nature are subject to condemnation, what do those deserve who have made no efforts to avoid sterility?

The laws of the Hebrews[8] awarded this privilege to marriage, that one who had taken a bride would not be compelled to go to war that same year. The state is in danger unless there are those to protect it by force of arms, but its destruction is assured unless there are those who through the benefit of wedlock make up for the loss of young manhood diminished by death. Roman laws also inflicted a penalty upon those who were unmarried, and excluded them from the offices of the state.[9] But those who had enriched the state with children were decreed a reward from public funds as having served it well. Proof of this is the law of three children,[10] not to mention others.

The early laws imposed penalties on the unmarried, which, though modified by the emperor Constantine[11] in deference to the Christian religion, still prove how detrimental it was to the republic that the state either be reduced in numbers through the desire for the single life or be populated with bastards. Moreover, Augustus as censor[12] took proceedings against a soldier on the grounds that he had disobeyed the laws in taking a wife, and his life would have been in danger had he not shown that he was the father of three children. The laws of the Caesars show favour towards the married state by the fact that they abolished the imposition of widowhood introduced by Miscella,[13] and, removing all penalties, declared that agreements of this kind should be considered null and void because they had been entered into contrary to justice and equity. There is in addition the statement of Ulpian[14] that dowry suits were always and everywhere awarded unique status, which would not have been so if there were no special advantages inherent in the state of matrimony. Wedlock was held in honour but fertility even more so. As soon as one acquired the name of father, he was made eligible for inheritance and every bequest, even one that had been rendered void, as is evident from the words of the satirist:[15] 'Through me you may become an heir / To all bequests, e'en those that fall by escheat.' The three children's privilege brought more advantages, including exemption from serving on public missions. Five children secured exemption from personal obligations as well, such as guardianship. To those who had thirteen children the emperor Julian granted exemption not only from serving as decurion,[16] but from any duties whatsoever. The wisest legislators make no secret of the reason for such great favour. What is more blessed than immortality? This gift, denied by nature, is bestowed artificially on the state by marriage as far as it lies in its power. Who does not wish to be remembered by posterity? No arches, pyramids, or inscriptions prolong our memory more surely than does the begetting of children. Albinus[17] won his case before the emperor Hadrian with nothing else in his favour except that he had bequeathed numerous offspring to his country. For this reason the emperor, at the expense of the public treasury, allowed the children to inherit their father's property in its entirety, because he perceived that the empire received greater support from the begetting of children than from the accretion of money. Finally, other laws are not suited to all places and all times; the law of wedlock alone concerns all nations in the world for all time.

Lycurgus[18] passed laws that those who did not take wives should be excluded in summer from games and public shows, and in winter should go about the forum without clothing, and admit with curses upon their own heads that they were suffering a just penalty for not obeying the laws.

If you now want to know the value placed on marriage by the ancients, consider the penalty for a violated marriage. The Greeks once decreed that the violation of the rights of marriage had to be vindicated by a ten years' war. In addition, not only Roman law but the laws of the Hebrews[19] and the barbarian nations prescribed capital punishment for adulterers. A thief was penalized by a fourfold repayment; an adulterer's crime was expiated by execution. Among the Hebrews stoning at the hands of the people was the fate of one who violated the institution without which the people would no longer exist. Not content with this, the severity of the laws allowed for an adulterer caught *in flagrante* to be stabbed to death without trial and without legal rights, evidently according to a husband's indignation what it grants only reluctantly to a man defending his own life from danger, which shows that the taking away of a wife was viewed as a more grievous wrong than the taking of a life. Certainly wedlock must be considered an institution of the greatest sanctity if its violation must be expiated by human blood, and the avenging of it need not await laws or judgment, a right that does not exist even in the case of parricide.

Yet why be concerned with written laws? This is the law of nature, not inscribed on any bronze tablets, but deeply implanted in our minds; if anyone does not obey it, he should not even be considered human, much less a good citizen. For if, as the Stoics, the most perceptive of philosophers, maintain, to live rightly is to follow the instigations of nature, what is so consistent with nature as marriage? For nothing has been so firmly implanted by nature, not only in mankind but in all living things, as the instinct in each of them to preserve its own species from destruction and render it in some way immortal by the propagation of offspring. Everyone must know that this cannot come about without the bond of wedlock.

It seems all the more shameful that dumb herds should obey nature's laws, but men, like the giants, should declare war upon nature. If we look at creation with eyes that are not blinded, we shall understand that nature intended that there should be some kind of marital union in all species. I shall say nothing about trees, in which on the sure authority of Pliny[20] sexual union is found with a clear distinction of sex, particularly in palm trees,[21] so that unless the male tree rests the weight of its branches upon the female trees around it as if with the urge for intercourse these will certainly remain barren. The same writer points out that there are authorities who believe that there is a male and female sex in everything the earth produces. I say nothing about precious stones, in which the same author says sex is to be found, and he is not alone. Has not God linked all things by certain ties so that they seem to need each other? What of the heavens turning with continual motion? Does it not play the part of a husband as it fructifies the earth, parent of all things, beneath it, making it produce every manner of thing by the infusion of its seed?

But it would take too long to run through every detail. What is the point of all this? Simply to have you understand that all things exist and are bound together in the association of wedlock; that without this they all dissolve, perish, and fall away. The tale is devised by those wise poets of antiquity, who took pains to clothe the teaching of philosophy in the wrappings of fable, that giants,[22] the serpent-footed sons of earth, piled up mountains to the sky and waged war with the gods. What is the meaning of this story? Evidently it signifies that some monstrous, savage, and uncivilized men felt a great loathing for the harmony of wedlock, and for this were hurled down by a thunderbolt, that is, they perished utterly, since they shunned the sole means of preserving the human race. The same poets record that Orpheus, poet and lute-player, moved the hardest of stones with his singing. What did they mean? They meant to show that men as unfeeling as stone, who were living after the manner of wild beasts, were rescued from promiscuity by this wise and eloquent hero and initiated into the holy laws of marriage. It is clear that one who is not affected by the love of matrimony is more like a stone than a human being; he is an enemy of nature, a rebel against God who brings destruction upon himself by his own folly. For a man who plots the destruction of his race is crueller than one who plots only his own destruction.

Come then, since we are entering into fables that have nothing of the fabulous about them, when the same Orpheus in the underworld had induced Pluto himself and the shades to allow him to carry off Eurydice, what was the poet's[23] intention but to commend to us conjugal love, which even in the underworld was held to be holy and sacred? For this same reason antiquity set Jupiter Gamelius over the rite of marriage and named Juno Lucina as divine *pronuba*,[24] to be present with her divine assistance to those in childbirth. They erred, of course, in the names of the deities, owing to their superstitious beliefs; but they did not err in judging marriage to be a holy and worthy institution that is of concern to the gods. Rites and laws varied among peoples and nations, to be sure, but no race was ever so barbarous, so remote from all human feeling, that the name of wedlock was not regarded as holy and worthy of veneration among them. It was held sacred by Thracians, Sarmatians, Indians, Greeks, Latins, even by the 'Britons who dwell at the ends of the earth,'[25] or others even more remote than these, if they exist. Why is that so? Because all must share in common what was implanted by the common parent of men, so deeply implanted that this instinct is felt not only by pigeons and turtle-doves, but even by the wildest of beasts, since even lions are gentle towards their mates, and tigers fight for their cubs. The instinct to protect their young drives donkeys through fires that stand in their way. This is called the law of nature, and it is both efficacious and all-embracing. Therefore, just as a conscientious grower is not one who, content with things as they are, manages his fully grown trees with sufficient care but does not bother about propagating or grafting, with the result that within a few years his orchards, however carefully cultivated, must come to nothing; so a man must be reckoned as less than a conscientious citizen of his country who, content with the population as it is, takes no thought about adding to its number. No one has ever been held to be an outstanding citizen who has not made it his concern to produce children and educate them properly. Among the Hebrews and Persians it was to one's credit to have as many wives as possible, as if the country owed most to the man who had enriched it with the most numerous offspring.

Surely you are not anxious to appear holier than Abraham himself? He would not have been called 'the father of many generations'[26] and that with God's own blessing, if he had shunned cohabitation with a wife. Surely you do not seek to be considered more scrupulous than Jacob, who did not hesitate to purchase the embraces of Rachel by such a lengthy servitude;[27] or wiser than Solomon – yet what a large flock of wives[28] he kept at home! Or more chaste than Socrates, who, we read, put up at home with the shrewish Xanthippe not so much, as he jokingly used to say, that he might learn tolerance at home but that he might not seem to have been delinquent in the service of nature. For the one man judged to be wise by the oracle of Apollo[29] understood that he was begotten under this law, born for this law, and owed this debt to nature. For if what the ancient philosophers said was correct, if it was approved with good reason by our theologians, and if it was deservedly repeated everywhere in the form of a saying that neither God nor nature does anything without purpose, then why did nature assign us these members and add these incitements and this power of reproduction, if celibacy is to be considered praiseworthy? If someone gave you a splendid gift, a bow, or fine raiment, or a sword, you would

seem unworthy of what you received if you were unwilling or unable
to use it. Since everything else has been designed with a purpose, it
hardly seems probable that in this one matter alone nature was asleep.

I have no patience with those who say that sexual excitement is
shameful and that venereal stimuli have their origin not in nature, but
in sin. Nothing is so far from the truth. As if marriage, whose function
cannot be fulfilled without these incitements, did not rise above blame.
In other living creatures where do these incitements come from? From
nature or from sin? From nature, of course. It must be borne in mind
that in the appetites of the body there is very little difference between
man and other living creatures. Finally, we defile by our imagination
what of its own nature is fair and holy. If we were willing to evaluate
things not according to the opinion of the crowd, but according to nature
itself, how is it less repulsive to eat, chew, digest, evacuate, and sleep
after the fashion of dumb animals, than to enjoy lawful and permitted
carnal relations?

'But one must obey virtue rather than nature.' As if anything that is
at variance with nature could be called virtue! For if it did not proceed
from nature, there would be nothing that could be further perfected
by training and discipline. But you are attracted by the mode of life of
the apostles, who both embraced celibacy themselves and encouraged
others to that kind of life. Indeed, let the apostles be imitated by
apostolic men, who, since it is their mission to teach and instruct the
populace, cannot at one and the same time satisfy both a flock and a
wife. Yet it is known that some of the apostles had wives. Let us leave
celibacy for bishops. Why do you observe the practice of the apostles
when you are far removed from the apostolic function, being in fact a
layman and a private individual? They were allowed the privilege of
being free from the duties of wedlock, so that they might have more
opportunity to produce a more plentiful offspring for Christ. Let that
be the prerogative of priests and monks, who evidently have succeeded
to the regimen of the Essenes.[30] Your situation is quite different. 'But
Christ himself,' you will say, 'declared blessed those who became
eunuchs[31] for the kingdom of God's sake.' I do not reject the authority
of this statement, but I offer an interpretation of its meaning. First, I
consider that this dogma of Christ pertains to those times when it was
right for an ecclesiastic to be kept as free as possible from all worldly
affairs. He had to run about from one country to another, threatened

by persecutors on all sides. But nowadays conditions and times are such that you would not find anywhere a less defiled purity of morals than among the married. Let the swarms of monks and virgins exalt their own rule of life as they will, let them boast as much as they like of their liturgical functions and their acts of worship, in which they excel all others; the holiest kind of life is wedlock, purely and chastely observed. Besides, it is not only the one who lives unmarried who makes himself a eunuch, but one who in chaste and holy fashion carries out the duties of wedlock. I only wish those who conceal their vices behind the high-sounding name of castration, and under the pretence of chastity gratify worse lusts, were truly castrated. I do not think that it becomes my sense of modesty to describe the disgraceful actions that those who oppose nature often fall into. Lastly, Christ does not impose celibacy on anyone; he does, however, openly forbid divorce.[32] In my view it would not be ill advised for the interests and morals of mankind if the right of wedlock were also conceded to priests and monks, if circumstances required it, especially in view of the fact that there is such a great throng of priests everywhere, so few of whom live a chaste life. How much better it would be to turn concubines into wives, so that the women they now keep dishonourably and with troubled conscience might be retained openly with honourable reputation; then they could beget children whom they could love as truly legitimate offspring and educate conscientiously, to whom they would not be a source of shame, and by whom they might be honoured in turn. And indeed, I think the representatives of the bishops would have seen to this long ago, were it not that concubines are a greater source of revenue[33] than wives.

'But virginity is a divine and angelic prerogative, while wedlock is merely human.' I speak now as one man to another, as one commoner to another, as one weak mortal to another. Virginity is certainly worthy of praise, but on the condition that this praise is not transferred to the majority of mankind. If it were to become a general practice, what could be mentioned or imagined more destructive than virginity? Besides, if virginity were to merit special praise in all others, in your case it cannot escape censure, since the duty of preserving from distinction a family that is supremely worthy of immortality will devolve upon you alone. Finally, there is very little distinction between the praise due to virginity and that due to the man who keeps the laws of wedlock unsullied, who keeps a wife for bearing offspring, not for the purpose of lust.

If a brother is bidden to raise up seed for a brother[34] who has died without children, will you allow the hope of your whole line to perish, especially when it has fallen on you alone? I am not unaware that the praise of virginity has repeatedly been sung in huge volumes by the early Fathers, among whom Jerome[35] admires it so much that he all but abuses marriage, and was summoned to recant by some orthodox bishops. However, let us make allowance for the fervour of those times; at the present time, I should wish that those who indiscriminately encourage to celibacy those who are not mature enough to know their own minds should direct similar efforts to presenting a picture of chaste and pure matrimony. The same individuals who are so pleased with virginity are not displeased with warring against the Turks, who outnumber us by so many; if their judgment is correct, it will follow that it should be considered especially right and honourable to strive with all one's might to produce children, and thus provide enough young men to serve in the war. Unless perhaps they think that artillery, missiles, and ships should be provided for this war, but that men are not needed. The same people approve of slaying heathen parents by the sword, so that it may be possible to baptize their children, who are unaware of their newly acquired religion. If that is true, how much more civilized it would be to obtain the same result by the office of wedlock! No nation is so barbarous that it does not execrate the killing of infants. The laws of princes punish with almost equal severity the inducing of abortion and sterility brought on by drugs. Why is that so? Because there is very little difference between the one who cuts short what has begun to be born and one who sees to it that there can be no birth. That which withers away within your body, or is destroyed at great risk to your health, or is ejected in sleep, would have been a human being if only you had been human. The literature of the Hebrews curses the man[36] who, when told to consort with his dead brother's wife, spilled the seed upon the ground so that nothing would be born, and was judged unworthy of life as he had grudged life to a foetus yet to be born.

How very little difference there is between him and those who impose perpetual sterility upon themselves! Does it not seem that they kill as many human beings as would have been born if they had attended to the begetting of children? I ask you, if anyone has a farm with naturally fertile soil that he allows to remain forever uncultivated and barren, should he not be punished by the law, as it is in the country's interests that each one should manage his property well? If a man is punished for neglecting a field that, even if fully cultivated, bears only wheat, or beans, or peas, what penalty does he deserve who refuses to cultivate a farm that when cultivated produces men? In the former case long and hard toil is required, in the latter cultivation is short, and also has the reward of pleasure as an added inducement. So if you are influenced at all by natural feelings, goodness, respect, piety, duty, and virtue, why do you shun what has been instituted by God, sanctioned by nature, prompted by reason, praised in divine and human writings alike, laid down by the law, ratified by the consensus of all peoples, and encouraged by the example of all good men?

But even if many unpleasant things are to be sought after by a good man for no other reason than that they are honourable, then marriage, concerning which it is difficult to determine whether it contains more honour or pleasure, is all the more greatly to be desired. For what is sweeter than living with a woman with whom you are most intimately joined not merely by the bonds of affection but by physical union as well? If we derive much spiritual delight from the kindness of other close relatives and acquaintances, how much more pleasant to have someone with whom to share the secret feelings of the heart, with whom you may talk as if with yourself, to whose loyalty you can safely entrust yourself, who regards your fortune as her own! What happiness there is in the union of husband and wife, than which none greater nor more lasting exists in all of nature! For while we are linked with our other friends by benevolence of mind, with a wife we are joined by the greatest affection, physical union, the bond of the sacrament, and the common sharing of all fortunes. Moreover, how much pretence and bad faith there is in other friendships! Those whom we think to be our dearest friends fail us when fortune's breezes change, like swallows flying away at the end of the summer. At times a more recent friend displaces an old one. I have heard of few whose faithfulness persisted until life's end.

The affection of a wife is not spoilt by faithlessness, is veiled by no pretence, is shattered by no change of fortune; in the end it is severed by death alone, or rather not even by death. She disregards her duties to her parents and sisters and brothers out of love for you, she looks up to you alone, she depends on you, with you she would fain die. If you have wealth, you have someone to look after it and increase it; if you have none, you have someone who can seek it for you. In times of prosperity, happiness is doubled; in adversity there will be someone to console and assist you, to show her devotion, to wish your misfortune hers. Do you think there is any pleasure to be compared with so close a union? If you are at home, she is there to dispel the tedium of solitude; if abroad, she can speed you on your way with a kiss, miss you when you are away, receive you gladly on your return. She is the sweetest companion of your youth, the welcome comfort of your old age. By nature any association is pleasant for man, seeing that nature begot him for kindness and friendship. Then how can this fail to be the most pleasant of all, in which there is nothing that is not shared? On the contrary, if we see that even the wild beasts dread loneliness and are pleased by companionship, in my view anyone who shuns this most honourable and joyful association should not be accounted as human.

For what is more hateful than a man who, as though born for himself alone, lives for himself, looks out for himself, is sparing or lavish for himself, loves no one, and is loved by no one? Indeed, should not such a monster be thought fit to be driven away from the general fellowship of mankind into the midst of the sea along with the notorious Timon[37] of Athens? I should not presume at this point to set before you those pleasures, the sweetest that nature has bestowed upon mankind, which men of great genius, for some reason or other, have chosen to ignore rather than despise. Yet, who has been born with so stern, not to say stolid, a nature as not to be attracted by pleasures of that kind, especially if they can be enjoyed without offence to God or man and without loss of reputation? Truly I should call him not a man, but a stone, even if bodily pleasure is but a small part of the benefits conferred by wedlock. Suppose, however, that you despise this as unworthy of a true man (though without it we do not deserve the name of true man); let it be set, if you wish, among the least advantages of wedlock, then what could be more lovely than chaste love, or, I should say, what more holy and more honourable?

Meanwhile the pleasant throng of relatives grows larger. The number of parents, brothers, sisters, and nephews is doubled. For nature can grant only one mother and one father. By wedlock a second father and second mother are added, who cannot but attend you with unusual devotion, as one to whom they have entrusted their own flesh. Then what joy it will bring you when your beautiful wife makes you the parent of beautiful offspring; when some tiny Aeneas[38] will play in your hall, who will recall your countenance and that of your wife and will call you by the name of 'father' with sweet stammering? To the affection of wedlock there will be added a bond as adamant as steel, which not even death can sever. 'Happy those,' says Horace,[39] 'three or more times over, / United by an unbroken bond / Whose love, unmarred by bitter strife / Will not release them till their dying day.' You have those who will give delight to your old age, close your eyes and perform the obsequies, in whom you may seem to be born again, in whose survival you may even be thought not to have died. What you have amassed for yourself does not pass into the hands of alien heirs. Thus when one has the sense of having performed all of life's duties, not even death itself can seem harsh. Old age threatens all of us willy-nilly. In this manner nature has provided that we should grow young again in our children and grandchildren. For who would find old age a burden when he has seen in his son the very features he had as a young man? Death awaits us all. But in this way alone the providence of nature devises a kind of immortality, as it creates one thing from another in such a way that, just as when a shoot springs up again after a tree has been felled, one who dies leaving offspring behind him does not seem to have perished altogether.

Yet I am well aware of the objections you are raising in the meantime. Wedlock is a blessed institution if all turns out favourably, but what if you end up with a difficult or shameless wife, or the children grow up to be disloyal? Cases of wedlock that brought ruin will come to mind. Magnify them as much as you will, these will prove to be faults of human nature, not of wedlock. Believe me, as a rule, only a bad husband gets a bad wife. Besides, it is within your power to choose a good one. What if she should be corrupted? A good wife can certainly be corrupted by a bad husband; a bad wife is usually reformed by a good husband. The accusations we bring against wives are false. No one, if you have faith in my words, ever had a wicked wife except through his own fault. Further, from good parents similar children are born, as a general rule. In fact, whatever their condition of birth, they turn out very much as one shapes them by education. There is no reason to be afraid of jealousy. That is the disease of those who love foolishly.

Chaste and lawful love is innocent of jealousy. Why do tragic examples come to mind? This adulteress[40] struck down her husband with an axe; this one got rid of hers by poison; that one through the repugnance of her character drove a man to his death. Why instead does not Cornelia, the wife of Tiberius Gracchus, come to mind?[41] ... Why not countless others whose virtue and good faith towards their spouses could not be altered even by death? You say, 'An upright women is "a rare bird"[42] upon the earth.' Make yourself worthy of a rare wife. As the wise man[43] says, 'A good woman is a good inheritance.' Dare to hope for one worthy of your character. Much lies in the choice you make, what you make of her, and how you behave towards her.

'But freedom is pleasanter,' you will say. 'Whoever takes a wife receives fetters that only death can shake off.' But what pleasure can there be for a man who is alone? If freedom is pleasant, I think you should take a partner with whom you may be willing to share that benefit. Yet what is more free than a servitude in which each is so subject to the other that neither wishes to be set free? You are bound to one whom you admit to your friendship, but no one claims that his freedom has been taken away on this account. You are afraid that when your children are taken away by death, you may be plunged into grief in your bereavement. If you are afraid of bereavement, you should take a wife for that very reason, since she alone can guarantee your not being childless. Yet why do you inquire so thoroughly, nay, so anxiously, into all the disadvantages of marriage, as if celibacy had no disadvantages? As if there were any form of human existence not liable to all the hazards of fortune! One who wishes to suffer no ills must depart from this life. But if you are thinking of life in heaven, this mortal life must be called death, not life. If, however, you limit your considerations to the life of man, nothing is more secure, more tranquil, more pleasant, more attractive, or more blissful than wedded life.

Consider the matter from its results. How few are there in your experience who, having once made trial of wedlock, are not eager to try it again! My friend Maurice,[44] whose exceptional wisdom is well known to you, entered into matrimony with a new bride a month after the death of the wife whom he dearly loved. This was not because of his inability to resist sexual desire, but he said that life did not seem real to him without a wife to share all his fortunes. Is not our friend Jovius[45] looking for a fourth wife? He was so deeply in love with them when they were alive that he seemed to admit of no consolation. Notwithstanding, when one died, he was quick to fill the loneliness of his marriage bed, as if he had felt little love for them. But why are we discussing goodness and pleasure when not only advantage induces us, but necessity impels us to wedlock? Take away marriage, and within a very few years all of mankind must perish utterly. They say that when Xerxes,[46] the famous king of the Persians, was gazing from a high place on his mighty array of men, he could not restrain his tears because sixty years from then not a single one of so many thousands would be alive. Why can we not perceive concerning the whole human race what he understood concerning his troops? If wedlock is taken away, of so many regions, provinces, kingdoms, cities, and assemblies how few will be left a century later!

Let us go then and pay our homage to celibacy, since it is destined to visit eternal destruction on our race! What plague or pestilence sent by the gods above or below could be more pernicious? What more bitter consequences could be feared from any flood? What greater tragedy could be expected even if Phaethon's conflagration should return? In calamities of this kind much remains unharmed, but from the effects of celibacy nothing will be saved. We see what a procession of maladies, how many dangerous situations lie in wait for the meagre race of mankind night and day. How many are carried off by disease, swallowed up by the sea, or snatched away by war? I do not mention the deaths that occur every day. Death hovers all around us: it strikes, seizes, and hastens with all speed to end our race; and yet we admire celibacy and flee from wedlock! ... From the bosom of the earth many things are born without our cultivating them. Young shoots often sprout up beneath their parents' shade; but for man nature has willed that there should be this single method of propagation, that by the co-operation of husband and wife the race of mortals should be saved from destruction; but if men were to shun this after your example, not even what you so admire would be able to exist.

Do you admire celibacy and respect virginity? But if you take away the practice of wedlock there will be neither unwedded nor virgins. Why then is virginity preferred and honoured if it involves the abolition of mankind? It has received praise, but in a given period of time and in few individuals. For God wished to show men a kind of picture and likeness of that life in heaven where no women marry or are given in marriage. But for an example a small number is suitable, a large one useless. Not every field, however fertile, is sown to sustain life; but some are neglected, others cultivated to please the eye; for the very abundance allows that in such a vast extent of arable land, a small part may be left barren. But if none were sown, who would not see that we should have to return to acorns? Similarly, amid such a great multitude of men celibacy in a few certainly merits praise, but if extended to all would deserve grievous censure.

Now if in others virginity were to be esteemed a virtue, in your case it would definitely be a vice. For the others will seem to have been interested in leading a pure life; you will be judged the murderer of your line, because, when you were able to have offspring by honourable wedlock, you allowed it to die out through vile celibacy. It would be permissible from a large brood to consecrate a virgin to God. Countrymen offer the first fruits of their crops to the gods, but not the whole yield; you must remember that you are the sole remnant of your line. There is no difference between killing it off or refusing to preserve it, since you are the only one who could preserve it, and easily at that.

But you protest that your sister's example encourages you towards celibacy. This very reason that you cite should have deterred you most of all from the state of celibacy. You are aware that the hope of your family, which previously was divided between the two of you, has now devolved entirely upon you alone. Some indulgence should be granted to her sex and her years. The girl did wrong because she was overcome with grief; at the instance of foolish women or foolish monks she threw herself into it headlong. You who are the elder must remember that you are a man. She has wished to die together with her ancestors; you will make sure that they do not die. Your sister has withdrawn from her duty; consider now that you must play the part of two. The daughters of Lot[47] did not hesitate to consort with their drunken father, judging it better, even through unholy incest, to take thought for the race than to allow it to die off. Will you not, by a marriage that is honourable, holy, modest, without offence, and that promises great satisfaction, take thought for your family, which otherwise is doomed to extinction?

So let us allow those to imitate the example of Hippolytus[48] in the pursuit of celibacy who can be husbands, but not fathers, or whose slender means are insufficient for rearing children, or whose line can be continued through the instrumentality of others, or else is of such a kind that the country is the better for its extinction rather than its continuance, or who by some special favour of the eternal Godhead have been set apart from the general lot of mankind and marked out for some heavenly function – and their number is amazingly small. In your case, on the evidence of a doctor who is quite skilled and honest, you seem to give promise of a large posterity; you have means that are abundant, and an excellent and distinguished line, which cannot be blotted out without the commission of a wicked crime and without grave consequences for the country. Then, too, your age is sound, good looks are not wanting, and you have the opportunity to take as a wife a girl as virtuous and distinguished as your fellow citizens have ever seen, pure, modest, respectful, divinely beautiful, with an abundant dowry. Although your friends beg you, your kinsfolk shed tears, your relatives press you, your country requests it, and the very ashes of your ancestors implore this of you from the tomb, do you still hesitate and still contemplate celibacy?

If what was asked of you were something dishonourable or difficult, still the prayers of your kin or the affection of your family should have prevailed over your desire. How much more reasonable it is that the tears of your friends, respect for your country, and your affection for your ancestors should win from you a decision to which you are urged by laws divine and human alike, impelled by nature, led by reason, drawn by honour, attracted by so many advantages, and even compelled by necessity itself? But this is more than enough argument. I am certain that you have long since changed your mind at my prompting, and have turned your thoughts to more useful plans.

NOTES

1 Legendary and biblical lawgivers
2 Mark 10:7
3 Eph. 5:32
4 Heb. 13:4
5 Implied in Exod. 23:26; Deut. 7:14; Mal. 3:11
6 Gen. 29:31
7 Ps. 127:3
8 Deut. 20:7

9 The *lex Julia de maritandis ordinibus* (18 B.C.) and the *lex Papia Poppaea* (A.D. 9), both passed under the emperor Augustus. The *lex Papia Poppaea* restricted the rights of bachelors, spinsters, and childless couples to inherit property. They were also given a low priority as candidates for office.

10 Those who had three legitimate children were accorded certain privileges by Augustus' marriage legislation, including seniority for holding magistracies. Under later emperors these privileges came to be granted as a favour regardless of the number of children.

11 'The Great,' emperor 306–37 A.D. The reference is to *Codex Theodosius*, 8.16.1 (320 A.D.). This constitution is usually ascribed to Christian influence.

12 He was not actually censor, but was granted censorial powers in 29–8 B.C. The legislation banning marriage for soldiers was probably introduced by Augustus (Suetonius, *Augustus*, 24.1). This law was not revoked until 536 A.D.

13 The two Augustan laws mentioned above, which established the *ius trium liberorum*, were referred to as the *lex Julia Miscella* (*Codex Justinianus*, 6.40.2-3).

14 Roman jurist (third century A.D.). The passage refers to *Digest*, 24.3.1.

15 Juvenal, 9.87–8

16 *Codex Justinianus*, 5.66.1. If no guardians of children were nominated by will, this duty fell to the nearest agnate. See *Institutiones Justiniani*, 1.16.7; *Codex Theodosianus*, 12.1.55. The decurion was a councillor in a country town; the office was obligatory on all appointed to undertake it.

17 Personage and anecdote unknown. It is mentioned by Dio Cassius, 69.23.3, that Hadrian lightened penalties in proportion to the number of offspring. The classical source is *Digest*, XLVIII, 20.7.3.

18 Plutarch, *Lycurgus*, 15

19 Prior to Christianity Roman law did not impose capital punishment on citizen adulterers, but sanctioned their execution *in flagrante delicto* by injured husbands (or fathers). Augustus' *lex Julia de adulteriis* re-enacted this, but also imposed economic sanctions and relegation to an island. For the laws of the Hebrews see Deut. 22:22.

20 Pliny, *Natural History*, 13.7.31

21 Ibid 13.7.34–5

22 Cf Ovid, *Metamorphoses*, 1.184, a metaphor for rebellion.

23 For instance Virgil, *Georgics*, 4.454ff.

24 Epithets of classical gods protecting marriage and childbirth

25 Horace, *Odes*, 1.35.28–30

26 Gen. 12:3

27 He served his uncle Laban for seven years in hopes of receiving Rachel in marriage.

28 1 Kings 11:1–3

29 In reply to the enquiry of his friend Chaerephon

30 A small community of Jews who lived mostly around the Dead Sea, practised extreme asceticism, and were firm believers in celibacy; Erasmus often refers to monks by this term, intended as pejorative.

31 Matt. 19:12

32 See Matt. 19:6.

33 Erasmus repeats this accusation in commenting on 1 Tim. 3:2 (LB VI 934C) and in *De interdictu esu carnium* (LB IX 1201F). The Fourth Lateran Council and the Council of Basel explicitly condemned this abuse.

34 Deut. 25:5

35 He exalts virginity over marriage, especially in the tracts against Jovinian and Helvidius. Jerome wrote a long justification of these views in a letter to his friend Pammachius, *Letters*, 49.

36 Onan; see Gen. 38:9.

37 The Athenian misanthrope; Erasmus translated Lucian's dialogue *Timon sive misanthropos*.

38 Virgil, *Aeneid*, 4.328–9

39 *Odes*, 1.13.17–20

40 Possibly referring to Clytemnestra, who murdered her husband, Agamemnon

41 Second daughter of Scipio Africanus, mother of the Gracchi, a very cultured woman who embodied all the ideals of the virtuous Roman matron; the list of 'good women' that begins here corresponds closely to one found in Valerius Maximus, *Facta et dicta memorabilia*, 4.6. Erasmus continues with a long list of classical heroines considered paragons of womanhood.

42 Horace, *Satires*, 2.2.26; Juvenal, 6.165; *Adagia*, II, i, 21; *Colloquia*, ASD I-3, 698

43 Jesus, son of Sirach; Prov. 12:4; 18:22

44 Probably a reference to Thomas More, who married Alice Middleton after a one-month widowhood. Cf Le Chevalier de Berquin, *Declamation des louanges de mariage*, ed. Emile Telle (Geneva 1976) 52 n2.

45 Telle, ibid, interprets the name as perhaps a reference to Mountjoy, already married to his fourth wife when the *Encomium matrimonii* was published.

46 In 480 B.C., when leading his army into Greece. The story is told in Herodotus, *Histories*, 7.45–6; and Nepos, *Themistocles*, 2.4.

47 Gen. 19:30–5

48 Vowed to the chaste goddess Artemis, he rejected women.

WIVES

1. *The Institution of Marriage*

The Institution of Marriage was published in Basel in 1526. It was dedicated to
Catherine of Aragon, queen of England, soon to be divorced by her husband,
Henry VIII. With unforeseeable irony Erasmus refers to her 'most sacred and
fortunate marriage' as exemplary (Allen, Ep 1727:18–19). Erasmus' treatise
on marriage is a detailed and painstaking examination of the institution. It
includes a wealth of citations from classical, biblical, patristic, and medieval legal
sources. In sharp contrast to the painfully realistic depiction in the *Colloquies*
of a relationship gone sour (see 131), we find here the portrayal of the ideal
marriage.

When the treatise appeared, the relative merits of marriage and celibacy were
the subject of intense scrutiny. Martin Luther had married the previous year;
monks and nuns everywhere had abandoned their cloisters; Erasmus himself
had suggested in a letter to the Paris theologian Noël Béda that clerics who were
unable to observe their vows should be allowed the 'remedy of marriage' (Allen,
Ep 1620:52). In patristic literature and throughout the Middle Ages marriage
had been considered inferior to celibacy. The reformers, however, overturned
this value-judgment. Many traditional theologians regarded Erasmus as one
of their sources of inspiration. His criticism of monasticism, his unfavourable

comparison of celibacy with matrimony, his apparently paradoxical theory of 'matrimonial chastity,' and his liberal views on divorce (see 89), gave offence to traditionalists and in their eyes linked Erasmus to the reformers. All of Erasmus' works were placed on the Index of Prohibited Books by Pope Paul III in 1559. It is notable, however, that the Council of Trent, which revised the Index and lifted some of the prohibitions against Erasmus' works, kept the *Institution* on the list of forbidden texts.

The translation is by Michael Heath.

a) Choosing the Right Mate

Much depends on the judgment of both sides, parents and children ...

The first thing to do is to pray to God for correct and wise judgment. Next you must decide upon your aims, and this above all will determine whether your judgment will be sound or faulty. If in choosing a son- or daughter-in-law the principal consideration is beauty, youth, wealth, nobility, or political influence, you will usually end by arranging an unfortunate match, not a happy one, since the chief source of happiness lies in an appropriate choice of partners, whose virtue and compatibility will ensure lasting harmony.

The Lord will provide the rest, and he will ensure that what is best for you will also prove most successful. Nothing done with God's approval can be called unsuccessful, whatever the outcome. All too often what the world calls the height of success is in fact utter disaster. I can understand why Pittacus' dictum, 'Marry an equal,' is so well known among scholars, since, as the proverb says, 'like attracts like, and they stick together.'[2] Equality is not to be measured simply in terms of wealth but of every kind of attribute. The proper order must not be reversed, as it usually is by ordinary people: 'Money first, morals last!' In a proper account, the first entry in the ledger should be the good things of the mind, then those of the body, and finally those called external. Moreover, there is a hierarchy among the attributes of the mind; some do not infallibly make their owners virtuous. Willingness to learn, for example, or a good memory, scholarship, eloquence, ingenuity, promptness can all be perverted to immoral ends. But chastity, sobriety, self-restraint, moderation, truthfulness, prudence, reticence, honesty, and vigilance make their owners virtuous whenever they are present. If your partner seems inclined towards these qualities, it is a very hopeful sign that she can be moulded to your character, and an even more hopeful one if a naturally virtuous disposition is reinforced by a sound upbringing. You should use a similar process to judge of her faults.

Now there are some moral attributes that are, as they say, written on the forehead, such as modesty, chastity, kindness, and self-restraint, but speech still gives the most reliable indication of character. 'Speak, young man,' said Socrates, 'that I may see you.'[2] The philosopher's eyes are in his ears, not in his face. Many people think it enough to have seen the girl whose hand they seek, but if they really want to see her, they should talk to her. To avoid disappointment, careful enquiries must be made as to how and by whom she was brought up. It is important, of course, to be well born, but much more important to be properly brought up. It is not at all uncommon to see young men and women of excellent family, endowed with remarkable natural abilities, deteriorate, if their upbringing is neglected, until they seem worse than by-blows and foundlings. By contrast, some bastards, given a liberal upbringing by virtuous tutors, surpass legitimate children in the probity of their character.

Here again, it is important to look not only for natural abilities, but also for a temperament that will make for a harmonious union; too close a resemblance is not always a good thing. If the young man is rather lethargic by nature, he will need a bride with a more active disposition; if the husband is inclined to extravagance, he will need a thrifty wife who is better at looking after the pennies. If he is a hot-tempered young man, he will be best suited by a more restrained wife, who will know the time to give in and obey. Since such temperamental differences are to be found even in the best natures, a marriage may be none too happy unless appropriate provision is made for them.

However, the most important of all the moral qualities to be observed in a partner are the amount of their respect for their parents and the extent of their devotion to God. If they have learned this respect and devotion, they can acquire all the other virtues. But you must take care not to marry someone who is superstitious rather than pious; if true piety implies an agreeable flexibility, superstition means a harsh inflexibility, and it tends to infect women more often than men. Of course, there are some trifling superstitions that a husband may as well tolerate until his wife knows better ... It seems advisable that a husband should bear with his wife, or a wife with her husband, since perhaps the one can correct the other, should they disagree somewhat on those doctrinal questions that are today a subject of controversy throughout the world. This does not apply if impiety has driven one of them so mad as to deny Christ entirely, along with the holy Scriptures and the Apostles' Creed, which is manifest apostasy. It would be imprudent to make a match if one of the partners were a zealous adherent of some reprobate sect. The apostle teaches that mixed marriages must be upheld if they were contracted through no fault of our own, but that they must not be contracted in other circumstances.

It is up to the individual to decide whether it is more advisable to marry an untutored virgin or a widow with experience ... A man who chooses a well-favoured but untutored bride will try, if he is a good craftsman, to fashion himself a wife to suit his own temper, and will succeed, with God's aid, so long as his own character reflects the moral code. Conversely, a man who wants to escape the drudgery of educating her, which is a long and not always successful job, may prefer a widow who is already broken in and formed. It is not a bad idea, so long as he takes into account her behaviour towards her previous husband and what means and methods he used to instruct her. You may be fairly sure that she will be compliant and docile towards you if she showed herself obedient to her dead husband ...

Just as only a craftsman can properly judge his craft, so only a virtuous man – and a man of experience too – can properly judge questions of virtue. Anyone who wants to choose himself a virtuous wife must first make himself virtuous. On this point the advice of older relatives and of parents will be more than valuable, not only because young men and women are usually led astray by love, which is, as they say, a blind judge, but also because people of more mature years, with all their experience, weigh things up more carefully than young people, who are guided more by desire than by reason. Their inexperience, as a laudable ancient maxim has it, makes them over-confident – and scorn for danger will bring the danger closer.

Love often mistakes the worst things for the best, as Theocritus wrote;[3] it deceives itself and will see a suitor's violence and arrogance as strength, his extravagance as generosity, and use a euphemism, such as *gynaecophilia* [being fond of women], to describe his unbridled lust. Similarly, love will call a girl's loose chatter polite conversation and will claim that the lewdness of her looks, walk, and gestures merely shows that she is friendly. Some people think that good behaviour is merely a matter of making the right gestures. If a girl has learned, let us say, to be forever curtseying, joining her hands, and pursing her lips in a prim smile, if she will touch as little food and drink as possible at a party (having stuffed herself in private beforehand), not stick out her left hand when it should be the right, touch food only with her fingertips, not show her teeth when laughing: if she has mastered such trifles as these they think she has learned enough to earn a husband. But on the contrary virtue should have been so deeply inculcated in her that it shines out candidly from her brow, her eyes, her face and in her every movement, in the same way that physical fitness is revealed unconsciously in the healthy glow and alertness of someone's body.

In reaching the right decision, a not unimportant role will be played by the girl's reputation. Of course, hearsay is often wrong, but a young man will justifiably refrain from marrying a girl who, though innocent, is the subject of widespread rumours. If a husband repudiates his wife, he stains her reputation forever; if a suitor withdraws from his engagement, it appears merely that he has not gone through with it, and the girl retains the right to marry another ...

Another point to be considered in choosing a husband or wife is whether they have learned or practised some skill. If their means are slender, knowing a craft is essential; even if they are comfortably off, possessing a skill will have two advantages. Firstly, should some mischance suddenly deprive them of their substance (and such possessions are particularly vulnerable to fortune's whims), they will have some means of escaping poverty without resorting to crime. Not only will 'skill fit your hand, in any land,' as the proverb says, but also any position in life; or, put a better way, skill will support any position in life. Secondly, it will leave less room for idleness, so often the ruin of morality ... There are of course differences between the arts ... Many girls think they have made a splendid match if they marry one of these Carian mercenaries whose only motive is profit, a butcher for hire, who will abandon his wife and children at the first sniff of a war. Yet women think it heroic to be united to a man who is defiled by sacrilege, pillage, carnage, rape, and other wickedness; they even expect a reward from heaven for putting up with such husbands, if they cannot change their ways. If I had my way, no girl would ever marry such a man if anyone else, however humble, were available, so long as he knew some harmless trade.

As for the arts that are both healthy and profitable, the Ancients all agreed in awarding the prize to agriculture; in days gone by it was an honourable calling even for mighty kings and aristocratic senators, but now it is turned over to the lowest members of society, who do all the work while their idle masters reap all the rewards. We have sunk so low that nowadays a girl married to a farmer is considered beneath contempt. But if physical fitness, which must surely be considered one of our greatest assets in life, is our aim, there is no healthier life than this; if it is thrift, no one lives more economically; if it is profit, there is no more harmless way to earn money; if – and this is the most important consideration – our aim is to live an upright life, nowhere is there less temptation ...

This way of life is so much happier and healthier – and safer – than the commercial business in which so many are engaged these days, which takes a man far from his family for much of the year, compelling him to flit over mountains and seas and roads infested with brigands, in danger of losing his life as well as all his goods. These men's wives are little more than widows; their minds are never free from anxiety and fear for their husbands, or their goods, and usually for both! All may be well in fact, but they are terrorized by the slightest rumour and often by nightmares. It is safer – and also harmless to others – to 'do business' with your trusty farm, which returns with interest whatever it receives. This is a respectable kind of usury, and the greater the effort you put in, the larger the return; should one harvest disappoint your hopes, the next will make good the loss. Not only does the land take the farmer and return him safe but, if he arrives a little under the weather, it sends him back fighting fit.

This business knows nothing of deceit, whereas normal commerce can barely survive without trickery; only the slippery and the sly find easy pickings there. For a Christian dishonest profit is no profit but a loss; no Christian can be happy with something that gnaws away at his conscience ... How often do we see great riches, painstakingly acquired by usury, monopoly, and other dirty tricks, destroyed in a moment by fire or storm, or confiscated by princes, who cunningly sell a monopoly, let the buyer soak up cash like a sponge, and then, at the right moment, squeeze him dry. I need hardly mention charlatans and hucksters, like those who make their money from paste jewellery or pinchbeck gold, or trick the gullible with alchemy or bogus magic, or those who cater for our lower appetites, such as confectioners, pastrycooks and pimps, or flute-players and rope-dancers. What about card-sharps and gamblers? Some people make their living that way. Any girl who knowingly marries one of these deserves to suffer, as an accessory to evil. If she says: 'I cannot be a spinster all my life, and no one else was available,' I can promise her more happiness if she marries the meanest cobbler than one of these fine 'craftsmen.'

But enough of these male professions! A girl whose parents have taught her to manage a household has acquired a skill that is by no means to be disdained. She will never find any shortage of jobs to do in the home, and will get enough exercise to keep her healthy if she visits the various parts of the house regularly – the kitchen, the men's and women's quarters, the bedroom, the attics – and either does the housework herself or tells others what needs to be done. Spindle and distaff are indeed the ideal female instruments for discouraging idleness, which is bad for anyone but particularly harmful to young people and women. Some men deal with important business by mental activity alone; unless a girl is given something to occupy her mind, her thoughts turn inevitably towards evil.

Families who will not let their daughters learn a trade because of their status and position in society or because they are already well off are nonetheless quite right to instruct them in tapestry work, silk-weaving, or playing an instrument, to enable them to cheat boredom; they would do even better to have them instructed in the humanities. Weaving, for example, is an occupation that leaves the mind free to listen to young men's chatter and to reply to their banter, but a girl intent on her books has no thought for anything else. What is more, once she begins to enjoy study, it will sharpen and stimulate her mind more than any other occupation; others may discourage idleness, but study has the advantage that the more you do the greater the pleasure you obtain, and it will keep you occupied even into old age. Finally, reading good books not only forestalls idleness but also fills girls' minds with the best of principles and inculcates virtue ...

To sum up: in judging your bride's moral qualities, the first thing is that you should know what you are talking about. Generally speaking, someone who is himself virtuous will recognize and appreciate virtue.

In this area, as I have said, the assessment of parents or elders will be
more reliable than the children's; it is better to trust them, since they
have learned from their own and others' misfortunes what to look for
and what to avoid, rather than to give youthful inexperience the chance
to learn wisdom from its own mistakes. Secondly, reasoned advice
must prevail over mere whim: here again, it is preferable that children
should defer to their parents' judgment, as the latter are beyond the
reach of Cupid's darts, which all too often afflict the young. Thirdly,
moral qualities themselves must be sifted: some are better than others,
but the greatest of all is piety. There are some that do not immediately
make their possessor virtuous: a good weaver is not necessarily a
good woman, and a good lawyer can be a bad man. Fourthly, you
should not look just for attractive qualities but for appropriate ones.
Although to a Christian nothing will appear suitable unless it is also
good, yet even some attractive quality will not always suit everyone.
Compatibility is so important that sometimes people who are dissimilar,
but right for one another, will live in greater harmony than those who
are more alike, despite the very proper saying that similarity breeds
goodwill; not everyone, after all, likes the same things, and in fact
the variety of people's tastes is astonishing. Fifthly, in examining her
moral qualities, you must rely less on your eyes than your ears and,
in order to appraise the girl's character and temperament, use every
scrap of information: about her family, since normally virtue breeds
virtue; about her upbringing, even more important than her family;
about her earlier life and her reputation, which her family should guard
as jealously as her virginity, since their main concern must be to hand
her unsullied to her husband; even if her body is untouched, she will
not be unsullied if her reputation is besmirched. Such considerations
will enable you to see your future much more clearly than any flight
of birds or sacred chickens gobbling corn;[4] clear thinking is the best
prophet.

Now although I would want you to investigate all this very thoroughly, I would expect you still to show consideration for other people's
honour and reputation, especially those of young girls. For some suitors, seeing that someone else is preferred to them, invent and spread
damaging rumours about the girl; they cannot have her, so they would
rather appear contemptuous of her than rejected by her. Would it not
be more in keeping with Christian charity to dissemble, and conceal

anything untoward that you might find out about the way of life or character of a marriageable girl? It is no disgrace for a young man to go looking for a partner, but a girl cannot, and it does no great harm to his reputation if he fails, since she cannot marry more than one suitor.

For this reason, whenever a girl has several suitors it would be better to leave the choice to her parents and thus reduce the chances of ill-feeling against her. If, on closer acquaintance, the girl fails to please the suitor, it will not be hard to invent some reason why he should not go through with the wedding. A customer who disparages the jewels for sale in front of everyone else is considered most uncouth: if the price is right, why disparage them? If not, it costs nothing to keep silent. But it is much more churlish to invent slurs upon the reputation of a girl you cannot have, simply to prevent her marrying another. A good way to avoid this would be for the parents to exclude other people from these negotiations and conduct them in private; if something goes wrong, there will be less scope for backbiting and ill will, and the quest will be more likely to succeed than if the news gets out and produces a crowd of rivals.

Now someone will ask: 'Since there is always a great shortage of good people, what is to become of all the bad ones, if only the good are allowed to marry one another?' Why, let the punishment fit the crime, and those who sinned outside marriage repent within it. Surely those who have wickedly enticed innocent girls to fornicate with them should be urged by all honest citizens to marry those they have defiled, or at the very least be compelled by law to find them a husband and provide a dowry. Why are Christian laws so reluctant to do this? Because fornication is a daily sport among the great men whose opinions make and unmake our laws. But divine law will continue to press for it, and that should carry more weight, with Christians at least, than human laws.

I feel that I have said enough about choosing a wife according to her moral qualities; now I must deal briefly with physical qualities ... On this subject, ordinary people's judgment is nearly always topsy-turvy; they prize youth and beauty above all else, but where these alone are the motives for love there can be no lasting affection. The flower of youth is fleeting and beauty fades, not only with the passing of the years but from many another cause; affection also must perish if its source dries up. Thus if we wish friendship to last it must be based on things that are not exposed to the buffets of fortune nor withered by age...

However, since matrimony is a union of body and soul, some thought must be given even to physical suitability, to ensure that here too some equality or similarity exists. A philosophical nature will ignore completely outward appearance, however unfortunate, provided that intellectual and moral gifts compensate for these shortcomings. We see deep marital affection continuing to flourish between decrepit old folk, though not a trace remains of their former good looks. Should not reason produce the same effect in a wise man that habit has produced in these others? Someone who marries only to beget children or curb his lust will find his wife quite acceptable simply because she is a woman; someone who is not philosopher enough to be content with moral qualities should choose a girl of only moderate looks, such as might be called regular or wifely, neither so loathsome as to put him off nor yet so charming as to attract adulterers or ugly gossip. But if he should happen to find a girl of outstanding beauty, ideal character, perfect thriftiness, and simple demeanour, he can easily avoid or reduce these dangers: the jewel of beauty is nowhere safer than at home, and no place is more appropriate for a virtuous wife to live ...

Ancient wisdom gives pride of place among physical qualities to good health, and the second place to beauty. Thus the most discerning judges will observe first of all how healthy, active, and temperate their partner's body is, whatever their age. A woman married to an invalid has taken on an old man; a man married to a sickly wife has taken on an old woman. Some illnesses, such as fevers and colds, do not last long, and sometimes even leave the body stronger afterwards; others, such as gout, dropsy, epilepsy, apoplexy, or paralysis, never leave their victims entirely. Some conditions are more distressing than any ordinary illness, such as leprosy or what is commonly called the Neapolitan pox [syphilis], probably worse than any leprosy. There are also diseases of the mind: frenzy, derangement, lethargy. Other things cannot be called diseases, but debilities or handicaps, such as blindness, lameness, mutilated or missing limbs (a squint is more damaging to the appearance than to the health). There are also minor defects that are nonetheless annoying in a partner, such as foul breath, a bad stammer, or partial deafness, but none of these is so terrible as to be intolerable in marriage, and if they appear after the wedding, both partners must accept them as their destiny, since no mortal can know what the future will bring. It is only right that a husband should tolerate in his wife something that, had the powers above so willed it, she might have had to tolerate in him.

However, I am still staggered by the folly of some parents, who will hand over a pure and healthy virgin to a husband riddled with the new leprosy. This pox differs from leprosy only in that it causes worse pain and greater danger to life, and is easier to catch. Shall an innocent virgin be joined to a walking corpse? If the girl had killed her father, I ask you, could anyone have devised a worse punishment? Does health not enter into the equation, when her age is reckoned, her looks inspected, her dowry counted? Has anyone ever deliberately married their daughter to a leper? What matter that the disease is not called leprosy, when it is more horrible than leprosy? What affection can a wife feel for a husband who hangs such a garland round her neck at the very start of their marriage? What respect will children feel for parents who have given them a life more loathsome than death? Again, since princes and their officials are supposed to take thought for everything that affects our health and well-being, I am truly astonished that they have ignored this plague for years and allowed it to spread far and wide, especially since in Holy Writ we are commanded to banish lepers and shown how to do it ...

Why should a marriage made with a man incapable of sexual intercourse be annulled, and yet a contract be valid with a man who produces pus instead of semen and begets pox instead of children? What are we to make of this, when a mind affected by bodily illness cannot be sound either, and yet parents, who consider themselves sane, thrust their sons and daughters upon such monsters and take less trouble over choosing a son-in-law than they would over a horse? With the latter, they flush out hidden defects and look carefully for things that the seller does not have to disclose; but in contracting a marriage, in our wisdom, we ignore the obvious.

Thus, after weighing up his character, our next concern must be his health. Some physical infirmities are not contagious, such as lameness, blindness, missing or mutilated limbs, or other unnatural deformities; in fact, if both have some defect it may add to the harmony of their marriage. I knew a priest in Britain, a tall, healthy, upright man, who told me that he had eleven brothers, all with an equally fine physique;

but their father had withered legs and had to be carried everywhere in a chair. He was also rather poor, so he married a blind woman and gave the following explanation: 'We shall be better friends because of it; we shall bear with one another, being united in misfortune, and neither of us will be able to find fault with the other.' And the man's judgment was perfect: every word they exchanged was friendly and fond. God rewarded their devotion with a happy issue; their life together was tranquil and blameless and their children numerous and well-favoured.

It remains to discuss external qualities, which are to some extent beyond our control (for example, being born of a distinguished or wealthy family) but can to some extent be obtained and improved by our own efforts. In this area the first place goes to family distinction, especially when it has been won by true virtue. All too often, 'nobility' is no more than inherited wealth, and it is not uncommon for wealth to be the proceeds of crime. By contrast, the true aristocrat, if he values more than a mere reputation for virtue, will have an example of the right way to live close at hand, from his ancestors, and if he fails to live up to it, his distinguished pedigree will serve no other purpose than to make his immorality all the more notorious.

In some countries nowadays a mere title of nobility can confer immunity on a criminal. If a commoner commits piracy or highway robbery, he is broken on the wheel; if he is a knight, or a claimant to some minor title, or the owner of some ruined castle (more like a den of thieves), then it is called war, which can apparently be declared by somebody without a foot of land to stand on. What gives such people the right to declare war? What gives them the right, under the pretext of some trumped-up 'war,' to rob anyone they please on the public highway or on other people's land? Whenever they run out of money for their gambling, whoring, and drinking, they rush to so-called war – making sure that their chosen enemy has something worth plundering. The princes, and the emperor in particular, would do humanity a great service if they would get rid of such monsters, with their horses and castles; when they are caught red-handed, let their titles give them just the one privilege – of being hanged higher, as their exalted status demands!

Parents must be mad if they imagine it to be in their daughter's best interests to marry her to one of these knights rather than an honest farmer or a skilled artisan. Bewitched by an empty parade of nobility, they prefer a son-in-law who will waste good money on bad living to one who will preserve and increase his portion by his own efforts. The girls themselves may be forgiven this mistake; their age and sex make them too eager for glory, unable to judge rationally or to look beyond the excitement of the moment. But no such allowance can be made for their parents, who to their shame bewail – afterwards – a calamity that they could have prevented. Given all the previous examples of such marriages, they should have learned from others' misfortunes.

Away then with these empty pretensions to nobility, acquired by crime, stained with sin, faked, or assumed! Only impostors will pass themselves off as noblemen, but some do so in order to commit their crimes with more safety and impunity; only fools who glory in shadows will buy nobility. The wise man will scorn even true nobility. There is some merit in being descended from distinguished and honourable forebears, but much more in being brought up and educated in a manner befitting your lineage ... Now, money should be the least important question, especially if both partners have enough income to live on decently, or a trade instead of an estate. In comedies, as it happens, marriages are called into question when an impoverished bride marries a rich husband, on the grounds that she is entering into slavery rather than matrimony. However, among Christians, whom Christ has made equal in so many ways, the size of the dowry should not be so important; in fact, as I have said, things usually turn out better if a rich husband takes a bride without a dowry, rather than the reverse. It is entirely laudable that a rich man should take in marriage a girl of slender means but of good character; the greater the disparity in their fortune, the more his generosity will be admired. However, financial equality may play a far from negligible part in establishing harmony between those of lesser means, if at the same time it is balanced against the other advantages and disadvantages, and if the order of priorities I have established is preserved.

If all marriages were made in this way, that is, with the support of the parents (or after due consultation with the older generation), by choosing with care and sound judgment, and above all by placing our hopes in God, then the world would not see so many unhappy and burdensome marriages, nor so many separations. It is God alone who joins human hearts in endless love and brings us success by his favour.

We cannot do better by him than to live according to his decrees, placing all our expectations of success in him, since he alone knows what is good for us. All that he sends us is truly blessed and auspicious, even if it sometimes appears calamitous to the superficial mind. Therefore, if you find a wife who fulfils your heart's desire, you must give thanks to God; if not, you must believe that, just as he draws some people to him and purifies them through illness or the loss of their worldly goods, so you have been given a shrewish wife to test your virtue ...

Finally, besides all that has been said, there is always that inexplicable element of liking – or dislike – between two people. Thus it happens that, for no apparent reason, a man is well-disposed towards one person rather than another, that he likes the first more than the second; similarly, he may recoil from someone but be quite unable to explain why he dislikes him. The Ancient sophists' theory was that people's presiding geniuses were either compatible or incompatible. Whatever we may think of this clever explanation, we do detect this unexplained affinity or disharmony between people's natures, as in the oft-repeated epigram:

I do not love thee, Doctor Fell;
The reason why I cannot tell;
But this alone I know full well,
I do not love thee, Doctor Fell.[5]

This instinct should not be entirely trusted, especially in women, because it is often thoughtless and merely temporary. But if it persists, if it is constant and unshakeable, then it is no use fighting the gods, in my view; we must give in to this inexplicable natural inclination, which is also observable in animals, plants and trees.

NOTES

1 Pittacus was one of the ancient Seven Sages. See Erasmus, *Adages*, I ii 20.
2 Erasmus, *Apophthegmata*, 3.70
3 Theocritus (Greek poet, c 300–250 B.C.) 6.18–19
4 Ancient methods of predicting the future; cf Cicero, *On Divination*, 1.15.28; 2.34.72.
5 Martial, 1.32. The free nursery-rhyme translation is by Thomas Brown.

b) Maintaining a Harmonious Relationship

Once a lawful marriage has been made with all due care and consideration, the next thing will be to ensure that harmony and goodwill are established and encouraged between the partners. For in some cases friendship disintegrates at the very beginning, before it has been cemented, before they have the chance to know and grow accustomed to one another. The parents and older members of the family have a primary responsibility here. They must warn the bride and groom beforehand that they will have to lay aside that aggressiveness that is so characteristic of inexperienced young women and hot-blooded adolescents, and that each will have to take up the common yoke with docility and make allowances for the other, until growing familiarity and intimacy enable each to understand the disposition and character of the other. If this is done, it will be none too difficult for them to avoid upsets by considerate behaviour and to lay the foundations of a lasting affection that, once established, will not easily be destroyed. You could compare them to little pots stuck together with glue. If you knock while the glue is still wet, they will break at a touch, but if you wait until the glue has hardened and they are firmly stuck, they will be very difficult to break, even with fire or a sword. Even things joined by nature are more easily broken than those that are glued together in this way.

Thus the girl needs to be told by her parents to be obliging and compliant towards her husband and, if he should upset her, to give him the benefit of the doubt, or at least put up with it. She must not rush headlong into recrimination and arguments, nor flounce out of the house: in time, when life together has bred intimacy between them, it will ensure that things that upset her at first will now amuse her, and that what once seemed intolerable will prove very easy to bear. However, it is best to try to avoid such problems altogether since, as Homer's epic tells us: 'Discord is swift, reconciliation is slow.'[1] It will not be difficult for one of them to make amends for some trifling offence, if it is done at once, but if they both retaliate the quarrel is likely to grow and become so deep-rooted that it will be very difficult to eradicate without leaving some traces of bitterness behind. It will be like a broken limb or a deep wound, which is rarely so completely healed by medical science that an occasional twinge of pain does not remind us of the accident, or an ugly scar allow us to forget the old wound. A mere bruise or a graze is easily healed and eventually quite forgotten.

Just as no one is blessed with a personality completely free from flaws, so almost no one can have a character so hopeless that there is not some admirable, or at least tolerable, trait among all the defects. Epictetus is worth listening to here: he says that we must always grab the handle that we can see, not look for another one that isn't there![2] There is a type of person who is disenchanted with every aspect of human existence, and no wonder, since they refuse to consider anything but the evils that beset our mortal condition. Take, for example, Heraclitus and Democritus:[3] whenever they went out into the world, the former would weep and the latter laugh; I don't know which of them was the madder. Somebody said: 'It would be best either not to be born, or to be snuffed out as soon as possible.'[4] On the other hand, Metrodorus, who managed to discern inherent advantages in everything, had nothing but praise for every aspect of life.[5] But the wise man will always weigh advantages against disadvantages, if he has the liberty to be dispassionate. If he is not free to change his way of life, he must turn his eyes from the disadvantages to the advantages, to help him bear what cannot be changed. You will find this easier to do if you will admit that other people may perhaps have to put up with a good deal from you. God, in whom there is no evil for others to put up with, nonetheless puts up with our errors and sins with immense forbearance; so how can you, a prey to so many vices, refuse to put up with some fault in your lifetime partner, whom you must tolerate, even if you find her intolerable?

If husband and wife are as bad as one another, then mutual forgiveness is more like appeasement than tolerance, more like a settling of scores than an act of generosity. The jurists define four types of contract: *I give that you may give; I give that you may do; I do that you may do; I do that you may give.*[6] What merit is there in someone offering forgiveness simply in order to be forgiven when he does something wrong? If yours are the worse misdeeds, it is merely cynical for you to shudder at the wart on your partner's face while expecting your own great tumours to be overlooked! If you surpass your partner in virtue and generosity, that is all the more reason, as Paul taught, to look after the weaker part.[7] Remember that your strength is a gift bestowed by God to enable you to help those weaker than yourself, and especially your partner. 'No man hates his own flesh' or shrinks from it, however corrupt, 'but instead cherishes and sustains it.'[8]

Now in some circumstances a husband should give in to his wife now and then, even though she is the 'weaker vessel,'[9] but the wife must defer much more to the authority of the head, 'for the husband is the head of the wife,' as Paul said.[10] The husband is to the wife what the spirit is to the body. The spirit is the greater of the two, but it is for the body's benefit; the spirit does not dominate and overwhelm it, but makes concessions to assist it. The affection the husband feels for his bride will enable him to recognize the right time either to tolerate or to correct the girl's inclinations. Similarly, if the girl gives her husband a wife's love together with appropriate respect for him, which nature's laws seem to require in view of his sex and position, she will not be tempted to argue with her husband but will win his affection by obedience and compromise.

At the outset, even the sweetest things may have their unpleasant side, a sort of bitter taste that, with the passage of time, turns to sweetness. What is more pleasant than wine? And yet it comes from grapes, which are bitter at first. Thus any man who recoils instinctively from his virgin bride, finding her unbearably sour and immature, is acting as irrationally as someone who tastes an unripe grape and disgusted by the acid taste, rejects it and leaves the sweet taste of the ripened grape to others. You are prepared to wait until new wine has lost its sharpness; you must also wait a little until your new bride has matured. Put the unripe apples to one side until in time they become more appetizing. Such rawness is often evidence of a natural vigour and firmness. People who mature too soon often have less strength and grow old before their time. As the proverb says: 'Neither honey nor bee.' If you require sweetness, you must accept that it may have its unpleasant side. Nature so frames human life that nothing is so sweet as to be free from all bitterness. Young men, too, not yet forearmed with any great experience of the world, can be somewhat rough and arrogant until the passage of a few years calms them down. Thus girls who recoil from their husbands and immediately begin to feud with them are acting as rashly as someone who is stung by a bee and therefore leaves the honey to others. The most beautiful rose grows among thorns. You do not dig up your rose garden as soon as a thorn pricks you; you accept the pain for love of the flowers.

They say there was a custom among the Boeotians[11] that a bride on her way to her husband was veiled – and crowned with a garland made of asparagus. This seems so absurd that of course it invites the observer to seek a hidden meaning. No doubt the Ancients intended it to signify that in the union of an inexperienced young man and an untutored and spirited virgin there was bound to be some friction and difficulty at first, but that, if they persevered, their difficulties would give way to a most agreeable way of life, just as asparagus is a prickly plant – all prickle, in fact, as it has no leaves – which nonetheless produces a fruit that is both delicious to eat and most useful in medicine. However, asparagus is always just asparagus, and does not bear fruit in every season, whereas the young couple's prickliness will change into endless sweetness and produce everlasting fruit, if only they will work together towards mutual harmony.

Even with the virtuous and the well-born, there are certain quirks of character, if not actual faults, that can be annoying unless you are used to them. It is the same with certain wines, which you cannot justly call sour or bitter, but which have their own peculiar taste, commonly called the tang of the soil, which may be somewhat unpalatable to anyone unused to it; but on a few days' acquaintance the distaste may be overcome. Would you begrudge doing for your wife what you do for your wine?

Again, there are minor blemishes, like moles on the skin, that it is best to ignore. That carping attitude which the Greeks call *micrologia* [pettiness] can cast a blight over all life's pleasures; it is like quarrelling over goat's wool, as the saying goes. One thing that will contribute much to preserving affection between you is an unfailing courtesy, striking a balance between indulgence and austerity so that it does not lose you respect, but equally does not mar the pleasures of family life. It should ensure that any necessary rebuke will not give offence, if it is timely, delivered in a pleasant manner, and tempered with praise and a little flattery.

Thus it will be essential, to avoid problems and to encourage total harmony between you, that each should study and be familiar with the character and disposition of the other; here again the parents could help by giving advice to the bride and groom. As Virgil put it: 'You know the tactful and the timely way to approach a husband.'[12] The slave in the comedy says something similar: 'I understand his disposition very well.' As the proverb has it: 'You should understand a friend's character, not hate it.'[13] All this will be even more necessary in marriage. Everyone has different tastes and a different temperament; people are attracted or repelled by different things. In this case, there is nothing wrong with friendship won by submissiveness. A modest silence or a pleasant soothing reply will often defuse a serious quarrel. Why should you refuse such things, which you would often grant a servant or an employee, to your spouse, with whom, willy-nilly, you are to spend the rest of your life?

However, although there must be mutual respect, both nature and scriptural authority lay down that the wife should obey her husband rather than the opposite. Paul recommends love and gentleness to husbands: 'You men,' he says, 'love your wives, and do not be harsh with them.' But what does he prescribe for the women? Obedience and submissiveness: 'You women,' he says, 'be subject to your husbands as to the Lord.'[14] For this very reason nature has endowed the male sex with a certain ruthlessness and fierceness, but the female with softness and gentleness. You may find the following comparison far-fetched, but it is apt enough to illustrate my point. The first thing that trainers of animals, wild beasts, or unbroken horses try to find out is what things will annoy or calm them. Lions are annoyed when they are looked at sideways; bulls are enraged by the colour red; lynxes are so maddened by the sound of drums that they will claw themselves to pieces; elephants are frightened by the squealing of a pig, and think it shameful to be caught in the act of coition. A plunging horse can be calmed by stroking and by clicking the tongue. There are countless other examples; animal trainers always know the best ways to avoid upsetting their charges, and use them to calm unsettled beasts. They are thus able to handle safely animals that are by nature dangerous and fierce.

If a married couple will do the same, they will soon begin to enjoy a life of tranquillity, and if some disagreement should arise, it will not be hard to resolve it peacefully. Some otherwise virtuous people are by nature quick to anger, but it soon evaporates if they are not opposed. What could be easier than to remain demurely silent in such cases, or to soothe them with appropriately amiable words? Some people cannot stand being answered back when they are upset, and even refuse words of comfort so long as the hurt is fresh in their minds. An easy and economical solution here is to postpone one's reply until such time as the wound is less sensitive. Some husbands enjoy boisterous parties; in this case a more serious-minded wife should not raise an eyebrow, but make some allowance for her husband, provided that her matronly modesty and the respect she should feel for her husband are not affected. Some people cannot bear to be told a lie, even in jest, some detest make-up, others like or dislike particular foods, or particular colours and styles of clothing. Even in such trivial cases, a measure of complaisance will avoid upsets and encourage affection. Certain kinds of story appeal to some tastes but not to others; an offensive tale can often be interrupted and toned down by a timely interjection. I knew a man, rather irascible by nature but easily placated, who never got so annoyed with his wife that he would not, if called on for a song or one of his poems, at once begin to recite or sing, apparently forgetting all that had gone before.

It is not too surprising that some wives do not get on with their husbands, when they take every opportunity to be contrary. If their husband is sad, their faces beam with joy; if he is happy, they look downcast; if he is laughing and joking, they will talk about something serious and sad; if the husband is feeling amorous, they suddenly become ostentatiously chaste and forbidding. No doubt this illustrates that witty saying: 'With a husband, life isn't very lively.'[15] But living together means sharing pleasures and cares, fun and seriousness, joys and sorrows. It is not enough for a wife to be honest and chaste unless she is also sympathetic to her husband's moods. No one would think much of a mirror, however crusted with gold and jewels, if it did not give a faithful reflection; similarly, a rich, noble, and beautiful wife is no use if she does not fit in with her husband. If a mirror showed a laughing face weeping or a happy face as sad, would it not be considered unreliable and useless? But a wife who is happy when her husband is sad or sad when he is happy, appears not only unsuitable but even hostile. Again, there are some women to whom nothing is so delightful as their husband's absence, while his presence makes them restless and foul-tempered; you could compare them to the moon, which is dull and dark when close to the sun, but ever brighter as it moves away. A good wife should do the opposite: when her husband is by her, she must share his joy; when he is away, she must stay indoors and behave as if she were a widow.

Similarly, some husbands make the bad mistake of being morose and stern at home and merry and gregarious everywhere else; by denying their wives a share in their pleasures at home, they are encouraging them to seek amusement and laughter elsewhere. However, a good wife will not revenge herself by imitating her husband's faults; instead, she will encourage him to appreciate home life by her pleasant and accommodating manner. When grafting new shoots onto a plant gardeners always take great care to meld the parts together, smearing them with a mixture of clay and oakum and, as Virgil elegantly put it: 'They teach the shoot to grow in the moist bark.'[16] This prevents even slight damage to the new graft; when in time a scar has covered the wound, they pull off the poultice and need give the graft no further special care. Similarly, there is a greater danger of discord in the very first stages of a marriage, when the union is still fresh and fragile, but each day's acquaintance makes it stronger. We may observe how animals of the same species, such as horses, do not necessarily get on until they have grown used to one another, but that we may see peaceful relations even between a dog and a cat, or a wolf and a lamb, once acquaintance has been established. We must surely expect even better of human beings, creatures born to social life, and still more of a man and a woman, whom nature has so fashioned that they cannot live without one another – unless a power greater than nature has breathed upon them.

Thus it is excellent advice that the first lovemaking between husband and wife should be made as easy as possible. This is believed to be the reason for the ancient marriage ritual in which the bride was taken into the husband's bedchamber in the dark. This custom was obviously exploited to deceive the patriarch Jacob, when Leah was substituted for her sister, Rachel.[17] Commentators suggest two reasons for the custom: the need to protect the girl's modesty, and to prevent anything in this first sexual act, which is often the most difficult, from offending the husband's eye.

Solon apparently made provision not only for fastidious eyes, but also for the most delicate nose.[18] He decreed that, before the bride was brought into the bedchamber for the intimate meeting with her groom, she should nibble a quince apple to purify her breath. Such attention to detail might seem unworthy of a legislator, were it not that the merest trifles all too often destroy human relationships. However, I am quite ready to accept the view that that wise man aimed to conceal a deeper meaning in his statute, namely that it is vital that a new bride should not, in their first conversation, let slip from her mouth anything that might offend the young man's ears or mind. Speech issues from the lips but is the most reliable image and witness of the soul; from her words he will see more clearly what she is like than by examining her whole body under a spotlight. When we send our children with a message to some worthy citizen, we teach them the correct form of address and the right answer to each question, so that nothing offends the company. How much more should parents ensure that the couple's first conversations be harmless, infused with modesty and politeness? They must learn that, whereas among close friends even insults can be laughed off, in a first conversation between strangers the most harmless observation may give offence. But no quince apple, no brand of perfume or unguent, smells as sweet to a wise young man as modest, sober, prudent and respectful words dropping from the lips of his new bride and bringing with them the reflection of a lovely nature.

Furthermore, there is nothing better than conversation to establish, confirm and maintain friendship. It was conversation that drew human beings, who used to roam the earth like wild animals, together in cities; it also joined city to city, people to people, kingdom to kingdom. It distinguishes the king from the tyrant, since the tyrant compels but the king persuades. Now marriage is rather like a kingdom, but must be far from any semblance of tyranny. Nothing is accomplished there by force; all is done by persuasion and goodwill. Plato will not let a law prescribe anything unless it can be defended on moral as well as practical grounds, and I do not see why Seneca attacks his view.[19] The husband is indeed the director and head of the woman and rules her: not, however, as the farmer drives his cattle, but as the spirit rules the body. His character provides unwritten laws for his wife's behaviour, as Aristotle rightly said,[20] but they are Platonic laws, persuading not compelling her, guiding her willingly, not dragging her along by force.

I wish that, among Christians, the lustful husband were not praised to the skies. Does it augur well for his marriage if he makes love to his wife for the first time as if he were raping a prisoner? He rips off her underwear, tears her clothes and anything else that impedes his stallion's lust. You would say that the groom behaves more like a madman than a lover, and that nothing could be less like a sacramental union. There is more dignity in the mating of most dumb animals. And it is not finished yet: the details of that first night are recounted and spread abroad ... How unchristian a marriage is this marriage between Christians! A wife must obey her husband, of course, but Mercury must also be there, to join their hearts before their bodies, to urge but not to force them to physical intimacy. While on the subject, we must remind the bride not to instigate their lovemaking herself, as this may diminish his affection for her; on the other hand, she must not show herself too unwilling or forbidding when he suggests it. The first attitude, for some reason, makes a woman cheap and less attractive to a man, the second changes love into hatred. A respectable married woman will not be provocative, a chaste woman will know how to refuse gently, but only a false wife will persist in her protests.

Let us make Christ the witness and sponsor of Christian marriage, so that no impurity may soil relations with a spouse; let the husband persuade his wife, through God's decrees and laws, to do willingly and joyfully what she has learned is pleasing to the Lord. Let both partners first pray to him in unison to bestow his favour on their marriage; after prayer, let them engage in pious conversation. Finally, let their lovemaking be modest and virtuous, the opposite of fornication and rape.

I know that there will be some – fine, witty fellows in their own estimation – who will find all this ridiculous, but let these fine unchristian fellows go hang: I am writing this treatise for good Christians. However, let those who think Christ's teaching worthless at least hearken to the old man in the pagan comedy, who said to his son: 'Go home, and pray to the gods that your bride may be brought to you.'[21] That pagan will not have the bride brought from her home, nor does he expect the marriage to be blessed by heaven, unless the bridegroom prays to the gods. But you consider it unfashionable, before you lay hands on your wife, to pray together to the one who first joined wife to husband, and to ask him to make your marriage stable, chaste and blessed. If you are not ashamed to be called a Christian, do not be ashamed to do what most befits a Christian.

Perhaps you need a form of prayer? I shall be pleased to provide one. It will be appropriate to pray along these lines: 'O creator, redeemer, and propagator of the human race, God, who first in paradise consecrated the marriage-alliance between the founders of our race; whose only begotten son commended this sacrament to us in many ways, first when in an inexpressible way he joined our nature to himself, as if in marriage, then again when he chose the congregation of all the saints as his bride, from which union were born things beyond human power; then when he honoured a wedding with the first of his miracles, turning water into the best wine; and finally, when he decreed that this holy union, to reflect its mystic origins, should be indissoluble, saying: 'What God has joined, let no man put asunder':[22] we pray that, since we have joined lawfully in this holy union, according to your decrees, you will deign to prosper with your perpetual favour what is yours, that we may obey your will with equal humility and equal zeal. May all uncleanness and all discord be banished from our home; give us that true peace the world cannot give; give us enough to satisfy our needs; give us offspring to bring up in your name, so that, continuing together under your commandments here below, we may deserve to come together into the inheritance of heavenly life.' If you can think of some better form of words, use that.

You can find a model for your conversation in the book of Tobit: 'We are the children of holy men,' he says, 'and we cannot be united in the manner of the pagans who know not God.'[23] You could also borrow a form of prayer from the same book, if you do not like mine. But the following exchange seems appropriate to Christian spouses; the husband begins as follows: 'My dearest one, my sister in religion, my partner in marriage: God has seen fit to join us together in the holy bond of matrimony and I have gained something I must prefer even to my parents whom, after God, I hold dearer than anything else; you too have been given something that you are told to hold dearer than your progenitors. We are closely joined to our parents by the ties of blood but, as the scriptural prophecy says, in matrimony we two have in a certain way been made one flesh, that is, a single person. We have accepted a yoke that cannot be lifted from us as long as we live; we must not even think of separation, but rather direct our energies towards establishing a tranquil and blessed partnership. If there is harmony between us, we shall live pleasantly and happily, however slender our means; on the other hand, if – God forbid – our bodies are united at bed and board, but our hearts disunited by discord, then, however abundant our wealth, we shall spend our lives in vexation and misery. Thus let there be between us that special love that unites the body and the soul, Christ and his church. If our friendship is based only on youth, or beauty, or physical attraction, or wealth, there will be no genuine or lasting harmony between us. But if our hearts are united by equal devotion to God and similar reverence for religion, then no earthly misfortune – not poverty, nor illness, nor age – can impair our joyous partnership through life. I shall try my hardest to be a husband you will not regret; I am sure that you on your side will strive to match or surpass my efforts. I have married you to beget children, not out of lust; if, as Paul admonishes, we wish our marriage to be honourable and our bed undefiled,[24] let our life together be pure and gentle, let our lovemaking be modest and infrequent; let us devote ourselves to bringing our children and the rest of the household to holiness, but in such a way that our greatest confidence and principal trust lies in help from God, who favours even the least favoured of his servants. The union of our hearts and the purity of our consciences will provide us with all the pleasure we need. We shall divide the management of the household into two parts: you shall have particular charge of matters pertaining to the home, and I to those outside, but in such a way that neither shall exclude the other. Since it is impossible that we mortals should always be wise, I hope you will believe that, if ever I admonish you, I shall be looking to your interests rather than my own and, if you should see me doing something wrong, I shall not resent admonition from her who shares all that is mine. But the authority nature has given to the husband, and that the apostles confirmed and sanctioned, will not harm you; our mutual affection will smooth every path. Let us therefore enter upon this holy enterprise, inspired by God, united in heart, and equal in resolve. Thus may we live a tranquil and innocent life, like a pair of doves: you shall guard the nest and I shall fly out to seek and bring home the necessities of life. We shall be one and, as it is written, "God shall have mercy on the two who are as one."'[25]

What shall the Christian bride reply to all this? Perhaps she might begin as follows: 'Best of husbands, whom I must not only love but honour, I count myself especially fortunate to have been given a husband who, beyond his other gifts, shows himself both wise and devout. I bring to you from my parents' house a body that is chaste and undefiled, I promise you a heart obedient to your wishes, to all your commands, concerning not only household tasks but also religion and worship. You must decide how to form and instruct me. I have the highest hopes that God will prosper all that we undertake in love.'

Christian matrimony should always begin with such preliminaries, with such exchanges; today, instead, we see many marriages that are no more honourable than concubinage, and not much less repulsive: as their beginnings are marked by impiety, so their course is full of troubles and their ending is despair.

The course of our discussion now almost compels me to deal with the separate duties of husband and wife. I shall indeed embark on that once I have given a few words of advice on the wedding ceremony, the prelude to marriage, in which ordinary Christians usually make worse mistakes than any pagans do, or ever did. There is more than one reason for these mistakes: people are led astray by ambition, extravagance, intemperance, and licentiousness. First of all, it is unacceptable to subject a bride and groom, who are about to embark on so important and so serious an undertaking, to so many ridiculous little rituals, devised in another time and place to cater for mere human caprice, as if it were a trivial and a frivolous matter for a young man to be united with a pure and chaste virgin. This sacrament need involve no more than the bride's journey to the church, the performance of the ceremony itself, and her return home. What then can justify the general rowdiness and merrymaking, the wanton frolics that go on from breakfast to suppertime, to which the blushing bride must admit all comers: open house for the whole town! The poor girl is obliged to shake hands with drunkards, syphilitics, sometimes with criminals, who have come with more of an eye to larceny than dancing; in Britain, she even has to kiss them! After a riotous supper, more dancing, another bout of drinking; the exhausted couple are not allowed to retire before midnight. Only a few hours later a mad din and tumult break out again outside their bedroom, everyone charges in to make obscene remarks, and the madness starts up all over again. In some countries this Corybantic frenzy[26] goes on for three days. What could be more inhuman, more uncivilised than to weary with such nonsense these anxious hearts, and these bodies about to take up new burdens? How much more pleasant it would be to hold the nuptial feast quietly and soberly with just the parents and few close relatives.

But here, as everywhere else, ambition, with extravagance in train, encourages a host of evils. The wedding will be considered beggarly unless a horde of aristocrats, grand ladies, plutocrats, and other notables is invited to the feast. A so-called respectable wedding is one where vast sums of money are squandered on frippery, where as many guests as possible throw up, or take a fever from intemperance and exhaustion, and where licence is freely granted to filthy language and silly pranks. What a splendid start to the life of chastity, self-denial, and sobriety on which the groom has embarked, tossing aside the follies of his earlier life! What an atmosphere in which to take a wife and teach her chastity and self-denial! Whose doctrine is it that the holy state of matrimony should begin with the Bacchanalia?[27] Is this the way to take a sacrament? Shall a girl on the threshold of matrimony be initiated into extravagance, wantonness, ambition, and the rest, all so incompatible with true marriage? Christians, it is like celebrating the festival of Flora in the temple of Vesta![28] Are these happy omens for a marriage? It used to be unlawful to speak words of ill omen at a wedding: what worse omens than filthy language, obscene behaviour, and lewd stories?

In ancient times the bride was brought to the groom with her face veiled; why show her to everyone now that she had found a husband? Only one man need set eyes on her, since she is allowed to please only one. In Italy they go to great lengths to keep unmarried girls at home. In Venice, they never go out without a chaperone and a veil down to their shoulders; you would think they were nuns. In fact it would be more acceptable for a girl who has not yet found a husband to be unveiled and paraded in public; but why on earth should a girl, to whom it is now forbidden to seek to please other men, be paraded bareheaded through the streets? For whose benefit is she unveiled now? For whom is she painted and prinked?

No less absurd is the custom of distinguishing a virgin from a woman of experience by letting her wear her hair loose. Is it not enough that her husband is satisfied as to her virginity, without the public being called to witness? What does such nonsense achieve, except to make impertinent tongues wag about a maiden who is, more often than not, quite irreproachable? The public is eager for scandal, and the envy provoked by this pointless display is a deadly sin. What awful things are sometimes shouted at young girls as they process back and forth in full view of everyone, with the cantor in the lead more or less inviting the public to see the show? What is the point of exposing the glory of virginity to the evil tongues and taunts of men? That treasure is safer if it is hidden. And again, what is the point of reproaching women about to remarry with their previous marriages? Granted, before marriage there is a distinction between married and unmarried, widow and virgin, but now that a marriage has been arranged, what use is this distinction? Those married once and those married twice will both be honoured before God. But it is humiliating, not honourable, for a blushing young virgin, her hair unbound, her head bare, painted and apparelled like a harlot, to be exposed to the lustful eyes of the young men and the slanderous tongues of the people. Is it an honour for a virgin, whose dowry is, above all, her chastity, to be attended by the sighs and catcalls of young men? It is no honour, but a kind of prostitution.

The gospel declares that anyone who has looked on a woman with lust has committed adultery,[29] and not the least part of virginity is an unsullied reputation. Thus a virgin has lost something of her chastity if she has delighted so many eyes, has awakened desire, has been pursued by lustful cries and perhaps appeared by night in someone's dreams and suffered defilement, so to speak, as the plaything of a phantom. Indeed, in the ancient myth Juno was offended merely because Jupiter subjected a cloud to Ixion in her place;[30] it was not enough that the adulterer had not touched her, but she judged it a kind of adultery to have been defiled even through an image and an illusion. Virginity is a fragile thing, like a milk-white rose that loses its fresh bloom in the gentlest breath of wind. Therefore, you parents, allow the bride to bring her virginity unsullied to her husband's chamber; she will be all the dearer to her husband, and her reputation will be all the safer.

Marriage is a holy and a chaste institution, and the ceremony should be equally pure and holy, to convince the bride and groom from the outset how sober, modest, and gentle are the ways that become marriage. Do you believe that marriage is a sacrament of the Church? You so believe. Do you believe that it was established by God in person? Of course, you so believe. Do you believe that the gift of the Spirit is poured out on those who perform this sacrament aright? You so believe. Why then is something so solemn and so holy accompanied by such unholy rites?

Come, tell me: when a virgin takes the veil of St Francis or St Dominic, who would allow the occasion to be celebrated with silly games, laughter, lutes, pipes, foolery, and dancing? On the contrary, the novice is purified by confession, prays, puts off the garments of worldly pride, prostrates herself, is veiled, and given the host, and with all that listens to a holy exhortation. Nothing indecent or foolish about these rites, although a girl entering this marriage is taking no new sacraments. And yet you approach the great sacrament of marriage, which God chose to establish and which the Lord so often commended to us both directly and through his apostles, with stupid nonsense and extravagant and immoral customs, as though it were a secular ceremony. If you receive a sacrament unworthily, your reward will be not grace, but God's wrath. Even in the church itself the nonsense continues: at the entrance the young men exchange blows with the bridegroom,[31] and during the service silly gestures and nods are exchanged and rude remarks are passed. Who would believe that a solemn act was being performed? Is it not a disgrace that the pagans who worshipped idols had holier marriage customs than Christians? Everyone seeks a bride who is thrifty, chaste, and unassuming – and at the very outset we show her extravagance, immodesty, and arrogance. When a deacon is ordained, he cleanses his conscience, he readies himself for worship, that he may receive the holy mystery in a holy frame of mind. How much more appropriate would such holiness be at weddings, instead of the goings-on we see now?

There is intense competition to see who can produce the finest clothes, the most sumptuous banquet, the best presents. It appears kind to give the newly-weds something for the house, but how has it become the custom that the bridegroom has to impoverish himself making gifts that nonetheless bring him more odium than thanks? Some think that these are presents not given but returned, while others think of them as the repayment of a debt. Many, seeing others get more expensive presents, angrily consider themselves slighted, and jealously increases among the recipients; as a result the bridegroom loses popularity and antagonises – at his own expense – the very people he has been trying to please. And thus Christians judge the quality of a wedding by the amount of money thrown away on presents! Not to mention the crazy cost of the bride's dress, and I mean crazy: I have seen people borrow so much money to deck the bride in her finery that within a couple of months they have been compelled to sell off their clothes and their crockery for a good deal less than they paid for them.

What is the point of all this costly display? Are you afraid that your bride will neglect her toilet or her appearance? Are you afraid to appear more intelligent than the last fellow to bankrupt himself by such extravagance? Are you really keen to make your less wealthy neighbours all too conscious of their poverty? Is not poverty enough of a burden in itself? You may think you risk humiliation if you lose this dire competition, but you cannot win; even if you surpass all your predecessors, the next man will cap even your insanity! Does not your affluence already expose you to envy, without you boasting and flaunting it before everyone? Even so, nothing is so thoroughly wasted as money laid out on food and drink: nobody really thanks you for laying on a public feast, and some even curse the host for giving them a fever and indigestion. Nonetheless, people splash out three years' income on such nonsense: do Christians have no sumptuary laws or censors[32] to restrain such behaviour? Marriages are arranged so that even people who are not very rich may, following Paul's advice, supply their family's needs by the work of their hands, and bestow something too upon those who are dogged by poverty.[33] And yet, outrageously, well-off Christians pour their money away on the doorstep of matrimony and leave nothing to pass on to the needy or to spend on their family.

Now the fact that girls from poor backgrounds also celebrate their nuptials with great pomp, though it is either hired or borrowed, will be recognized by the more clear-sighted as a kind of momentary respite from their poverty, which these days is not just a burden but also a humiliation. But why do rich girls ostentatiously display their good fortune, which they refuse, of course, to share with lesser mortals? They enjoy tormenting the needy instead of helping them. The rich should be content with their good fortune without reminding others of their poverty and increasing the burden they have to bear.

Indeed, the richer and more powerful you are, the more you should set an example of economy to others, which would have the dual effect of making the rich less envied for their luck and the poor less burdened by their poverty. What is so wonderful about some egregious prima donna strutting down the street exhibiting her expensive jewellery, gold, purple, and furs? She can play with them at home whenever she likes. In fact, she would be truly admirable and truly dazzling if she wore a simple, unadorned outfit and thus rebuked the ambition of the lesser mortals who use such things to advertise themselves beyond the domestic sphere. Which is the greater compliment: to hear foolish or vulgar women, gaping at your dazzling gold and jewels, say: 'How much of her money has she got on her back? The cheapest thing she's wearing is the gold!' – but nothing about your figure or your mind? Or to hear wiser spirits saying: 'What honesty and modesty in a wealthy woman! How little are her ways affected by her fortune!'? This homespun simplicity does her more credit than all the sumptuous display of others. Will not ordinary people, who have barely enough to live on, be ashamed in the future recklessly to throw around money that exists more in their minds than in their wallets?

Such examples of sobriety and economy will be all the more striking if they are set by you, princes and noble ladies, rather than by anyone else. Your inferiors readily copy whatever example you set them and thus the less well-off will be shamed into restraint, as it were, from shameful indulgence in luxury, when they see that you disapprove strongly of flaunting one's wealth. They will realize that it is done on purpose, since otherwise the size of your fortune and the independence of your life would make extravagance quite justifiable in the people's eyes – but you have decided against it. Christians must always be mindful of thrift and moderation. So far from wasting money on riotous living, they should rather spend even less on essentials and set aside a portion to relieve the needs of their neighbours.

Even if there appears to be some excuse for pomp, extravagance, and wantonness in other areas, surely they must be entirely excluded from a wedding, which sets the pattern for married life. But these days the poison has crept even into this holy remedy – for what else is the profession of matrimony but the abjuration of a young man's dissipation, debauchery, gluttony, prodigality, and gambling and (if applicable) a young woman's haughtiness, excessive pride in her appearance, or wantonness? And yet in our society marriage is an initiation into these evils!

What is baptism but an abjuration of Satan? But nowadays, even there, pride makes people competitive. The godparents are chosen either because of their social standing or because they may bring expensive presents. But Paul taught that anyone under instruction in the faith should give a share of all his worldly goods to his teacher;[34] these days, perversely, those who play the catechist's part[35] make the gifts, though more out of habit than out of conviction. If you wanted to show kindness to the poor, it could be done in secret, or under another pretext; why tarnish a sacrament with self-advertisement? At the very least death, which levels rich and poor, high and low, should teach us moderation and thrift. But what could be more ostentatious and less frugal than our funerals?

But enough of this lengthy criticism of ordinary people's behaviour: if only I could improve it and turn my reproaches into praise! My discussion will now return to the subject I interrupted earlier. I have set out the rules for embarking upon matrimony clearly enough, I think, and shown that the final result nearly always corresponds to the beginning. As I said earlier, people who throw themselves into wells, or fall in by accident, will get badly hurt, but those who climb down step by step, even into the deepest well, will emerge unscathed. Similarly, men who marry in haste, without thinking, usually end up complaining – far too late – about their unhappy marriage, but you will find very few people disappointed in marriage who, with the advice of their elders, have made a careful and deliberate choice and taken a wife whom they can love forevermore. Anything that is the result of a whim will not last; any decision based on reason and judgment will be stable and lasting.

Now, to prevent the discussion wandering off too aimlessly, I shall confine the rest of this discourse to just three subjects, but in such a way that I shall not diverge from the plan I established at the beginning. Paul considers three things supremely valuable: faith, hope, and charity,[36] and these three words also seem to contain the secret of any successful marriage. And the greatest of these is charity; if it is present, all the rest is easy and straightforward. Closely allied to it is faith, without which mutual goodwill cannot subsist between the partners. Finally there is hope – the hope of a happy issue. The reward of a truly Christian marriage is children who are obedient and virtuous.

First of all let us continue our discussion of charity, or love. It must first be born, then nourished and strengthened, and finally healed and restored if it should happen to break down. It is born, nourished, and maintained mostly by the following: natural disposition, similarity of character, equality, mutual deference and service, worthy advice and exhortation, and children; it is destroyed by their opposites. Love that changes to hatred for some trivial reason was not true love. Just as a blazing fire made with hares' fur or dry straw will quickly go out unless there is more solid material underneath to keep the flames going, so love that is based on physical attraction or some other trivial cause, though it may seem overwhelming for a while, cannot last, any more than the things on which it was based. Denser material, such as iron, is slower to ignite, but once alight it retains heat for a long time. Again, some materials make a fire smoky or crackly, and others produce an unpleasant smell; such is the 'love' established between immoral people for shameful reasons; soured by quarrels and brawls, life together is impossible, and then it is time for infamy's trumpet to sound. We can observe this sort of noise and smoke in certain ill-fated marriages that reach the point where the husband is driven from the house, and sometimes the wife, too; both become the subject of general mockery. A clean fire is made with woods called for this reason *acapnos*, smokeless. A sweet-smelling fire is made with cedar wood. You will get a quiet, bright flame from pure wax smeared on clean linen, or from asbestos cloth (called 'quick flax' because it is not consumed by fire) dipped in oil that has been thoroughly aged to remove any watery residue. This is not the kind of love that is bred in sinful and foolish hearts by sensuality, ambition, the thirst for riches, or a shared predilection for evil, but the kind that virtue cements between those who are devout and temperate. Nothing is more truly lovely nor more lovable than this, and if it were visible to our physical sight it would inspire many more to love it than any physical beauty or adornment. Again, certain materials are quicker to put out fires than to kindle from them. Some people have personalities like that, being so rebarbative that they cannot even love themselves, let alone maintain a friendship with someone else.

It is no wonder that relationships are brief and unhappy if they are bred by Cupid, since he is both blind and winged. I am speaking of the earthly Cupid, son of the terrestrial Venus, who impudently inspires shameless and immoral love in first one and then another. He is depicted as blind, because such feelings are the product not of reasoned judgment but of heedless physical passion; he is winged because his tainted love changes rapidly to hatred. By turns it brings war, peace, a truce, war again, but nothing constant, nothing peaceful and enduring. For this reason the poets call the violent passions of lovers 'frenzy' rather than love. And rightly so, for when reason is dead and buried, what is left but madness?

However, the philosopher says that there is another Cupid, the child of the heavenly Venus, and that none is more clear-sighted than he.[37] He does not blind those whom he strikes with his darts, but instead cures their blindness and gives them sight. He shows them the beauties of the spirit, which reflect the Supreme Beauty. Once it is glimpsed, the lover is transported by love for it; it creates and fosters those faultless relationships that grow ever deeper and better. There can be no doubt that the source of all true beauty is God himself; everything in him is unalloyed goodness, absolute purity, complete wisdom. He does not begrudge his beauty to others, but shares it generously, as James the apostle teaches: 'Every good gift and every perfect gift comes not from the earth but from on high, from the father of light.'[38] For he showers sparks of his light upon the hearts of his chosen ones, and from them is kindled among the virtuous a kind of loving and chaste fire of mutual affection, reflecting its source. For just as God's light knows no clouds, nor the play of passing shadows, so the love it inspires is always cloudless and serene, and knows nothing of transient quarrels and jealousies. There is no need for contracts, witnesses, and documents between those whom this bond has united; true virtue can never perish.

Thus it is inward beauty, inward riches, inward nobility that must inspire Christian marriages, and if affection should arise from some other cause, it must nonetheless be transferred from there to ensure that it survives. The order of nature decrees that we move on from things that are accessible to our physical senses towards those that can only be perceived through the workings of the mind. Christian piety must not reject entirely this order of things; it gradually pulls feeble humankind away from these physical preliminaries and leads it by the hand towards the things of the mind. Thus someone enraptured by some example of physical beauty is being made aware, as if in a dream, of that other, truly supreme, beauty of which Plato thinks some memory is awakened in us,[39] since humans seem to have an innate inclination towards good that apparently does not exist in animals. When the dream has been shattered, the lover will turn his mind's eye towards the hidden beauties of the soul, and the phantom of insubstantial beauty will yield to the truly beautiful.

The newborn child is nourished by its mother's milk, and adults too thrive best on such basic food; similarly, true love is nourished by much the same things as gave it birth. Love that is inspired by sensuality or wealth is no more true love than those are truly desirable things. A man who takes a wife with a large dowry, but would never have married her without this inducement, is in love with money not his wife. A man who marries a beauty out of lust is motivated by love of himself not of his wife. Nobody calls it friendship when people cultivate childless old folk in the hope of an inheritance. It is no more justified to call a young man a lover if he ensnares a girl in order to rob her of her dearest possessions – her chastity and her good name. Tell me, could an enemy do more? Do enemy soldiers subject the girls they capture to worse outrage? Love must be born of honour, and nourished by honourable conduct.

The girl whom virtue makes lovable possesses the most effective of love potions. If you would be loved, be sure you are lovable – and nothing is truly lovable but virtue. This makes those women seem all the more insane who try to inveigle men into loving them by using cosmetics, or spells and sorcery. In Xenophon, Ischomachus cleverly used cross-examination to reprove his wife's vice.[40] He had noted that she was using white lead, antimony, rouge, and other cosmetic colours to prettify herself, and also built-up shoes, like those worn by goddesses and heroines in tragedy, to make herself taller. 'Tell me, wife,' he said, 'was not one of the conditions of our marriage that we should share all our possessions?' She nodded. 'Well, would you have been pleased if, after you had made your contribution as agreed, I had given you paste instead of jewels, pinchbeck instead of real gold, gold-plated glass instead of gold bracelets, and, instead of genuine necklaces, wooden beads covered with gold, silver, and jewelled coatings? Would you reckon such trumpery gifts more precious than the possessions – all I own – that I have in fact put into our pool?' When his wife replied that she could not possibly love a husband who would use her so deceitfully, he continued: 'But of course the major point of our agreement was that we should surrender our bodies to one another: true?' The wife nodded once more. 'Am I more agreeable to you,' he asked, 'will I be dearer to you, if I give you my body as it is, untouched by artifice, or if I offer you lips and eyes bespattered with red dye?' She declared that her husband's eyes could not be any dearer to her painted with red than in their natural state, and he concluded: 'Believe me, I feel the same, and take more pleasure in your natural complexion than I do in that unnatural face you put on with white lead and antimony.' Accepting this timely advice, the woman threw out all her warpaint and other supposed aids to beauty.

A made-up face is not a face but a mask, and no husband, however complaisant, will allow his wife to wear a mask. Moreover, when a woman knows what her husband likes, but paints her face and does her hair in some other way, she is admitting a desire to please other men: not the action of a virtuous woman, whose greatest achievement is to satisfy just the one man to whom she was betrothed and given in marriage, for whom she put on her veil. For a marriageable girl to have her face painted is a sort of confidence trick; for a married woman to be made up is a kind of adultery. What husband is so foolish as to be taken in by his wife's cosmetics, if he knows she is wearing them? And is any husband so unobservant as to miss the fact, either in the morning, when she is at her toilet, or when she takes a bath, or sweats, or on some other occasion when the make-up comes off, as in Galen's story?[41] A game of 'follow my leader' was being played at a party, he tells us; each guest had a turn at being the leader. A little harlot called Phryne, seeing that many of the women present were wearing layers of nail varnish and rouge, ordered that everyone should put both hands in a basin of water she had brought in and should at once rub them over their face, then wipe off the water with a towel. When it was done, the women's make-up was ruined and their faces looked hideous; the make-up had peeled off in some places, but patches of it remained in others, and it was smeared and blotchy. Only Phryne looked clean, and seemed even prettier than before, because she was wearing no make-up.

This was probably sufficient punishment for the whores who were, I imagine, the guests at that party; but a Christian wife who tries to deceive her husband with cosmetic tricks deserves something more severe. Either she is extremely foolish, or she takes her husband for a complete fool, if she expects to hoodwink him, and she shows scant respect for her husband's tastes if she believes that this bogus complexion will give him any pleasure. What would a man say if he asked his wife for a kiss and she offered him a cheek smeared with tar? You might as well look at your husband through a glass screen as through a film of antimony. Even if she has managed to find a husband so stupid that he enjoys being taken in by all these cosmetic lies, it is indecent for a Christian bride (who has chosen to be a wife, not a mistress) to pander to the desires of such a husband. She must give her husband modest physical satisfaction, not the exotic services of the harlot.

Thus marriage should have no truck with love potions, drugs, pills, and paint; unadorned beauty and a wholesome appearance are all that is needed. Love based on deception or constraint is not love. If the husband is easy to please, her sex alone will be sufficient recommendation; if he is more fussy, pleasant manners and cheerful conversation will be the most effective spell or induction.[42] At the court of Olympias, mother of Alexander the Great, a certain woman, with whom Philip was desperately in love, was accused of using magic potions to enrapture the king. The queen ordered her to appear, but when she came and proved to be handsome, self-assured, and well-spoken, Olympias said: 'We can forget the charges of witchcraft; the only potion you need is yourself.'[43] How much more easily can a wife, who lives constantly at her husband's side, arouse his love. Circe, after all, is supposed to have been a skilled enchantress; she used to turn the men she attracted into various kinds of beast.[44] But in so doing she could not accomplish her desires, nor would they love the woman who had wronged them, should they return to their senses. Ulysses' companions, whom she turned into pigs, did not make very agreeable company – unless perhaps she was a devotee of grunting! She truly loved Ulysses alone (whom she failed to bewitch), struck by his character and his words rather than his appearance; but he could never love Circe or Calypso[45] for long, since both used magic on him. He was steadfast in his love for Penelope, who, instead of make-up and magic, used modesty.

Christians should not waste much time on their physical appearance; our self-restraint should be apparent not only in the naturalness of our appearance and the sobriety of our meals, but also in our dress. The body is a kind of clothing for the soul, and dress is a covering for the body; just as the body projects a certain image of the mind, through gesture and expression, the brow and the eyes, so dress can be a sure sign of physical chastity and modesty. What an outcry there would be if the dress of a man entering Benedict's or Francis' order did not correspond to his profession! It would be no less shocking if someone who has in baptism renounced the world and all of Satan's trappings, should in his attire parade the world and the trappings of Satan! If a woman were married to a man who had not yet confessed Christ, perhaps Paul would forgive her for dressing a little too ostentatiously, in deference to her husband's ways.[46] She could echo Esther: 'Lord, you know the compulsion I am under, and that I hate the symbol of pride and glory that I wear on my head when I must appear in public.'[47] But when a Christian woman has married a Christian, she must reckon that nothing pleases her husband more than to see her dress as a professed Christian should; and if the husband happens to forget Christian principles himself, she must adjure him to remember them. If she cannot persuade him to change at once, she must acquiesce, but within certain limits, helping him gradually to see the truth; if he cannot be won over by shock tactics, he may be swayed by constant reminders. Virtue is a powerful weapon if you persevere with it. If a monk puts on a soldier's tunic instead of his Franciscan habit, he is called an apostate. If instead of everyday clothes a Christian wears all-silk garments, which even the Roman emperors found distasteful, or, worse, cloth of gold studded with jewels, then he has thrown off the dress of *his* order and is thereafter in some sense an apostate, unless his soul protests that he is under duress.

There is a good way for a wife to soothe a husband who is annoyed by the modesty of her attire: she could address him in the following words: 'My dearest husband, did we not agree that we would both practise, with equal zeal, the religion in which we were baptized?' 'Yes.' 'Now, where can we find better religious principles than in holy Scripture?' 'Nowhere better.' 'And you will not insist that I obey you, if you tell me to do something that is plainly contrary to its teaching?' 'I'm not so wicked as to ask you to do anything of the kind.' 'That's exactly what I thought ... and yet St Paul, writing to Timothy, clearly laid down rules about the appearance expected of respectable women: "Similarly," he says, "women must dress in an appropriate manner, modestly and soberly, without elaborate hair-styles, gold, pearls or costly clothes, but as befits women professing godliness through good works."'[48] Paul here requires a wife to conceal her body, not parade half-naked through the streets, and to conceal it beneath a dress befitting a woman who professes godliness. Decorous appearance does not consist in carefully styled or dyed hair, in necklaces of gold or jewels, or in costly purple and fine linen, but in the true adornments of the heart – your virtues.

Peter makes the same point still more clearly: 'Similarly, women are to be subject to their husbands, so that even if the latter do not believe, they may be won over without a word being said, by their daily contact with their wives, as they observe with respect your holy way of life. Your beauty should reside not in your hair-style, your gold bracelets, or your fashionable clothes, but be hidden in your hearts, in a spirit that is imperturbably calm and modest, a most precious ornament in the eyes of God. Thus too in days gone by the best of women placed their hopes in God and adorned themselves with obedience to their husbands.'[49] If the prince of the apostles counselled simplicity in their attire even to women who had married unbelievers, to help in their conversion, how much more unseemly it is for a Christian husband to demand of his Christian wife an appearance that is neither suitable for a respectable woman nor effective in safeguarding her modesty. Would it not be infinitely preferable that the money squandered on adorning her body be spent in relieving the poor?

The Ancients were quite right to say that similarity, especially of character and temperament, was the father of love. But the precise nature of this similarity is very important. It is no good if people are brought together because they have the same faults. There will be little stability in a union based on things that are subject to the whims of fortune, to mishap, or to the passing of time, such as physical attraction, youth, beauty, a dowry, health, or strength. Only a set of shared virtues will tie the 'Herculean knot' used, we are told, in ancient wedding ceremonies.[50] The Greek proverb, too, is not far wide of the mark: 'People are brought together less by misdeeds than by misfortune.' For example, a bastard will get on well with another, or an exile with an exile, a maid with a serving-man, a lame woman with a cripple, a monster with a monster.

By similarity, we really mean equality. Of course, there can be similarities between those who are not equals, and equality between those who are not alike. When a pauper marries a millionaire, there is neither similarity nor equality between them, and we may rightly consider her sold into slavery, not given in marriage. Again, when a woman of noble birth marries a commoner, the match is unbalanced and exposed to scandal. When people are matched in wealth, age, family, and appearance, then both similarity and equality are present. But when the daughter of a noble but impoverished house marries a plutocratic plebeian, there is no similarity, but a certain equality between them. Again, when an eminent scholar marries a nobleman, or a distinguished doctor weds a wealthy woman, there is a certain equality between these dissimilar people, so long as they put their different qualities to equally profitable use.

But in any case Christians should not bother with these niggling calculations, since the Lord Jesus, who presides at weddings, made us equal in so many ways. He redeemed us by the same death, he washed us in the same blood, he justified us with the same faith, he refreshes us with the same spirit, he strengthens us with the same sacraments, he honours us with the same name, calling us his brothers and the children of God, and he has summoned us all to share the same inheritance of heavenly life. Why, then, are you calculating her income? Why are you consulting the annals about her family tree? Forget about your birth, and hers: what about your rebirth? Can you consider her beneath you, when God accepts her as a daughter, and Christ as a sister? How can she be poor, when she shares Christ's inheritance? An honest Christian will appreciate his wife by scrupulously weighing her good points. If she happens to be less than beautiful, observe the beauty of her soul; she is pretty enough if she is chaste, restrained, and modest. She may be penniless, but hard-working and thrifty, quick to acquire property and careful to look after it; her dowry will be large enough if she is endowed with these qualities.

Here, of course, you must view her with the honest dovelike eyes of the gospel, not with the squinting, devious gaze of the Pharisee.[51] There are certain optical instruments that enlarge objects, and others that make them seem smaller; some make things lighter, others darker, and still others make it easier to see things in the distance though they make closer things indistinct. But the eye of the Pharisee is inconsistent and looks askance, since even the smallest faults in other people appear very large to him, while his own faults, however great, appear very small when he turns his gaze on them. Indeed, either he fails to see them at all, like a blind man, or else he hallucinates or, to use a more expressive Greek word, παραβλέπει, he sees things wrong, judging a vice to be a virtue and condemning others' virtues as vices. He is perspicacious, even lynx-eyed, about things that are at a distance but purblind to those closer to him; he reminds us of those vampires[52] who were said to blunder into things at home, whereas outside nothing could be concealed from their eyes. Very different are the kind and dovelike eyes mentioned, which will wink at many of their neighbour's faults, either by giving him the benefit of the doubt or by making light of them; but they are harsher judges of their own faults. If you have eyes of this kind, then inequality will not trouble you too much.

However, experience suggests that inequality will matter less if it is the husband who outshines his wife; he is more powerfully swayed by reason whereas feelings have a stronger hold on her. Given the slightest excuse, a woman's feelings will rapidly bring her to despise her husband. But a truly charitable Christian will treat his wife with even greater consideration, if she happens to be much poorer than him in the things ordinary people prize, than if they were on an equal footing. The less well-off are always apt to be touchy, so that often they take an unguarded remark or a joke as an insult. If you playfully call a pretty girl an old hag, she will not mind; but it might offend an older or less pretty woman. Paul taught us that those parts of the body considered less honourable must be treated with greater respect,[53] to do so is to increase our respect for ourselves. By analogy, is not a husband who disparages his wife also demeaning himself? Each partner must always show respect for the other, but especially in the presence of other people or when their partner is absent. No one will look down on a wife, however lowly her origins, if it is clear to all that she is precious to her husband, that she is dear to him above all else. You must not say to yourself: 'She is of low birth; she brought me almost nothing.' Say instead: 'She is my wife.' Still less should a wife be thinking: 'This man does not deserve my loyalty and obedience.' She should instead be saying: 'He is my husband; the allegiance I give him, I give to the Lord.'

Again, a husband may defer to his wife in the sense that he will sometimes swallow his pride, but he will never surrender his authority; he will be consistently friendly and obliging, but he will never grovel. Nature has ordained this, the Scriptures teach it, and indeed it works to the advantage of women themselves. Even among the persons of the Trinity, there is a hierarchy, though it demeans none of them. Where there is no order, there is no respect. If the plough drives the ox – if, that is, the established order is overturned – the result will be disaster.

It is possible to err in two different ways here. Some husbands are so inept in handling their rich and well-born wives that they try to repress them and bring them down until they are sufficiently humiliated to be dominated without difficulty. This strikes me as altogether inadvisable: you might as well teach a large and spirited horse to bend its knees to let you mount because you are too short, weak, or clumsy with horses to get on by yourself. You can also find friends and rulers of this kind. People belittle and humiliate their friends to make them more deferential, and certain princes enhance their own power by attacking and enfeebling their subjects and their neighbours. Anyone treating friends that way quickly changes from a friend to a master, and ends up with slaves and flatterers instead of friends. Similarly, any prince who manages to enhance his power only at the expense of his subjects and neighbours has clearly sunk from king to tyrant; citizens and allies have now become bondsmen and covert enemies. If the nation he is called on to govern is insignificant, a skilful prince will work to raise its prestige; if it is already rich and renowned, he will accept the challenge to match or even outshine the glories of his new realm by the noble virtue and diligence with which he rules it. These principles are still more vital in friendship; without some measure of equality the very notion of friendship cannot survive. Thus, if your wife possesses outstanding qualities, do not try to bring her down, like a muleteer trying to flatten a pack-saddle by putting rocks in the part that sticks up; instead, you should yourself strive for moral improvement and rise to your wife's level. In any case, no one will begrudge a wife her glory if he bears in mind that, legally, in marriage all property belongs to the husband rather than the wife!

These insecure husbands show a similar attitude towards their household, envying it as they would an individual; they cannot bear independent spirits and will put up only with the most abject toadies: to these alone will they give houseroom. I can well believe that they would like to turn their servants into asses; it would make them that much easier to enslave. The famous playwright is relevant here: 'Misgovernment will bring down the best government.'[54] It is no great feat to govern asses, or people who are little different from asses, but it is a noble achievement to govern properly a community of independent, free, and lofty spirits. In this sphere the wife yields to her husband, but takes a share in the government and protects his flank. Thus husbands are quite wrong to try to turn their wives into mere maidservants.

No less misguided are spineless husbands who allow their wives to become their rulers, as Epictetus, in rather simple terms but nonetheless truthfully, warns us.[55] Physical passion prompts them to indulge their wives' every whim while they are young and beautiful. They court them with gifts, which was forbidden, not without reason, even by the laws of the pagans.[56] They allow them to do as they please: wear whatever clothes and make-up they like, eat what they like, go where they please. They flatter and grovel, calling them 'mistress,' and themselves 'willing slaves.' By the time their wives' youthful beauty has withered, they have in fact become mistresses, and tyrannical ones at that, but the husbands cannot really complain, since they were responsible. It smacks of tyranny to undermine your wife's self-esteem so you can order her about like a maid, but to surrender to a wife's rule is the height of foolishness. A spirited horse will repeatedly throw a rider who cannot rein him in, but a skilful horseman will be safe on his back.

Thus many husbands err in one of these two ways, and it is the same story with the women. Some of them are discontented, envious, it may be, of their husband's distinction, and keep complaining that they have been sold into slavery, not given in marriage; they could avoid this if they would only buck up and remember that a husband's good fortune is shared by his wife. Whom do you envy, woman, if you envy your husband? Why, no one but yourself! Most people will confess their hates, but no one will admit to jealousy, because to be envious is to admit your inferiority. If it is so shaming to envy someone else, is it not much worse to envy yourself?

By contrast, some women aim to bend their husbands to their will, and to lead them by the nose like oxen. They unhinge them with drugs, called *philtres* in Greek, which they think will force the man, however unwilling, to love them. But what in the end do they gain by these black arts? They spend their lives like Circe with her pigs and asses: how else to describe men bewitched by drugs and magic incantations? What sort of mentality have such women, who prefer to rule over senseless, dumb madmen than to obey wise and sensible husbands? On a journey, any rational person will prefer to follow someone who can see and who knows the way, rather than to lead a blind man. If lethargy, mental derangement, or some accident has impaired a husband's faculties, will not his wife complain that she is the most wretched of women, condemned to spend her life with a lunatic? And yet these women think themselves lucky if they can make a sane man lose his mind!

I said a few words earlier about flexibility. There is no personality so completely rounded that one could not wish it changed in some way or other. Nor will you easily find a pair of human beings so completely reconciled to life together that a certain weariness with one another's company will not arise – unless each in turn give way to the other when appropriate. As the father in the comedy says: 'It is not essential that a husband should have things all his own way.'[57] Still less is this true of a wife. A little rain often stills a mighty wind, and similarly a quarrel, which may get out of hand if both parties stand their ground, may be patched up and settled by a soft and conciliatory answer, sometimes even by a timely witticism. A soft answer turns away wrath, and silence sometimes does the same. Some people are easily moved to anger, but their anger subsides as quickly as it arose, unless they are provoked further. With them the simplest way to avoid the worst trouble is to keep quiet for a while, until they return to their normal selves. As a result, friendly relations are not only preserved intact but actually improved; the man, regaining his senses, realizes that he has been upset for no good reason, and is annoyed with himself; he is thus even better disposed towards a wife whose gentle nature compensates for his pointless tantrums. Therefore, if something crops up that requires a warning to her husband, a wife will find him much more willing to listen at an opportune moment. Also, she will be ill-advised to recall any particularly unpleasant thing he may have said while angry, especially as he may not remember saying it! Instead, she should tell herself: 'That was anger speaking, not my husband.'

In such situations keeping silence, always an ornament in a virtuous wife, will also provide a ready cure. Not the kind of silence where her tongue is still but her face speaks volumes, betraying her obstinacy and her disregard for her husband; such eloquent silence is worse than any words. No, her face should be respectful and grave, reflecting the feelings in her heart, but without a trace of resentment or scorn. However, although some people do not like to be answered back, others find silence more than a little offensive. In this case, as the Greek proverb says, the best doctor for a hurt mind is gentle but salutary advice, a few well-chosen words, halfway between silence and a full riposte. You could say, for example, that things are better than they seem, or that it will be easy to put things right, or that what is done cannot be undone by shouting. But if there is a danger that your words, however soothing, will upset him, the safest course is to keep silent.

In any case, even when your husband is entirely calm, you must not give him the rough edge of your tongue. A wife who makes war on her husband is making war on God, who said: 'You shall be in your husband's power, and he shall be lord over you.'[58] Charity softens this rule, but it does not remove the husband's power; thus Paul commands women to be silent in church, 'because they have a sign of authority on their heads.' He also calls the man the head of the woman. Thus religious obligation makes the woman subject to the man. But even if this had not been laid down in Holy Writ, reason alone would convince us that soft words or silence will be more effective than rage. An intelligent wife will naturally want her husband to grant her wish: if a gentle and modest request will achieve this more surely than a harsh and haughty demand, why start a quarrel, which will usually do no more than turn his anger into fury? Not to mention that sometimes hard words are answered by hard blows. The north wind is the fiercest of the winds: he drives the clouds, calls up thunder, shatters the oaks, and heaves up earthquakes. By contrast, the south wind is the gentlest of the winds: his breath coaxes the flowers from the earth. Yet when Boreas tries to snatch a traveller's cloak, what happens? The traveller pulls it tighter or puts on a thicker coat. But when the gentle breeze begins to blow, he will take off both cloak and jacket of his own accord. A wife should learn from this example how much better it is to deal gently with her husband than to quarrel and brawl. 'Do not strike fire with a sword,' said Pythagoras, and the noble playwright was right when he said: 'A good woman rules her husband by obeying him.'[59]

The most honourable victory is that won by patience, and for a woman the best way to rule is through obedience. If the wife is upset by that streak of cruelty that nature instilled in the male sex, she should remind herself that this harshness, however unpleasant at times, could be the salvation of the household. It is a kind of seed-bed of the courage a husband needs when he must risk his life for his wife and children. Would a wife want her husband to be lacking in manly spirit then? When his wife's honour is at stake, what will a husband not dare? Therefore you women must put up with your husbands' innate roughness in everyday life; you may find that it will save your lives if the need arises for a man of courage. When you and your children, your lives, and your possessions must be saved from an enemy's assault, would you rather have a monkey or a lion for a husband? A lion, of course. Give your lion the respect he deserves, careful not to stir him to justified anger against you. More people will treat you, the lion's wife, with respect if you always show respect for your lion. It is better to be a lioness, the obedient mate of a friendly lion, than to be the playmate of an ape. In ancient times, it was customary for the bride, when first brought into the bridegroom's house to say: 'Wherever you are, my lion, there shall be your lioness; where you are the master, I shall be the mistress; where you are the lord, I shall be the lady; where you are ruler of the house, I shall rule by your side.' But if you try to be Caius and not Caia, there will soon be no house and no household.

Nonetheless, there are some areas in which the husband should yield to his wife now and then, either because they are unimportant, or because they fall within the province of womankind, or because they are specifically domestic matters. An example of the first kind would be if the wife preferred some particular form of dress (so long as there was nothing indecorous about it), or if she had her own special fasts or prayers. A husband might well wink at these for a while, although it is generally safer to get the wife accustomed to fall in with her husband's wishes in small matters as well as in great. Thus it will be more a matter of winking at them than of yielding to her explicitly. But in matters that are the province of women, such as cooking, shopping, looking after the small children, and supervising the maids, the husband will not be too quick to intervene, unless he sees something that really needs to be rectified, and he will not mind giving way if he sees that his wife knows better than he does.

In more important areas, too, the female sex can sometimes give advice worthy of a man, for example, in urging him to abandon some feud of his. The philosophers grant that women are often ready with the sort of impromptu advice they would not manage after long deliberation, as a man might; in fact, a man's judgment is often impaired if he yields to a sudden impulse. In such a case, a man should not be ashamed to listen to good advice from his wife. Abraham deferred to his wife Sarah and allowed her opinion to prevail when they disagreed: he sent away the maidservant and her son.[60] At first he found it hard to accept: 'Send away your son and his mother.' But the Lord told him: 'Do not think it hard on your son and your maidservant; listen to Sarah and all that she has told you.' You husbands must accept that the Lord says the same to you, whenever your wife's advice affects your reputation or your welfare; you must believe that God dictates whatever reason tells you to do. Many have found it profitable to follow their servants' advice, and so you should be all the more eager to accept your wife's. Of course, some people are so contrary that if something seems right to their partner, they will oppose it for the very reason that the other supports it; there is no matter so trivial that the one will deign to give way to the other. No wonder that 'charity grows cold'[61] between such people.

Now, there is embedded in human nature a certain ἀψίκορον, a sort of fastidious impatience with things as they are, which means that nothing pleases them for very long, and that they quickly get tired even of the most agreeable things. There are two remedies for this affliction: temporary separation and service. To break off marital relations for a while may serve to renew the pleasures of friendship, whilst performing little services for one another may rekindle your mutual affection, like blowing gently on a fire.

Temporary separation is a useful way to improve a relationship that is becoming tedious. However, total separation of husband and wife is not the aim; for many, such as businessmen and courtiers, it comes with the job, and in their case wedded bliss is imperilled more by these lengthy absences than by constant companionship. Paul laid down precise rules about sleeping apart;[62] if it is done tactfully and by mutual consent, it may contribute much to preserving the freshness of the couple's affection for one another.

Giving small presents is a crude way of gaining affection. Love cannot be bought, unless perhaps the gifts commend themselves not so much by their cost as by their symbolism or the evidence that some thought has gone into them, or if they make a tasteful joke: things like letters, poems, antique medallions, original drawings. However, it is rather risky to introduce such ideas into a discussion of matrimony, as I may open a window on things prohibited by the law. The very word 'service' includes all the things that a husband must do for a wife, and a wife for a husband. Such obligations also exist between parents and children, masters and servants, and this will be touched on later; without them, harmony cannot reign in the household. At the moment I am thinking of less weighty kinds of service, but ones that will increase and preserve mutual affection and help to soothe potential hostility. For example, send your husband off on a journey with a kiss and good wishes, and greet his return with a smiling and eager face; when he is off to business or the court, accompany him to the door, and welcome him joyfully when he returns; include words of love and respect in any complaint you have to make. A wife should not say too much about her absent husband, not even in praise of him; if she must, she should make it brief and respectful, either concealing or making light of any fault in him. Again, if she knows that something is precious to him, a little bird, a dog, or anything else, she must take special care of it. These are small things, but of no small importance in maintaining affection between husband and wife. The husband will compete with his wife in performing these little services. If something goes wrong, these services will make things better; if nothing is wrong, their affection will be aroused and renewed by them.

Again, any children married couples have together bind chains of adamant around their married love. Of course, anyone can perform little services for another, but not everyone can have children. We have a natural instinct to show love and devotion to them. Moreover, the more they love their children, the less a husband and wife will find to quarrel about. Those nations who lived with nature as their sole guide called children 'pledges.' Now a pledge is normally something given to guarantee a contract, in the same way that hostages are exchanged; indeed, princes attempting to make a lasting treaty will give and receive as hostages those who are dearest to them, and sometimes it is the worse for them if one of the parties goes back on his word. But how much more sacred is the pledge devised by nature! When a wife has a child by her husband, each gives the other a hostage in which both of them live and breathe, like two beings made one; the child will be dearer to each than they are to themselves. Artful nature ensures that the husband gives a hostage to the wife, and the wife to the husband. Thus they refuse to be parted, from innate love of their children, and they cannot be parted, since the possession of children is indivisible. When people go different ways, they can usually say: 'Take what belongs to you.' But when it comes to children, who shall say to whom: 'Take what belongs to you'? In this case neither of you can take what belongs to you without taking what belongs equally to both of you.

Here we may contemplate nature's marvellous attention to detail: both partners are delineated in the same face, both are represented in the same little body. The husband sees a portrait of his wife there, the wife sees an image of her husband. Often some feature of a grandparent's face will reappear in the child, or it may be the image of its great-uncle or great-aunt: all the more reason for feeling affection and obligation towards your children. Anyone who turns a deaf ear to nature's message here has not merely ceased to be a Christian but has ceased to be human; he has fallen to a level below the beasts, become fiercer and wilder than a lion or tiger.

I believe that this is why there is no special injunction to parents to love their children, in the same way that no one is ordered to love himself. Solon was asked why he had decreed no punishment for parricide, although he had prescribed punishments for much less serious crimes. He replied that he never thought that so heinous a crime would be committed in his city.[63] Nature has so engraved this law in the innermost hearts of all that a man-made law seems quite superfluous. It is indeed wonderful that nowhere are more examples of devotion to duty to be found than in areas where there is no law to prescribe one's duties. The historians recount such things of friends, though not so many; human history overflows with examples of fathers who did not hesitate to lay down their own lives to save their children. We read of Aeneas that 'all the loving father's thoughts were for Ascanius.'[64] The Lord cries out in Isaiah: 'Can a woman forget her infant, and not take pity on the child of her womb?'[65] But alas, for human wickedness! There are women in Christendom who will murder newborn babes, who will procure abortion and kill the unborn child.[66] But let us dismiss from this discussion what are more like rare and terrible freaks than true examples. Thus, if you have children, you have hostages for your love for one another; but even if you have not, where there is love there is no barrenness. Remember how Elkanah consoled his wife: 'Why is your heart full of grief? Am I not more to you than ten sons?'[67]

NOTES

1 Homer, *Iliad*, 9.502
2 Epictetus, *Enchiridion*, 43
3 Pre-Socratic Greek philosophers proverbial for their contrasting reactions to the spectacle of humanity
4 A venerable utterance reported in this form by Pliny, *Naturalis historia*, 7.1.4; cf *Adagia*, II iii 49.
5 Cf Plutarch, *Moralia*, 142A. Metrodorus, a physician, was a disciple of the laughing philosopher Democritus.
6 On these basic forms of contract see, for example, Justinian's *Digest*, 45.1.75 and *Institutes*, 3.15.1.

7 This conveys Paul's meaning in such chapters as 1 Cor. 7 and Eph. 5, but is closest textually to 1 Pet. 3:7, cited a few lines later.

8 Eph. 5:29

9 1 Pet. 3:7

10 Eph. 5:23, a principle enshrined in canon law with the approval of Augustine and Jerome.

11 This example and the preceding one of the rose are found in Plutarch, *Moralia*, 138D–E. The Boeotians were proverbial for their stupidity, but Plutarch and Erasmus do their best to rehabilitate them here. Judging by the subsequent description of the plant, there may be some confusion with the *aspalathus* a prickly shrub that yielded a fragrant oil: Pliny, *Naturalis historia*, 12.24.110.

12 Virgil, *Aeneid*, IV 423; Dido is addressing her sister Anna.

13 Terence, *Adelphi*, 533

14 The quotations are Col. 3:19 and Eph. 5:22.

15 A wordplay: *conviva non conviva*

16 Virgil, *Georgics*, 2.77

17 Gen. 29:23–5

18 Solon, the celebrated Athenian law-giver, as quoted in Plutarch, *Moralia*, 138D and 280A

19 Plato, *Laws*, 4.722–3 and Seneca, *Epistulae morales*, 94.38

20 Ps-Aristotle, *Oeconomica*, 3.1

21 Terence, *Adelphi*, 699

22 Matt. 19:6; the preceding allusion is to the wedding at Cana (John 2:1–11).

23 Tob. 8:5 in the Vulgate; English versions are rather different. The prayers of Tobias and Sara follow in vv 7–10 (5–8 in English versions).

24 Cf Heb. 13:4.

25 Tob. 8:19 in the Vulgate

26 The Corybantes were priests of Cybele, proverbial for the abandon of their rituals.

27 The Bacchanalia were riotous festivals in honour of the wine-god Bacchus.

28 The *Floralia*, were an extremely licentious Roman celebration of the goddess of spring, supposed originally to have been a courtesan; Vesta was the goddess of fire and the hearth, and the patroness of the celebrated Vestal Virgins, whose shrine no male might enter. These references to pagan festivals have an obvious satirical edge.

29 Matt. 5:28

30 Ixion, king of Thessaly, was transported to heaven by Jupiter; attempting to seduce Juno, he was beguiled by a cloud made in her image, from which the centaurs were born. Ixion was hurled into hell.

31 A widespread custom attested as early as the 14th century and as far afield as Scandinavia; the blows were presumably intended to impress on the young men that the bride was now beyond their reach.

32 The Romans in particular imposed severe legal restrictions on consumption. The censors were the officials enforcing these laws.

33 Cf Eph. 4:28.

34 Gal. 6:6

35 I.e., the godparents

36 See 1 Cor. 13:13.

37 Plato, *Symposium*, 180d

38 James 1:17

39 An allusion to Plato's theory of reminiscence, expounded in the *Meno* 80–6 and the *Phaedo* 72–7

40 Xenophon, *Oeconomicus*, 10.1–9. 'Cross-examination' translates *isagoge* literally 'bringing a case to court.' White lead (*cerussa*) was used to whiten the face and antimony (*stibium*) was the equivalent of mascara.

41 The story is told in Galen's *Exhortatio ad artium liberalium studia*, translated and published by Erasmus in April 1526 (CWE 29:225–39). The cosmetics mentioned here are *purpurissa* (rouge) and *anchusa* (ox-tongue), another red dye obtained from the plant of the same name and used for painting both the nails and the face.

42 Erasmus uses the rhetorical term, *epagoge*, an opening statement or preamble presenting the facts of the case.

43 The story is told in Plutarch, *Moralia*, 141B–C.

44 The Homeric sorceress

45 Calypso was the nymph who detained Ulysses for seven years on her island: *Odyssey* 5.

46 Cf 1 Cor. 7:13–4.

47 Esther 14:16

48 1 Tim. 2:9–10

49 1 Pet. 3:1–5

50 The bride's girdle was knotted at the ceremony, and untied only by the bridegroom in the nuptial chamber. This was apparently a fertility ritual, since Hercules had seventy children.

51 For Erasmus, the Pharisees of the gospels frequently represent bigotry, legalism and lack of charity.

52 *Lamiae*: cf *Adagia*, I vi 85, based on Plutarch, *Moralia*, 515F. In some versions of the legend, the monsters actually removed their eyes when at home.

53 Cf 1 Cor. 12:33.

54 Publilius Syrus, *Sententiae*, 380

55 Epictetus, *Enchiridion*, 40

56 See, for example, *Digest*, 24.1.1–67; but Erasmus is probably following Plutarch, *Moralia*, 143A and 265E.

57 Terence, *Adelphi*, 51–2

58 Gen. 3:16

59 Publilius Syrus, *Sententiae*, 108

60 See Gen. 21:10–12.

61 Matt. 24:12

62 See 1 Cor. 7:5.

63 See Diogenes Laertius, 1.59.

64 Virgil, *Aeneid*, 1.646

65 Isa. 49:15

66 See another passage on this topic in Erasmus' letter-writing manual, CWE 25:138–9.

67 1 Sam. 1:8

2. *Marriage*:
A Counselling Session

This dialogue was first printed in the 1523 edition of the *Colloquies* (for the publication history of this work see 25). *Marriage* was one of the most popular colloquies and was soon translated into all major vernacular languages. The first English version was published anonymously in 1557 under the title *A Merry Dialogue Declaring the Properties of Shrewd Shrews and Honest Wives*. It may have inspired Shakespeare's *Taming of the Shrew*. Echoes of the Erasmian dialogue can also be found in the popular Spanish *Coloquios matrimoniales* by Pedro de Luxan.

The translation is by Craig Thompson.

EULALIA, XANTHIPPE[1]

Eulalia Greetings, Xanthippe! I've been dying to see you.

Xanthippe Same to you, my dearest Eulalia. You look lovelier than ever.

Eulalia So you greet me by making fun of me right away?

Xanthippe Not at all; I mean it.

Eulalia Maybe this new dress flatters my figure.

Xanthippe Of course it does. I haven't seen anything prettier for a long time. British cloth, I suppose?

Eulalia British wool with Venetian dye.

Xanthippe Softer than satin. What a charming shade of purple! Where did you get such a marvellous gift?

Eulalia Where should honest wives get them except from their husbands?

Xanthippe Lucky you to have such a husband! As for me, I might as well have married a mushroom when I married my Nicholas.

Eulalia Why so, if you please? Are you falling out so soon?

Xanthippe I'll never fall in with the likes of him. You see I'm in rags: that's how *he* allows his wife to appear. Damned if often I'm not ashamed to go out in public when I see how well dressed other women are who married husbands much worse off than mine.

Eulalia Feminine finery, as St Peter the apostle teaches[2] (for I heard this in a sermon recently), consists not of clothes or any other adornment of the person but of chaste and modest sentiments and embellishments of the mind. Harlots are decked out for vulgar eyes. We're sufficiently well dressed if we please one husband.

Xanthippe But meanwhile that fine gentleman, so stingy towards his wife, squanders the dowry he got from me – no slight one – as fast as he can.

Eulalia On what?

Xanthippe On whatever he pleases: wine – whores – dice.

Eulalia That's no way to talk.

Xanthippe But it's the truth. Besides, when he comes home drunk in the middle of the night, after being long awaited, he snores all night and sometimes vomits in bed – to say no worse.

Eulalia Hush! You bring reproach on yourself when you reproach your husband.

Xanthippe Hope to die if I wouldn't rather sleep with a brood sow than with such a husband!

Eulalia Don't you welcome him with abuse then?

Xanthippe Yes – as he deserves. He finds I'm no mute.

Eulalia What does he do to counter you?

Xanthippe At first he used to talk back most ferociously, thinking he'd drive me away with harsh words.

Eulalia The bickering never came to actual blows?

Xanthippe Once, at least, the argument grew so hot on both sides that it very nearly ended in a fight.

Eulalia You don't say so!

Xanthippe He was swinging a club, yelling savagely all the while and threatening terrible deeds.

Eulalia Weren't you scared at that?

Xanthippe Oh, no. When it came my turn, I grabbed a stool. Had he laid a finger on me, he'd have found I didn't lack arms.

Eulalia A new sort of shield! You should have used your distaff for a lance.

Xanthippe He'd have found he had an Amazon to deal with.

Eulalia My dear Xanthippe, this won't do.

Xanthippe What *does* do? If he won't treat me as a wife, I won't treat him as a husband.

Eulalia But Paul teaches that wives should be obedient to their husbands in all subjection.[3] And Peter sets before us the example of Sarah, who would call her husband Abraham 'lord.'[4]

Xanthippe So I've heard. But this same Paul teaches that husbands should cherish their wives as Christ has cherished his spouse the Church. Let him remember his duty and I'll remember mine.

Eulalia All the same, when things have come to such a pass that one person must yield to the other, the wife should give way to the husband.

Xanthippe Provided he deserves to be called husband. He treats me like a servant.

Eulalia But tell me, my dear Xanthippe, did he stop threatening to beat you after that?

Xanthippe Yes – and he was wise to do so or he'd have got a cudgelling.

Eulalia But you haven't stopped brawling with him?

Xanthippe No, and I won't stop.

Eulalia What does he do all this time?

Xanthippe Do? Sometimes he sleeps, the lazy lout. Occasionally he just laughs; and at other times grabs his guitar, which has hardly three strings, and plays it as loud as he can to drown out my screaming.

Eulalia That infuriates you?

Xanthippe More than I could say. At times I can hardly keep my hands off him.

Eulalia Xanthippe, my dear, may I speak rather frankly with you?

Xanthippe You may.

Eulalia You may do the same with me. Our intimacy – which goes back almost to the cradle – surely demands this.

Xanthippe That's true. You've always been my dearest friend.

Eulalia Whatever your husband's like, bear in mind that there's no exchanging him for another. Once upon a time divorce was a final remedy for irreconcilable differences. Nowadays this has been entirely abolished; you must be husband and wife till the day you die.

Xanthippe May heaven punish whoever robbed us of this right!

Eulalia Mind what you're saying. Christ so willed.

Xanthippe I can scarcely believe it.

Eulalia It's the truth. There's nothing left now but to try to live in harmony by adjusting yourselves to each other's habits and personalities.

Xanthippe Can I reform him?

Eulalia What sort of men husbands are depends not a little on their wives.

Xanthippe Do you get along well with your husband?

Eulalia Everything's peaceful now.

Xanthippe There was some turmoil at first, then?

Eulalia Never a storm, but slight clouds appeared occasionally: the usual human experience. They could have caused a storm had they not been met with forbearance. Each of us has his own ways and opinions, and – to tell the truth – his own peculiar faults. If there's any place where one has a duty to recognize these, not resent them, surely it's in marriage.

Xanthippe Good advice.

Eulalia It frequently happens, however, that goodwill between husband and wife breaks down before they know each other well enough. This above all is to be avoided, for once contention arises love is not easily recovered, especially if the affair reaches the point of harsh abuse. Things glued together are easily separated if you shake them immediately, but once the glue has dried they stick together as firmly as anything. Hence at the very outset no pains should be spared to establish and cement goodwill between husband and wife. This is accomplished mainly by submissiveness and courtesy, for goodwill won merely by beauty of person is usually short-lived.

Xanthippe But tell me, please, by what arts you drew your husband to your ways.

Eulalia I'll tell you in order that you may imitate them.

Xanthippe If I can.

Eulalia It will be very easy if you want to; and it's not too late, for he's a young man and you a girl, and the marriage isn't a year old, I believe.

Xanthippe You're correct.

Eulalia I'll tell you, then, but only if you'll keep it secret.

Xanthippe Of course.

Eulalia My first concern was to be agreeable to my husband in every respect, so as not to cause him any annoyance. I noted his mood and feeling; I noted the circumstances too, and what soothed and irritated him, as do those who tame elephants and lions or suchlike creatures that can't be forced.

Xanthippe That's the sort of creature I have at home!

Eulalia Those who approach elephants don't wear white, and those who approach bulls don't wear red, because these beasts are known to be enraged by such colours. Likewise tigers are driven so wild by the beating of drums that they tear their own flesh. And trainers of horses have calls, cluckings, pattings, and other means of soothing mettlesome animals. How much more fitting for us to use those arts on our husbands, with whom, whether we like it or not, we share bed and board for our entire lives.

Xanthippe Go on with what you've begun.

Eulalia When these matters were looked after, I would adapt myself to him, taking care to avoid any unpleasantness.

Xanthippe How could you do that?

Eulalia First of all, I was vigilant in my management of household affairs, the special province of wives. I made certain not only that nothing was omitted but that everything was suited to his taste, even in the slightest details.

Xanthippe What details?

Eulalia For example, if my husband were unusually fond of this or that dish, or if he liked his food cooked, or the bed made, in a certain way.

Xanthippe But how could you adapt yourself to one who wasn't at home or was drunk?

Eulalia Just a moment; I was coming to that. If ever my husband seemed quite depressed and I had no chance to appeal to him, I wouldn't laugh or joke, as some women like to do, but I too put on a sombre, worried look. As a mirror, if it's a good one, always gives back the image of the person looking at it, so should a wife reflect her husband's mood, not being gay when he's sad or merry when he's upset. But whenever he was more upset than usual, I'd either soothe him with pleasant conversation or defer to his anger in silence until he cooled off and an opportunity came to correct or advise him. I'd do the same whenever he came home tipsy: at the time I'd say nothing except what was agreeable; I'd just coax him to bed.

Xanthippe Wives have an unhappy lot for sure if they must simply put up with husbands who are angry, drunk, and whatever else they please.

Eulalia As if this putting up with things didn't work both ways! Husbands have much to endure from our habits as well. On occasion, however – in a serious matter, when something important's at stake – it's right for a wife to reprove her husband; trivial matters are better winked at.

Xanthippe What occasion, pray?

Eulalia When he's at leisure and not disturbed, worried, or tipsy, then she should admonish him politely, or rather entreat him – in private – to take better care of his property, reputation, or health in one respect or another. And this very admonition should be seasoned with wit and pleasantries. Sometimes I'd make my husband promise in advance not to be angry if I, a foolish woman, reproved him about something that seemed to concern his honour, health, or welfare. After reproving him as I intended, I'd break off that talk and turn to other, more cheerful topics. For as a rule, my dear Xanthippe, our mistake is that once we've started to talk we can't stop.

Xanthippe So they say.

Eulalia Above all I was careful not to scold my husband in the presence of others or to carry any complaint farther than the front door. Trouble's sooner mended if it's limited to two. But if something of this sort does prove intolerable, or can't be cured by the wife's reproof, it's more polite for her to take her complaint to her husband's parents and relatives than to her own, and to state her case with such restraint that she won't seem to hate her husband but his fault instead. She should refrain from blabbing about everything, though, so that her husband may tacitly acknowledge and admire his wife's courtesy.

Xanthippe Whoever could do all this must be a philosopher.

Eulalia Oh, no; by such practices we'll entice our husbands to similar courtesy.

Xanthippe There are some no courtesy would improve.

Eulalia Well, I don't think so, but suppose there are. In the first place, remember you must put up with your husband, whatever he's like. Better, therefore, to put up with one who behaves himself or is made a little more accommodating by our politeness than with one who's made worse from day to day by our harshness. What if I were to mention examples of husbands who improved their wives by courtesy of this kind? How much more fitting for us to do the same for our husbands!

Xanthippe Then you'd tell me of an example very different from *my* husband.

Eulalia I'm well acquainted with a certain nobleman, a learned and remarkably clever[5] man. He married a girl of seventeen who had been reared wholly in her parents' country home (since nobles generally like to live in the country, for the sake of hunting and hawking). Her lack of sophistication recommended her, because he would fashion her to his tastes the more readily. He undertook to teach her literature and music and gradually to accustom her to repeating what she had heard in a sermon, and by other devices to train her in what would be of later use. Since this was all new to the girl, who had spent her time in her own home in complete idleness and been brought up amidst the chatter and pranks of servants, she began to grow bored. She became balky, and when her husband grew insistent she would cry and cry, sometimes throwing herself down and dashing her head against the floor as though she wished she were dead. Because there was no end to this, her husband, hiding his vexation, invited his wife to accompany him on a visit to the country, to his father-in-law's house, for a holiday. She accepted eagerly. When they arrived there the husband left his wife with her mother and sisters; he himself went hunting with his father-in-law. Then and there, when they're out of hearing, he tells his father-in-law he had hoped for an amiable partner but now had one who was forever weeping and tormenting herself and could not be corrected by any reproofs. He begs for help in curing the daughter's fault. The father-in-law replies that he gave him his daughter once for all; that if she refused to obey his commands, he should exercise his rights and correct her by blows. 'I know my rights,' says the son-in-law, 'but rather than resort to this desperate remedy I'd prefer to have her cured by your skill or authority.' The father-in-law promised to attend to the matter. A day or so later he seizes an opportunity to be alone with his daughter. Then, putting on a stern look, he begins to recall how homely she was, how ill-mannered, how often he had feared he would be unable to find her a husband. 'But,' he says, 'with the greatest difficulty I've found you a husband such as any girl, however favoured, would long for. And yet, not recognizing what I've done for you, nor realizing that you have such a husband – who would scarcely think you fit for one of his maidservants if he weren't the kindest of men – you rebel against him.' To make a long story short, the father's speech grew so heated that he seemed barely able to keep his hands off her. (For he's a man of marvellous cunning, capable of playing any comedy without a mask.) Moved partly by fear, partly by the truth, the girl promptly went down on her knees before her father, begging forgiveness for the past and swearing she would be mindful of her duty in the future. He pardoned her, promising to be a most affectionate father if she carried out her promise.

Xanthippe Then what happened?

Eulalia After the conversation with her father, the girl went to her bedroom, met her husband privately, fell on her knees before him, and said, 'Husband, up to this time I have known neither you nor myself. Hereafter you shall see me a different person; only forget the past.' Her husband received this speech with a kiss and promised her everything if she kept her word.

Xanthippe Well? Did she keep it?

Eulalia As long as she lived. And there was nothing, however lowly, that she did not do promptly and willingly when her husband wished. So strong was the love born and confirmed between them. After some years the girl often congratulated herself on her luck in marrying such a husband. 'If it hadn't been for this,' she said, 'I'd have been the unhappiest woman in the world.'

Xanthippe Husbands like that are as scarce as white crows.

Eulalia If you don't mind, I'll tell you something about a husband reformed by his wife's kindness: something that happened recently in this very city.

Xanthippe I've nothing to do and I enjoy your conversation very much.

Eulalia There's a certain man[6] of no mean rank who, like most of his class, used to hunt a good deal. In the country he came across some girl, the daughter of a poor peasant woman, with whom he – a man already fairly well along in years – fell passionately in love. On her account he'd often spend the night away from home, his excuse being his hunting. His wife, a woman of exceptional goodness, suspected something, investigated her husband's secret doings, and, after discovering the facts (I don't know how), went to their rude cottage. She found out everything: where he slept, what he drank out of, what dinnerware he had. No furniture there – just sheer poverty. The wife went home but soon came back, bringing with her a comfortable bed and furnishings and some silver vessels. She added money, too, advising the girl to treat him more handsomely on his next visit – all the while concealing the fact that she herself was his wife and pretending to be his sister.

Some days later the husband returns there secretly. Noticing the new furniture and the more expensive household utensils, he asks where this uncommon luxury comes from. Some good lady (he's told), a relative of his, had brought it and had left orders to entertain him more properly thereafter. He suspected at once that his wife had done this. Back home, he asks her; she doesn't deny it. And why, he asks finally, had she sent the furniture to him? 'My dear husband,' she replies, 'you're used to a pretty comfortable life. I saw you were shabbily treated there. I thought that since you're so fond of the place, I ought to see that you're entertained more elegantly.'

Xanthippe Too good a wife! I'd sooner have made him a bed of nettles and thistles.

Eulalia But hear the conclusion. In view of so much gentleness and kindness on the part of his wife, the husband never again engaged in secret amours but enjoyed himself at home with his own wife. – I know you're acquainted with Gilbert the Dutchman.[7]

Xanthippe I know him.

Eulalia As you're aware, when he was in the prime of life he married a woman already in her declining years.

Xanthippe Perhaps he married the dowry, not the wife.

Eulalia Yes. Despising his wife, he doted on a mistress with whom he would often enjoy himself away from home. He seldom lunched or dined at home. What would you have done in this situation?

Xanthippe What? I'd have flown at his sweetheart's hair; and when my husband was going to her I'd have emptied the chamber pot on him, so he'd be perfumed for his party.

Eulalia But how much more sensible this woman was! She invited the girl to her own home and received her cordially. Thus she enticed her husband home too, without sorcery. And whenever he went out to dinner at the girl's, she sent over some fancy dish, bidding them have a good time.

Xanthippe I'd rather die than be bawd to my husband.

Eulalia But just consider the case. Wasn't this far better than if she had simply alienated her husband by her fury and spent her whole time in brawling?

Xanthippe It's the lesser evil, I admit – but I couldn't do it.

Eulalia I'll add one more example; and this will be the last. One day a neighbour of ours, a good, honest man but a little short-tempered, beat his wife, a most worthy woman. She withdrew to an inner room and there, weeping and sobbing, cried out her grief. Some time later her husband happened to go into that room and found her weeping. 'Why are you crying and sobbing here like a child?' he said. 'What?' she answered discreetly. 'Isn't it better to bewail my misfortune here than to scream in the street as other women usually do?' The man's heart was so touched, so overcome by such wifely speech, that he solemnly promised her he would never lay a hand on her again; and he didn't.

Xanthippe I got the same promise from my husband by a different method.

Eulalia But meanwhile there's constant warfare between you.

Xanthippe What would you have me do, then?

Eulalia First of all, keep to yourself any wrong your husband does you and win him over gradually by favours, cheerfulness, gentleness. Either you'll triumph at last or certainly you'll find him much more affable than you do now.

Xanthippe He's too savage to soften under any favours.

Eulalia Oh, don't say that. No creature's so fierce that he can't be tamed. Don't despair of the man. Try for several months; blame me if you don't find this advice has helped you. There are even some failings you ought to wink at. Above all, in my judgment, you must be careful not to start an argument in the bedroom or in bed, but try to see that everything there is pleasant and agreeable. If that place, which is dedicated to dispelling grudges and renewing love, is profaned by any contention or bitterness, every means of recovering goodwill is clean gone. Some women are so peevish that they even quarrel and complain during sexual intercourse and by their tactlessness render disagreeable that pleasure that ordinarily rids men's minds of whatever vexation may be therein – spoiling the very medicine that could have cured their ills.

Xanthippe That's often happened to me.

Eulalia Yet, even though a wife should always be careful not to offend her husband on any occasion, she should take special pains to show herself wholly complaisant and agreeable to him in that union.

Xanthippe Husband! My business is with a monster.

Eulalia Do stop talking in that horrid fashion. Usually it's our fault that husbands are bad. But to return to the subject. Those well read in ancient poetry say that Venus, whom they make the patroness of married love, has a girdle fashioned by Vulcan.[8] Woven in it is some drug to arouse love. She puts on this girdle whenever she's going to sleep with her husband.

Xanthippe That's a mere story.

Eulalia A story, yes, but hear what the story signifies.

Xanthippe Tell me.

Eulalia It teaches that a wife must take every precaution to be pleasing to her husband in sexual relations, in order that married love may be rekindled and renewed and any annoyance or boredom driven out of mind.

Xanthippe But where shall I get that girdle?

Eulalia You don't need sorcery or charms. No charm is more effective than good behaviour joined with good humour.

Xanthippe I can't humour such a husband.

Eulalia Yet it's important to you that he stop being such. If by Circe's arts you could turn your husband into a swine or a bear,[9] would you do it?

Xanthippe I don't know.

Eulalia Don't know? Would you rather have a swine than a man for a husband?

Xanthippe I'd prefer a man, of course.

Eulalia Well, now, what if by Circe's arts you could change him from drunk to sober, spendthrift to thrifty, idler to worker? Wouldn't you do it?

Xanthippe Indeed I would, but where can I find those arts?

Eulalia But you've those very arts in yourself if only you're willing to make use of them. He's yours whether you like it or not; that's settled. The better you make him, the better off you'll be. You have eyes only for his failings. These intensify your disgust, and with this handle you're simply catching him where he can't be held. Mark the good in him, rather, and by this means take him where he *can* be held. The time to weigh his faults was before you married him, since a husband should be chosen not only with eyes but with ears too. Now's the time for improving him, not blaming him.

Xanthippe What woman ever picked a husband by ear?

Eulalia The one who sees nothing but good looks chooses him with her eyes. The woman who chooses by ear is the one who considers his reputation carefully.

Xanthippe Good advice – but too late.

Eulalia But it's not too late to try to improve your husband. If you present your husband with a child, that will help.

Xanthippe I've already had one.

Eulalia When?

Xanthippe Long ago.

Eulalia How many months ago?

Xanthippe Almost seven.

Eulalia What do I hear? Are you reviving the old joke about the three-months' baby?

Xanthippe Not at all.

Eulalia You must be if you count the time from your wedding day.

Xanthippe Oh, no, we had some conversation before marriage.

Eulalia Are children born from conversation?

Xanthippe Chancing to find me alone, he began to play, tickling me under the arms and in the sides to make me laugh. I couldn't stand the tickling, so I fell back on the bed. He leaned over and kissed me – I'm not sure what else he did. I *am* sure my belly began to swell soon afterwards.

Eulalia Go on! Belittle a husband who begot children in sport? What will he do when he goes to work in earnest?

Xanthippe I suspect I'm pregnant now, too.

Eulalia Fine! A good ploughman's found a good field.

Xanthippe He's better at this than I would like.

Eulalia Few wives join you in that complaint. But were you engaged?

Xanthippe Engaged, yes.

Eulalia Then your sin was the lighter. Is the child a boy?

Xanthippe Yes.

Eulalia That will reconcile you two if you meet him halfway. What do others – his friends and business associates – have to say about your husband?

Xanthippe They say he's very easy to get along with, cheerful, generous, a trusty friend.

Eulalia And this makes me confident he'll be the way we want him.

Xanthippe But to me alone he is different.

Eulalia Now behave towards him as I've told you, and call me Pseudolalia[10] instead of Eulalia if he doesn't begin to be such to you too. And just remember this: he's still a young man; not over twenty-four, I believe. He doesn't know yet what it's like to be head of a family. You must not even think of divorce.

Xanthippe But I've often thought of it.

Eulalia Whenever the notion comes into your head, consider with yourself, first of all, what a paltry thing a woman is if separated from her husband. A woman's highest praise is to be obedient to her husband. It's the order of nature, the will of God, that woman be entirely dependent on man. Only think what the situation is: he's your husband; you can't get a different one. In the second place, think about the little boy you two have. What will you do about him? Take him with you? You'll rob your husband of his possession. Leave him with your husband? You'll deprive yourself of the one dearest to you. Tell me, finally: have you any enemies?

Xanthippe I have a stepmother – the genuine article – and a mother-in-law just like her.

Eulalia Do they hate you so very much?

Xanthippe They'd like me to drop dead.

Eulalia Have a thought for them, too. How could you give them greater pleasure than by letting them see you parted from your husband, living like a widow, nay worse than a widow? For widows may at least remarry.

Xanthippe Well, I like your advice, but a long-drawn-out job I don't like.

Eulalia But consider how much work it took before you taught this parrot here to talk.

Xanthippe Plenty, to be sure.

Eulalia And do you shrink from working hard to reform your husband, with whom you might spend your life pleasantly? How much labour men put into training a horse! And shall we be hesitant about labouring to make our husbands more tractable?

Xanthippe What should I do?

Eulalia I've already told you. See that everything at home is neat and clean and there's no trouble that will drive him out of doors. Show yourself affable to him, always mindful of the respect owed by wife to husband. Avoid gloominess and irritability. Don't be nasty or wanton. Keep the house spick and span. You know your husband's taste; cook what he likes best. Be cordial and courteous to his favourite friends, too. Invite them to dinner frequently, and see that everything is cheerful and merry there. Finally, if he strums his guitar when he's a bit tipsy, accompany him with your singing. Thus you'll get your husband used to staying at home and you'll reduce expenses. At long last he'll think, 'I'm a damned fool to waste my money and reputation away from home on a drab when I have at home a wife much nicer and much fonder of me, from whom I can get a more elegant and more sumptuous welcome.'

Xanthippe Do you think I'll succeed if I try?

Eulalia Look at me. I'll vouch for it, and meantime I'll approach your husband and remind him too of his duty.

Xanthippe I approve of the plan, but watch out he doesn't suspect this plot; he'd raise hell.

Eulalia Don't fear. I'll speak to him in such a roundabout way that he'll tell me himself what the trouble is between you. After that I'll draw him on very innocently, in my usual fashion and – I hope – make him more considerate of you. When I get a chance, I'll tell him a fib about you – how lovingly you spoke of him.

Xanthippe May Christ favour our effort!

Eulalia He will – if only you do your part.

NOTES

1 Eulalia means 'well-spoken'; Xanthippe is named after Socrates' wife, the proverbial shrew.

2 1 Pet. 3:3–4

3 Eph. 5:22–4, 1 Tim. 2:11–12

4 1 Pet. 3:6

5 A reference to Thomas More and his first wife, Jane Colt

6 The theme is also used in Marguerite of Navarre's *Heptameron* (story 38).

7 Erasmus' friend Pieter Gillis, town clerk at Antwerp, who was married three times.

8 In Homer, Vulcan fashioned a girdle for Venus that made the wearer sexually attractive (cf *Iliad*, book 14).

9 The Homeric sorceress

10 I.e., 'false-speaking'

3. A Marriage in Name Only

This dialogue, subtitled 'An Unequal Marriage,' was first printed in the 1529 edition of the *Colloquies* (for the publication history of that work see above 25). It elaborates on remarks in *The Institution of Marriage* that stress the importance of the physical health and compatibility of the marriage partners (see above 88–9). It was commonly believed that syphilis was imported into Europe from America by Columbus' sailors. This theory is disputed today, but there is no doubt that the disease spread rapidly in the first half of the sixteenth century. Its symptoms and treatment are discussed in many books. Among the most popular accounts was the Latin poem *Syphilis* by Girolamo Fracastoro, in which the disease is so named after a Greek shepherd who, according to legend, was stricken with a malady of this type by the god Apollo. Niccolò Leoniceno's *Book about the Epidemic* notes that Italians referred to the disease as the 'French pox,' while Frenchman used the term 'Neapolitan disease.'

The translation of the dialogue is by Craig Thompson.

PETRONIUS, GABRIEL

Petronius Where from, friend Gabriel, with such a dismal look? Not come out of Trophonius' cave,[1] are you?
Gabriel Oh, no – from a marriage.
Petronius A less marriageable face I've never seen. Wedding guests generally look happier and merrier for six whole days afterwards; greybeards grow ten years younger. So what wedding are you talking about? That between Death and Destruction, I suppose?
Gabriel No, between a young nobleman and a girl of sixteen in whom you'd find no lack of beauty, manners, family, or fortune – in short, fit to be the wife of Jove.
Petronius Huh! So young a girl for such an old fellow?
Gabriel Kings don't age.
Petronius Then why so glum? Maybe you're jealous of the groom who forestalled you and carried off the captured spoils?
Gabriel Pooh! Not at all.

Petronius It wasn't the sort of thing they say occurred at the feast of Lapithae?[2]

Gabriel By no means.

Petronius What? Did you run out of wine?

Gabriel On the contrary, there was more than enough.

Petronius No flute players on hand?

Gabriel Yes, fiddlers, harpers, flutists, and bagpipers.

Petronius What, then? Wasn't Hymen[3] present?

Gabriel He was summoned in vain by ever so many voices.

Petronius Nor the Graces?

Gabriel Not the slightest sign of one. Nor Juno, who presides over marriages; nor golden Aphrodite; nor Jove, the marriage god.[4]

Petronius Really, you describe a wedding simply unlucky and without benefit of clergy; or rather a marriage without marriage.

Gabriel Had you seen it, you'd go further than that.

Petronius No dancing, then?

Gabriel No, it was a wretchedly lame affair.

Petronius So no favouring deity was there to gladden the nuptials?

Gabriel No divinity at all, save one goddess the Greeks call Pox.

Petronius You tell of a scabby wedding, I think.

Gabriel An ulcerous and festering one, rather.

Petronius But why, my dear Gabriel, does this mention of it bring tears to your eyes?

Gabriel Petronius, this affair could draw tears from flint.

Petronius I believe it could – if flint had seen it. But please do tell me, what is this awful misfortune? Don't conceal it and don't keep me in suspense any longer.

Gabriel You know Lempridius Eubulus?[5]

Petronius There's no man better – or better off – in this city.

Gabriel Well, you know his daughter, Iphigenia?[6]

Petronius You've named the flower of the age.

Gabriel So she is. But do you know whom she's married?

Petronius I'll know if you tell me.

Gabriel She's married Pompilius Blenus.[7]

Petronius What? Not that Thraso,[8] who's in the habit of slaughtering everyone – in his bragging yarns?

Gabriel The very one.

Petronius But he's long been notorious in this city for two things: lies, and the pox that doesn't yet have an exclusive name, since it goes by such a variety of them.

Gabriel It's a most presumptuous pox. In a showdown, it wouldn't yield to leprosy, elephantiasis, ringworm, gout, or sycosis.[9]

Petronius So the medical tribe proclaim.

Gabriel Why should I now describe, Petronius, a girl already known to you? Though her attire added a great deal of charm to her natural beauty. My dear Petronius, you'd have said she was some goddess: altogether lovely. Meanwhile, enter our handsome groom: nose broken, one foot dragging after the other (but less gracefully than the Swiss fashion would be),[10] scurvy hands, a breath that would knock you down, lifeless eyes, head bound up, bloody matter exuding from nose and ears. Other men have rings on their fingers; this one even wears rings on his thigh.

Petronius What possessed the parents to trust their daughter to such a monster?

Gabriel I don't know, except that a great many people seem to have lost their minds these days.

Petronius Perhaps he's very rich.

Gabriel He's rich, all right – in debts.

Petronius If the girl had poisoned her grandparents on both sides, what worse punishment could have been inflicted on her?

Gabriel Had she defiled her ancestors' ashes, it would have been punishment enough to have to kiss such a monster.

Petronius I agree.

Gabriel To my way of thinking, this treatment is more cruel than flinging her naked to bears or lions or crocodiles. Wild beasts would have spared one so beautiful, or a quick death would have ended her torment.

Petronius What you say is true. In my opinion, this deed is worthy of Mezentius, who (according to Virgil) tied dead bodies to living ones, fastening hands to hands and mouth to mouth.[11] Though, unless I'm mistaken, not even Mezentius was so savage that he would yoke so lovely a girl to a corpse. And there's no corpse you wouldn't rather be bound to than such a stinking one, for his breath is sheer poison, his speech a plague, his touch death.

Gabriel Just imagine, Petronius, what pleasure she'll take in his kisses, his embraces, his lovemaking and caresses.

Petronius I've sometimes heard theologians discussing marriage between unequals. Surely this could be called with perfect justice a marriage of unequals – as though you set a jewel in lead. But I marvel at the young woman's recklessness. Usually such girls are scared almost to death at the sight of a ghost or a spectre. Will this one dare to embrace such a corpse at night?

Gabriel The girl has excuses: the authority of her parents, the entreaty of friends, and the innocence that goes with her age. For my part, I can't sufficiently marvel at the parents' madness. Who has a daughter so homely that he'd be willing to give her in marriage to a leper?

Petronius In my judgment, no one with the slightest tinge of sanity. If I had a one-eyed daughter who was lame in the bargain and as deformed as Homer's Thersites,[12] and dowerless to boot, I'd refuse a son-in-law of that sort.

Gabriel Yet this plague is both more hideous and more harmful than every kind of leprosy, for it progresses quickly, recurs over and over again, and often kills, while leprosy sometimes allows a man to live to a ripe old age.

Petronius Perhaps her parents were unaware of the groom's disease.

Gabriel Not at all; they knew about it perfectly well.

Petronius If they hated their daughter so, why didn't they tie her in a sack and throw her into the river Scheldt?

Gabriel That would have been a milder form of insanity, to be sure.

Petronius What quality recommended the groom so highly to them? Does he excel in any profession?

Gabriel Many of them: he's an indefatigable gambler, an invincible boozer, a reprobate whoremonger, a past master of cheating and lying, a ready thief, a total bankrupt, an abandoned rake. Why elaborate? Universities teach only the seven liberal arts, but this fellow has more than ten illiberal ones.

Petronius Still, there must have been something to recommend him to her parents.

Gabriel Only his glorious title of knight.

Petronius What sort of knight is one whose pox scarcely allows him to sit in the saddle? But perhaps he owns splendid estates.

Gabriel He did have middling ones, but thanks to his extravagance nothing's left except one little tower, from which he sallies forth at regular intervals in search of prey; a tower so nobly furnished you wouldn't want to keep your hogs there. Yet all the while he prattles about castles, fiefs, and other fine-sounding names, and hangs up his coat of arms everywhere.

Petronius What insignia does his shield bear?

Gabriel Three golden elephants in a field of scarlet.

Petronius Elephant for the elephant – that's appropriate, surely.[13] Must be a bloodthirsty fellow.

Gabriel No, a wine-thirsty one, for he's wonderfully fond of red wine. That's your man of blood.

Petronius Then that snout of his would be useful for drinking.

Gabriel Indeed it would.

Petronius Thus his insignia proclaim a great and confirmed fool and wine-guzzler. For his colour isn't that of blood but of unmixed wine, and the golden elephant indicates that whatever gold he gets his hands on goes for wine.

Gabriel That's true.

Petronius What dowry will this Thraso bring to his bride, then?

Gabriel What? A very great –

Petronius How could a bankrupt give a very great one?

Gabriel Give me a chance to tell you: a very great, I say, and very bad pox.

Petronius Damned if I wouldn't rather have my daughter married to a horse than to such a horseman!

Gabriel But I'd rather have mine married to a monk. No, this isn't marrying a man but a man's corpse. If you had seen this sight – tell me, would you have held back the tears? ...

Petronius What madness it is willingly to hand over a daughter to one who's worse than leprous!

Gabriel More than madness. If a lord undertook to breed dogs, would he couple a scabby, spiritless dog with a full-blooded bitch?

Petronius No, he'd be very careful to match her with one purebred in every respect, so the litter wouldn't be mongrels.

Gabriel And if a general wanted to strengthen his cavalry, he wouldn't couple a diseased or broken-down horse with a prize mare, would he?

Petronius He wouldn't even admit a diseased horse into a common stable, lest infection spread to the other horses.

Gabriel But *they* think it doesn't matter whom they couple with a daughter and from what sort of stock come the children who will not only inherit all the wealth but even govern the commonwealth.

Petronius A farmer wouldn't mate just any bull and heifer, or just any horse and mare, or just any hog and sow, since bullock is bred for plow, horse for carriage, and pig for kitchen.

Gabriel Note how consistent men's judgments are: if some commoner dares to kiss a girl of noble birth, people think this insult must be avenged by war.

Petronius A most ferocious war, too.

Gabriel And yet these very people, having free choice, well aware of what they're doing, experienced in the ways of the world, give away their dearest possession to a repulsive monster. As private individuals, they're disloyal to their family; as citizens, to the state.

Petronius If a bridegroom otherwise normal has a slight limp, how the marriage is dreaded! Whereas *this* terrible evil is no impediment to betrothals.

Gabriel If someone has farmed out his daughter to a Franciscan, how great the horror, how loud the lamentation over the maiden foully placed! Yet remove the habit and she has a man of sound physique. But *this* bride passes her whole life with a corpse that is only half-alive. If a girl marries a priest, people joke about an 'anointed' man, but this girl married a man who's worse than smeared with ointment.

Petronius Enemies scarcely do this to girls captured in war, pirates to those they kidnap; and yet parents do it to an only daughter, and a magistrate doesn't put them under a guardian?

Gabriel How will a physician cure a lunatic if he himself is mad?

Petronius But it's amazing that princes, whose duty it is to look out for the commonwealth, at least in matters pertaining to the person – and in this regard nothing is more important than sound health – don't devise some remedy for this situation. So huge a plague has filled a large part of the globe – and yet they go on snoring as if it made no difference at all.

Gabriel One must speak guardedly of princes, Petronius. But bend your ear; I'll whisper a few words into it.

Petronius Alas! If only you were mistaken in what you say!

Gabriel How many types of disease do you suppose are caused by wine spoiled and decayed in a thousand ways?

Petronius Countless ones, if you believe the doctors.

Gabriel Aren't inspectors on the watch for this?

Petronius Certainly they're on the watch – to collect excise taxes.

Gabriel The girl who knowingly marries a diseased man perhaps deserves the trouble she's brought upon herself, though if I were head of the government I'd run them both out of town. But if she married this baneful pest when he misrepresented himself as sound – if I were pope I'd annul this marriage even if it had been made with six hundred marriage contracts.

Petronius On what pretext, since a marriage lawfully contracted cannot be annulled by mortal man?

Gabriel What? Do you think one made by a wicked fraud is contracted lawfully? The contract isn't valid if the girl is deceived into marrying a slave she thought a free man. Here the husband is slave to a loathsome mistress, Pox, and this slavery is the more wretched because she sets none free; no hope of release can mitigate the misery of the bondage.

Petronius You've discovered a pretext, clearly.

Gabriel Besides, marriage exists only between the living. Here the girl is married to a dead man.

Petronius That's another pretext. But I suppose you'd permit scabby to marry scabby, in accordance with the old saw 'like to like.'

Gabriel Were I permitted to do what would benefit the commonwealth, I'd let them marry, all right – but once they were married I'd burn them.

Petronius Then you'd be acting the part of a Phalaris,[15] not a prince.

Gabriel Does the physician who amputates some fingers or cauterizes a part of the body, lest the whole body perish, seem a Phalaris to you? I regard it as mercy, not cruelty. Would it had been done when this mischief first began to appear! Then the welfare of the whole earth would have been promoted by the destruction of a few. And we find a precedent for this in French history.[16]

Petronius But it would have been more merciful to castrate or deport them.

Gabriel What would you do with the women, then?

Petronius Put chastity belts on them.

Gabriel That would protect you against getting bad eggs from bad hens. But I'll admit this is the more merciful method if you'll admit the

other is safer. For even eunuchs experience lust. Besides, the disease is
transmitted not by one means alone but spread to other persons by a
kiss, by conversation, by touch, by having a little drink together. And
we observe that this disease is accompanied by a mortal hatred, so that
whoever is in its clutches takes pleasure in infecting as many others
as possible, even though doing so is no help to him. If deported, they
may possibly escape; they can fool others at night or take advantage of
persons who don't know them. From the dead there's no danger, surely.
Petronius It's safer, I grant, but I don't know whether it suits Christian
compassion.
Gabriel Come, tell me: which are the worse menace, mere thieves or
these creatures?
Petronius Money's much cheaper than good health, I admit.
Gabriel And yet we Christians crucify thieves, and that isn't called
cruelty but justice. And it's a duty, if you consider the public welfare.
Petronius In that instance, however, the penalty is paid by the one who
committed the crime.
Gabriel *These* fellows confer a favour, of course! But let's grant that
many people get this disease through no fault of their own (though
all the same you'd find few victims who hadn't invited it by their
own misconduct). Jurists hold that there are times when it is right for
innocent persons to be put to death if this is essential to the public safety,
just as the Greeks slew Astyanax, son of Hector, after the destruction
of Troy lest the war be renewed through his efforts.[17] And it is not
thought wrong, after a tyrant is killed, to butcher his innocent children
also.[18] What about the fact that we Christians are constantly at war
despite our realization that most of the evils in war befall those who
haven't deserved to suffer? The same thing occurs in what are called
'reprisals':[19] the one who did the injury is safe, and the trader, who
so far from being responsible for the deed never even heard of it, is
robbed. Now if we use such remedies in cases of minor importance,
what do you think should be done in the cruellest case of all?
Petronius I yield. It's true.
Gabriel Then consider this. In Italy, buildings are locked up at the
first sign of pestilence; those who attend the sufferer are quarantined.
Some call this inhumanity, though actually it's the highest humanity,
for because of this precaution the plague is checked with few fatalities.
How great the humanity of protecting the lives of so many thousands!

Some people accuse the Italians of inhospitality because, if pestilence is reported, they banish a stranger at evening and make him spend the night in the open air; but it is morally right to inconvenience a few for the sake of the public good. Some fancy themselves very brave and dutiful because they dare to visit a sufferer from pestilence even if they haven't any business there. But when, on their return, they infect wives, children, and the entire family, what is more foolish than that 'courage,' what more undutiful than that 'duty' of greeting somebody else to bring your nearest and dearest into imminent danger of their lives? Yet how much less is the peril from plague than from this pox! Rarely does the plague affect close relatives; as a rule it spares the aged; and those it does attack it either releases quickly or restores to health stronger than ever. *This* disease is simply slow but sure death, or rather burial. Victims are wrapped like corpses in cloths and unguents.

Petronius Very true. At least so deadly a disease as this should have been treated with the same care as leprosy. But if this is too much to ask, no one should let his beard be cut, or he should be his own barber.

Gabriel What if everyone kept his mouth shut?

Petronius They'd spread the disease through the nose.

Gabriel There's a remedy for that trouble, too.

Petronius What?

Gabriel Let them imitate the alchemists: wear a mask that admits light through little glass windows and allows you to breathe through mouth and nose by means of a tube extending from the mask over your shoulders and down your back.

Petronius Fine, if there were nothing to fear from contact with fingers, sheets, combs, and scissors.

Gabriel Then it would be best to let your beard grow to your knees.

Petronius Evidently. In the next place, make a law that the same men may not be both barber and surgeon.

Gabriel You'd reduce the barbers to starvation.

Petronius Let them cut costs and raise prices a little.

Gabriel Passed.

Petronius Then make a law to prohibit the common drinking cup.

Gabriel England would hardly stand for that!

Petronius And don't let two share the same bed unless they're husband and wife.

Gabriel Accepted.

Petronius Furthermore, don't permit a guest at an inn to sleep in sheets anyone else has slept in.

Gabriel What will you do with the Germans, who wash theirs barely twice a year?

Petronius Let them get after the washerwomen. Moreover, abolish the custom, no matter how ancient, of greeting with a kiss.

Gabriel Not even in church?

Petronius Let everyone put his hand against the board.[20]

Gabriel What about conversation?

Petronius Avoid the Homeric advice to 'bend the head near,'[21] and let the listener in turn close his lips tight.

Gabriel The Twelve Tables would scarcely suffice for these laws.[22]

Petronius But meanwhile what advice have you for the unhappy girl?

Gabriel Only that by being cheerful in her misery, she lessen her misery by that much; that she cover her mouth with her hand when her husband kisses her; and sleep with him armed.

Petronius Where do you hurry off to now?

Gabriel Straight to my study.

Petronius To do what?

Gabriel To compose an epitaph instead of the wedding song they ask for!

NOTES

1 A Greek god, who pronounced oracles from a cave

2 According to Greek legend, the centaurs, mythological beasts that are half human, half horse, attempted to rape the women of Lapith at a wedding feast.

3 In classical Greek weddings, the God Hymen was invoked for good luck.

4 Gods associated with marriage in classical mythology

5 'Eubulus' means 'one who gives good counsel.'

6 Her classical namesake, Iphigeneia, was sacrificed by her father so that the Greeks might have a prosperous journey to Troy.

7 Perhaps a pseudonym for Erasmus' correspondent Heinrich Eppendorf

8 A character in comedy, the proverbial bragging soldier

9 An ulcer of inflammation of hair follicles

10 An obscure reference to Swiss mercenaries

11 Virgil, *Aeneid*, 8.485–6

12 Proverbial for ugliness

13 Proverbial, like English 'birds of a feather'

14 Virgil, *Aeneid*, 5.344

15 Proverbial tyrant

16 Reference unclear

17 The child was killed to prevent any attempt to reestablish the dynasty on the throne of Troy.

18 It is not clear what historical incident Erasmus had in mind.

19 A medieval legal term denoting the right to regain stolen property

20 I.e., touching the pax board, a small disc that the priest normally kissed during the celebration of the Mass.

21 Homer, *Odyssey*, 1.157

22 The oldest Roman code of law

4. *The New Mother*

This dialogue was first printed in the 1526 edition of the *Colloquies* (on the publication history see above 25). It draws heavily on classical sources. Nearly everything the young mother is told by her visitor can be found in the tract *On the Education of Children* ascribed to the Greek essayist Plutarch, and in the *Attic Nights* of the Roman writer Aulus Gellius. The discussion of the nature of the soul is borrowed from Aristotle's treatise *On the Soul*.

The translation is by Craig Thompson.

EUTRAPELUS, FABULLA[1]

Eutrapelus Greetings, my dear Fabulla.
Fabulla Greetings in plenty to you too, Eutrapelus. But what in the world finally brings you here to say hello for a change? We haven't seen you these three years.
Eutrapelus I'll tell you. As I happened to pass by this house, I saw a crow tied with a white cloth and I wondered what the reason was.
Fabulla Are you such a stranger in this neighbourhood that you didn't know this is a sign of a birth in the house?
Eutrapelus Oh-ho, isn't it a marvel to see a white crow? But joking aside, of course I knew that; only I couldn't believe that you, a girl scarcely past her sixteenth year, had learned so early the very difficult art of bearing children, which some women scarcely learn before they're thirty.
Fabulla How you always live up to your name, Eutrapelus!
Eutrapelus How Fabulla is never at a loss for fables! So it was lucky for me, while I was wondering about this, that Polygamus turned up.[2]
Fabulla The man who recently buried his tenth wife?
Eutrapelus The very one. But what you missed, I suppose, is that he's eagerly courting a girl again as though he'd been a bachelor up to now. When I asked him what the news was, 'In this house,' says he, 'a woman's body was cut in two.' 'For what crime?' 'If the common gossip is true,' says he, 'a wife tried to skin her husband,' and off he went with a laugh.

Fabulla That fellow has a crude sense of humour.

Eutrapelus I'm coming straight inside to congratulate you on a happy delivery.

Fabulla Congratulate me on a safe delivery if you like, Eutrapelus; on a happy one when you see my offspring prove himself an honest man.

Eutrapelus Dutifully and truly spoken, my Fabulla.

Fabulla I'm nobody's Fabulla except Petronius'.

Eutrapelus Yes, you bear only for Petronius, but you don't live only for him, I dare say. I congratulate you further on having produced a boy.

Fabulla But why do you think it's luckier to have had a boy than a girl?

Eutrapelus Nay, Petronius' Fabulla (for now I'm afraid to say *my* Fabulla), *you* tell me why you're glad to have boys rather than girls.

Fabulla How other women may feel I don't know; for my part, I'm pleased now to have had a boy because it was God's will. Had he willed me to have a girl, I would have preferred it too.

Eutrapelus Do you imagine God has so much leisure that he even attends women in labour?

Fabulla What could he better do, Eutrapelus, than preserve by propagation what he created?

Eutrapelus What could he do, my good woman? On the contrary, if he weren't God I don't think he could get through so much business. King Christian of Denmark, a devout partisan of the gospel, is in exile.[3] Francis, king of France, is a 'guest' of the Spaniards.[4] What *he* thinks of this I don't know, but surely he's a man worthy of a better fate. Charles is preparing to extend the boundaries of his realm.[5] Ferdinand has his hands full in Germany.[6] Bankruptcy threatens every court. The peasants raise dangerous riots and are not swayed from their purpose, despite so many massacres. The commons are bent on anarchy; the Church is shaken to its very foundations by menacing factions; on every side the seamless coat of Jesus is torn to shreds. The vineyard of the Lord is now laid waste not by a single boar,[7] but at one and the same time the authority of priests (together with their tithes), the dignity of theologians, the splendour of monks is imperilled; confession totters; vows reel; pontifical ordinances crumble away; the Eucharist is called in question;[8] Antichrist is awaited; the whole earth is pregnant with I know not what calamity. The Turks conquer and threaten all the while; there's nothing they won't ravage if their undertaking succeeds. And you ask what could he better do? No, it's high time, I think, for him to look out for his own kingdom too.

Fabulla What men think most urgent may seem insignificant to God. But let's exclude God from this cast, if you will. Tell me: what are your reasons for believing it's more fortunate to have had a lad than a lass?

Eutrapelus It's a duty to consider this the best because God, who is beyond question best, gave it. Now if God gave you a crystal cup, wouldn't you thank him heartily?

Fabulla I would.

Eutrapelus What if he gave one of glass? You wouldn't thank him so much, would you?– But I fear I'm a bother instead of a comfort, wrangling over these questions here with you.

Fabulla Not at all. Fabulla's in no danger from fables. I've been in bed a month now and I'm strong enough to wrestle.

Eutrapelus Then why don't you fly out of the nest?

Fabulla The king forbade.

Eutrapelus King who?

Fabulla A tyrant, rather.

Eutrapelus Who, I ask?

Fabulla In a word, custom.

Eutrapelus Ah, how many unjust demands that king makes!– Let's go on discussing crystal and glass, then.

Fabulla I suppose you think man is naturally better and stronger than woman.

Eutrapelus So I believe.

Fabulla On the authority of men, to be sure. Men aren't therefore longer lived than women, are they? Not immune to disease?

Eutrapelus Not at all, but they generally excel in strength.

Fabulla But they themselves are excelled by camels.

Eutrapelus Well, but the male was created first.

Fabulla Adam was created before Christ. And artists usually surpass themselves in their later works.

Eutrapelus But God made woman subject to man.

Fabulla A ruler's not better merely because he's a ruler. And it's the wife, not the female, whom God made subject. Besides, he made the wife subject in such a way that, though each has power over the other, nevertheless the woman is to obey the man not as a superior but a more aggressive person. Tell me, Eutrapelus, which is weaker, the one who makes concession to the other or the one to whom concession is made?

Eutrapelus I'll yield to you in this if you'll show me what Paul means in his letter to the Corinthians when he says the head of the man is Christ and the head of the woman is the man; and when he says man is the image and glory of God, woman the glory of man.[9]

Fabulla I'll explain that if you'll show me whether it's granted to men only to be members of Christ.

Eutrapelus Heaven forbid! That's granted to all human creatures through faith.

Fabulla How does it happen, then, that since there is one head this is not shared by all members alike? In the next place, since God created man in his own image, did he express this image in man's bodily form or in mental gifts?

Eutrapelus In mental gifts.

Fabulla But in these respects what superiority, pray, have men over us? In which sex is there more drunkenness, more brawls, fights, killings, wars, robberies, and adulteries?

Eutrapelus But only we men go to war for our country.

Fabulla But quite often you same men desert your post and run away shamefully. And it's not always for your country, but more commonly for a paltry pittance, that you desert wife and children. You're worse than gladiators: you voluntarily surrender your bodies into the slavish necessity of killing or being killed. Now – though you make a special point of boasting of your martial valour – there's not a single one of you who, if he once experienced childbirth, would not prefer standing in a battle line ten times over to going through what we must endure so often. Battle doesn't always reach the stage of hand-to-hand fighting; and even if it does, not every part of the army is in danger. Your kind are stationed in the middle line; another man is in the reserves; another stays safely in the rear; and finally many are saved by surrender and flight. *We* must engage death at close quarters.

Eutrapelus Not the first time I've heard this – but is it true?

Fabulla Yes, very true.

Eutrapelus Then, Fabulla, would you like me to persuade your husband not to touch you hereafter? With that sort of bargain, you'll be safe from this danger.

Fabulla Yes, indeed, I'd like nothing better if you could do it.

Eutrapelus What reward will this negotiator have if he succeeds?

Fabulla I'll give you ten smoked calves' tongues.

Eutrapelus I'd prefer them to ten nightingales' tongues.[10] I don't reject the terms, but I wouldn't want this agreement ratified before a guarantee is inserted.

Fabulla Add it, if you like – and any other covenant.

Eutrapelus I will, depending on how you feel about it after one month.

Fabulla Why not on how I feel now?

Eutrapelus I'll tell you: because I'm afraid that after a month you may not feel the same. So you'd have to pay me double, and I'd have the double job of persuading and dissuading.

Fabulla Well, be it as you wish. But meantime go on with your demonstration of why the male sex is superior to the female.

Eutrapelus I see you're bent on single combat. For that reason I think I'd better yield for the present. I'll engage you at some other time, but fully armed with an auxiliary; for where wars are fought with words, not even seven men are a match for one woman.

Fabulla Yes, Nature armed us with this weapon, though even you men aren't tongue-tied.

Eutrapelus Maybe so. But where's your little boy?

Fabulla In the next room.

Eutrapelus What's he doing there? Cooking cabbage?

Fabulla Are you trying to be funny? He's with his nurse.

Eutrapelus What nurse are you talking about? Has he any other nurse than his mother?

Fabulla Why not? It's common custom.

Eutrapelus You name the worst authority on good behaviour, the common herd, Fabulla. Sinning is common, gambling is common, visiting brothels is common; cheating, boozing, folly are common.

Fabulla My friends advised it because they thought a person as young as I am should be spared nursing.

Eutrapelus But if Nature gave you strength to conceive, undoubtedly it gave you strength to nurse, too.

Fabulla Yes, probably.

Eutrapelus Tell me: don't you think the word *mother* is very sweet?

Fabulla I do.

Eutrapelus So if it were possible, you'd allow some other woman to be mother of your offspring?

Fabulla Not for the world!

Eutrapelus Then why are you willing to transfer more than half the name of mother to some other woman?

Fabulla Do mind what you're saying, Eutrapelus. I'm not dividing my son. I'm his sole, entire mother.

Eutrapelus No, Fabulla, Nature herself contradicts you on that score. Why is earth called the universal parent? Because it produces so much? Not at all; the real reason is that it nourishes what it brought forth. What water begets is reared in water. On land no kind of animal or plant is produced which that same land does not nourish by its own vitality. And there's no class of living creatures that does not nurse its own young. Owls, lions, and vipers bring up their own offspring; and do men reject theirs? I ask you, what is more cruel than those who are said to expose their children because bringing them up is a nuisance?

Fabulla Horrid!

Eutrapelus But people don't find the deed equally horrid. Or isn't it a kind of exposure to hand over the tender infant, still red from its mother, drawing breath from its mother, crying for its mother's care – a sound said to move even wild beasts – to a woman who perhaps has neither good health nor good morals and who, finally, may be much more concerned about a bit of money than about your whole baby?

Fabulla The woman chosen is in sound health.

Eutrapelus Physicians would be better judges of this than you are. But assume she's equal to you in this respect, or better, if you like. Do you suppose it makes no difference whether a delicate infant drinks in congenial and familiar nourishment and is cherished by the now familiar warmth or is forced to get used to somebody else's? Wheat sown in alien soil degenerates into wild oats or winter wheat; a vine transferred to a different hill changes its character; a young plant torn from its parent earth droops and dies, as it were; for that reason it is transplanted with native earth if possible.

Fabulla On the contrary, they say plants that are transplanted and grafted lose their wildness and bear better fruit.

Eutrapelus But not as soon as they're born, my friend. This time too will come some day, if God will, when you must send the boy out from home to learn his letters – and harder lessons, which are the father's responsibility rather than the mother's. Now his tender age should be cherished. Furthermore, while the nature of the food contributes much to bodily health and strength, this is especially true of the nourishment a soft and delicate little body is filled with. Here also Horace's saying applies: 'Once steeped when new, the jar its fragrance long will keep.'[11]

Fabulla I'm not worried so much about his body if only his mind will be the sort we hope for.

Eutrapelus Dutifully spoken, but dubious wisdom.

Fabulla Why?

Eutrapelus When you chop cabbage, why do you complain that the blade of the knife is dull and order it sharpened? Why reject a needle with a blunt point when that alone does not deprive you of skill?

Fabulla The skill's not lacking, but an unsatisfactory tool hinders it.

Eutrapelus Why do people who need keen eyesight avoid tares and onions?[12]

Fabulla Because they harm the eyes.

Eutrapelus Isn't it the mind that perceives?

Fabulla Yes, for dead men see nothing. But what would a carpenter do with a bad axe?

Eutrapelus You admit, then, that the body is the instrument of the mind?

Fabulla It is.

Eutrapelus And you grant that if the body's injured, the mind doesn't function or functions awkwardly?

Fabulla What you say is not far from the truth.

Eutrapelus Well, now, I seem to have met with a philosophical nature. So assume that the soul of a man transmigrates into the body of a cock:[13] would the cock speak like us?

Fabulla Of course not.

Eutrapelus Why wouldn't it?

Fabulla Because it lacks lips, teeth, and tongue like ours; and it has neither epiglottis nor the three cartilages moved by the three muscles to which the nerves from the brain extend; nor throat nor mouth like ours.

Eutrapelus What if it entered into the body of a swine?

Fabulla It would grunt like a swine.

Eutrapelus Into the body of a camel?

Fabulla It would sing as a camel sings.

Eutrapelus Into the body of an ass, as happened to Apuleius?[14]

Fabulla It would bray like an ass, I suppose.

Eutrapelus Yes, and he says that when he wanted to call out to Caesar, with his lips as tight together as possible, he could scarcely sound an 'O'; he simply couldn't utter 'Caesar.' The same chap, when he wanted to write down a story he had heard before it slipped from his mind, rejected so asinine an idea when he noticed his thick hoofs.

Fabulla Properly, too.

Eutrapelus Therefore when eyes are bleary, the mind perceives less; when ears are filled with dirt, it hears less; when you have a cold in the head, it smells less; when a limb is stiff, it feels less; when the tongue is infected by ill humours, it tastes less.

Fabulla Undeniably.

Eutrapelus And the sole reason is that the organ is faulty.

Fabulla I think so.

Eutrapelus You won't deny it's often injured by food and drink.

Fabulla Granted, but what has this to do with a clear head?

Eutrapelus In the same way, what have tares to do with keen eyesight?

Fabulla They damage the instrument of the mind.

Eutrapelus Well answered. But explain this: Why is it that one person has a quicker understanding than another and a more tenacious memory? That one gets angry sooner or hates more moderately?

Fabulla It's the way his mind's made.

Eutrapelus You shan't escape like that. Why is it that one who was formerly quick and alert and had a fine memory afterwards becomes forgetful and slow, either from a blow or an accident or disease or old age?

Fabulla Now you seem to play the sophist.

Eutrapelus Do the same for your own part: play the sophistress.

Fabulla I suppose you mean that just as the mind perceives and hears through eyes and ears, so it understands, remembers, loves, hates, grows angry, and is appeased through certain organs.

Eutrapelus Quite correct.

Fabulla Just what are these organs, and where are they?

Eutrapelus You see where the eyes are.

Fabulla I know where the ears, nostrils, and palate are too. And I perceive that the sense of touch pervades the entire body except when a member is numb.

Eutrapelus When a foot's cut off, the mind still understands.

Fabulla It does, and likewise if a hand is cut off.

Eutrapelus But one who is struck hard on the temple or on the back of the head falls down as though dead and is completely unconscious.

Fabulla I've seen that sometimes.

Eutrapelus From this you conclude that the organs of intellect, will, and memory are within the skull, less gross than eyes and ears but material nonetheless. Though the extremely rarefied spirits in our bodies are substantial, too.

Fabulla Are these also injured by food and drink?

Eutrapelus Certainly.

Fabulla But the brain is far away from the stomach.

Eutrapelus So is the top of the chimney far from the fireplace, but if you sit on it you'll feel the heat.

Fabulla I shan't try it.

Eutrapelus But if you don't believe me, ask the storks. And so it does make a difference which spirits and vapours fly up from the stomach to the brain and to the organs of the mind. For if these are crude and cool, they sink back into the stomach.

Fabulla You're really describing a still by which we draw off the juice evaporating from flowers and herbs.

Eutrapelus Not a bad guess. For the liver, to which the gall bladder is attached, serves as a fire, the stomach as a pan, the skull as the cap of the tube; and in the same fashion, if you like, the nose serves as the lead pipes. And so from this mutual flowing back and forth of the humours is generally produced whatever diseases there are, as one humour or another slips down now into the eyes, now into the stomach; at another time into the shoulders; sometimes into the neck or elsewhere. To make this more intelligible: why do intemperate wine-drinkers have poor memories? Why are those who feed on foods containing the lighter spirits less dull-witted? Why does coriander improve the memory?[15] Why does hellebore empty the mind?[16] Why does frantic cramming of oneself bring on an epilepsy that numbs all the senses at once, like a deep sleep? In short, as unusual hunger or thirst weakens boys' wits and memory, so overeating makes them stupid (if we believe Aristotle):[17] the tiny spark of reason is buried, so to speak, by the stuff heaped upon it.

Fabulla Is the mind corporeal, then, that it should be affected by corporeal things?

Eutrapelus The nature of the rational mind is not itself corrupted, but its power and activity are weakened if the organs are injured; as an artist's skill is useless if he's deprived of proper tools.

Fabulla How big is the mind and what does it look like?

Eutrapelus Ridiculous to ask about size or shape when you admit it's without body.

Fabulla I take 'body' to mean what is perceptible.

Eutrapelus Yes, but the imperceptible is the most perfect, as for example God and the angels.

Fabulla I hear God and the angels called spirits. But we perceive a spirit.

Eutrapelus In this expression sacred Scripture speaks obscurely, in consideration of human simplicity. It means mind free from all connection with objects of sense.

Fabulla Then what's the difference between angel and mind?

Eutrapelus The same as between slug and snail, or tortoise, if you prefer.

Fabulla Then the body is the dwelling rather than the instrument of mind.

Eutrapelus There's nothing to prevent us from calling the instrument attached a 'dwelling.' And, in fact, philosophers have different opinions on this subject. Some say the body is the 'garment' of the soul,[18] some the 'dwelling,' some the 'instrument,' some the 'harmony.'[19] Whichever of these names you use, it follows that acts of mind are curtailed by states of the body.

Fabulla If body is the dwelling-place of mind, I observe many whose minds are ill housed.

Eutrapelus Yes, namely in houses dripping, dark, and exposed to every wind; smoky, damp, damaged, dilapidated – in short, rotten and infected. And yet Cato holds that to be comfortably housed is the first requirement for happiness.

Fabulla There would be no complaint if moving into another dwelling were allowed.

Eutrapelus To depart is not permitted except when the landlord bids. But even if we aren't allowed to leave, we *are* allowed to make the dwelling of our minds more habitable through our skill and care, just as in houses the windows are changed, floor raised, walls plastered or hung with tapestries, dirt got rid of by fire and fumigation. In an old body on the verge of ruin, this is very difficult. What matters most is that the youthful body receive proper care from the minute it's born.

Fabulla You want the mother to be a medical nurse, too.

Eutrapelus Certainly I'd have her be so with regard to choice and regulation of food and drink, movement, sleep, baths, oilings, rubbings, clothing. How many persons are there, do you think, who are liable to the most serious diseases and defects – epilepsy, emaciation, feebleness, deafness, ruptures, crooked limbs, weak-mindedness, stupidity – for no other reason than careless treatment by nurses?

Fabulla I'm surprised you didn't become a Franciscan instead of a painter, you preach so eloquently.

Eutrapelus When I see you in the order of Poor Clares, then I'll preach to you as a Franciscan.

Fabulla I should very much like to know what *is* the soul of which we hear and talk so much, when nobody has seen it.

Eutrapelus On the contrary, nobody with eyes can miss it.

Fabulla I see souls painted in the form of little children. But why no wings, as angels have?

Eutrapelus Because, if Socrates' story[20] is to be believed, when souls came down from heaven their wings were broken.

Fabulla Then how can they be said to fly up to heaven?

Eutrapelus Because faith and charity cause their wings to sprout again. These wings he sought who, wearied of the habitation of his body, cried, 'Oh that I had wings like a dove! for then would I fly away and be at rest.'[21] For the soul has no other wings, since it is incorporeal, nor has it any shape visible to bodily eyes; but what we see by our minds we perceive with the greater certitude. Do you believe there is a God?

Fabulla Of course.

Eutrapelus But nothing is more impossible to see than God.

Fabulla He is seen in the creation.

Eutrapelus Likewise is the mind seen by its activity. If you want to know what happens in a living body, consider a dead one. When you see a man feel, perceive, hear, be moved, understand, remember, reason, you perceive the presence of the soul more certainly than you now see this tankard. According to Aristotle,[22] the soul does nothing except through the organs, that is, the instruments of the body ... Here, then, you can perform no mean service for your baby by seeing that his mind's instrument is well tuned, damaged as little as possible, lest it be slack from laziness or shrill with anger or hoarse with drunkenness.

Upbringing and the pattern of life sometimes plant these dispositions in us.

Fabulla I accept the advice, but I await your defence of Aristotle.

Eutrapelus He classified the soul as animating, vegetative, and sentient.[23] Soul gives life, but what is alive is not on that account animal. Trees live and age and die but don't feel, though some people do credit even them with a slight power of sensation. In clinging objects, scarcely any power of sensation is found. Sponge-gatherers find it in a sponge; woodchoppers find it in trees, if we believe them. It's said that if you strike with your palm the trunk of a tree you mean to fell, as woodchoppers are in the habit of doing, the tree is harder to cut, since it shrinks in fear.[24] What lives and feels is animal, but there is nothing to prevent what is incapable of feeling from being vegetative, for example mushrooms, beets, cabbages.

Fabulla If these live and feel somehow or other, if they have power of movement when young, why don't they deserve the name 'animal'?

Eutrapelus Our forefathers didn't approve of it, and we have no right to depart from their decisions. Also it's irrelevant to the present subject.

Fabulla But I won't accept the proposition that a beetle and a man have the same soul.

Eutrapelus Not the same, my good friend, but they have a common faculty up to a certain point. Your soul animates your body, causes it to grow, and renders it capable of sensation. A beetle's soul does the same in its body. What a man's soul does differently from a beetle's, or in addition, is due partly to material cause. A beetle doesn't sing or speak, because it lacks organs capable of doing so.

Fabulla Then what you're saying is that if a beetle's soul entered a man's body, it would act the same as a human soul does.

Eutrapelus No, no: it wouldn't act the *same* even if it were an angelical intelligence – as I've said. The only difference between an angel and human soul is that man's soul is created to move a human body furnished with natural organs, just as a beetle's soul moves only a beetle's body. An angel is not created to animate a body but to have understanding without bodily organs.

Fabulla Can't a soul do the same?

Eutrapelus When separated from the body, yes.

Fabulla Then it does not have this independence while in the body?

Eutrapelus No, indeed, unless something unnatural occurs.

Fabulla But in place of one soul you've dumped many into my lap – animating, vegetative, sentient, rational, remembering, willing, irascible, concupiscent. One was enough for me!

Eutrapelus The same soul has different functions; the various names are drawn from these.

Fabulla I don't quite follow.

Eutrapelus But I'll see that you do follow. In the bedroom you're a wife, in the shop a weaver of tapestries, in the store a seller of tapestries, in the kitchen a cook, among the menservants and maidservants a mistress, among the children a mother – and yet you're all these in the same house.

Fabulla You're a thickheaded reasoner,[25] all right! So the mind's in the body as I'm in a house?

Eutrapelus Yes.

Fabulla But while I weave in the shop I don't cook in the kitchen.

Eutrapelus You're not *only* a soul, but a soul bearing a body. The body can't be present in many places at the same time. The soul, since it is simple form, is in the whole body in such a way that all of it is in every part of the body; yet it does not perform the same action through all the parts, nor in the same manner through the parts, however affected they are. For it knows and remembers in the brain, grows angry in the heart, lusts in the liver, hears in the ears, sees in the eyes, smells in the nostrils, tastes in the palate and tongue, perceives in all parts of the body connected with the nervous system. It doesn't feel in hair or tips of the nails. Even a lung doesn't feel by itself, nor does the liver, nor (perhaps) the spleen.

Fabulla In some parts, therefore, it merely animates and causes growth.

Eutrapelus Evidently.

Fabulla If the same soul does all this in one man, it follows that as soon as the foetus begins to grow in the mother's womb – the sign of life – it perceives and understands; unless perhaps one man has many souls to start with, and then, after the others have given way, a single one does everything. So man will have been first a plant, then an animal, last of all a human being.

Eutrapelus To Aristotle, what you say might not seem far-fetched. To me it is more likely that the rational soul is infused along with life, but this soul, like a tiny flame stifled under damp wood, is not yet able to exert its power.

Fabulla Then the mind is bound to the body it acts on and moves?

Eutrapelus Just like a tortoise to the shell it bears.

Fabulla It moves the shell, certainly, but so that it is itself moved at the same time, as a pilot turns the ship whithersoever he pleases, yet he himself is moved along with the ship.

Eutrapelus Yes, and as a squirrel turns his cage, he himself on the jump all the while.

Fabulla So the soul both affects and is affected by the body?

Eutrapelus Clearly, so far as its workings are concerned.

Fabulla With regard to its essential nature, therefore, a fool's soul is equal to Solomon's.

Eutrapelus Nothing absurd about that.

Fabulla Consequently angels are equal too, since they have no substance (which you say is the source of inequality).

Eutrapelus Enough of philosophy for now. Let the theologians worry about these questions, while we resume what we began. If you would like to be a complete mother, take care of your baby's little body, so that after it has freed itself from vapours,[26] the spark of reason may have the support of good and serviceable bodily organs. Every time you hear your boy squalling, believe that he's asking this of you. When you see on your breasts those two little swollen fountains, so to speak, flowing with milk of their own accord, believe that Nature is reminding you of your duty. Otherwise, when your child is ready to speak and with his sweet baby-talk calls you 'mamma,' what will be your reaction, hearing this from him to whom you refused the breast and whom you banished to a hired nurse, just as if you had put him under a sheep or a goat? What if he calls you 'half-mother' instead of 'mother' when he can talk? You'll fetch the rod, I dare say. But the woman who refuses to nurse what she bore is scarcely a half-mother. The better part of childbearing is the nursing of the tender baby, for he's nourished not only with milk but by the fragrance of the mother's body as well. He needs that now familiar, recognized fluid that he absorbed in her body and by which he grew strong. And for my part, I'm convinced that children's characters are injured by the nature of the milk just as in fruits or plants the moisture of the soil changes the quality of what it nourishes. Or do you suppose the common saying 'He drank in his spite with his nurse's milk' has no basis? I doubt if the Greeks were wrong in their phrase 'like nurses,' in connection with someone who doesn't get enough to eat; for nurses put very little of the food they chew into the baby's mouth; most of it they swallow themselves. Hence one who presently rejects what she produced hasn't even borne a child; that's aborting rather than bearing. And for such women I think the etymology of the Greeks,[27] who derive μήτηρ from μὴ τηρεῖν 'not take care of,' is fitting, for simply to take on some wet-nurse for a baby still warm from its mother is a kind of exposure.

Fabulla I'd agree, unless the woman selected were one who met all your requirements.

Eutrapelus Even if it made no difference what milk a delicate child drinks, or what saliva it swallows with the pre-chewed food, or even if you came across a nurse of the sort I doubt exists, do you imagine anyone can put up with all the irksomeness of nursing as a mother can – the filth, the sitting up late, the bawling, the illnesses, the never sufficiently attentive watching? If there's any woman who loves like a mother, it will be one who cares like a mother. Yes, and what's more, your son may love you less, his natural affection being divided, as it were, between two mothers; and your devotion to him will cool in turn. The result will be that when he's older, he'll be the less willing to obey your commands and you'll care less for him – you'll see perhaps the nurse in the way he behaves. Now one of the main steps in the learning process is mutual affection between teacher and pupil. If, therefore, none of the sweet scent of natural devotion is lost, you'll instil principles of good conduct into him more easily. The mother is of no small importance in this respect, both because the material she moulds is most plastic and because it is responsive to every suggestion.

Fabulla So far as I can see, childbearing is not so simple an affair as people commonly suppose.

Eutrapelus If you doubt me, here's Paul speaking quite plainly of woman: 'She shall be saved,' he says, 'in childbearing.'[29]

Fabulla So she who bears a child is saved?

Eutrapelus Oh, no; he adds, 'if the children continue in faith.' You haven't fulfilled the duty of a childbearer unless you've first formed the delicate little body of your son, then fashioned his equally pliable mind through good education.

Fabulla But it's not in the mother's power to guarantee that her sons will persevere in righteousness.

Eutrapelus That may be, but vigilant instruction is so important that Paul thinks mothers should be blamed if children go wrong. In brief, if you do the best you can, God will join his help to your earnestness.

Fabulla Your eloquence has certainly persuaded me, Eutrapelus, if you could persuade my parents and husband likewise.

Eutrapelus I'll undertake this if you back me up.

Fabulla I promise.

Eutrapelus But may one see your boy?

Fabulla Of course. Syrisca, send for nurse and baby.

Eutrapelus A fine lad! They say one should overlook an initial attempt, but you've produced a masterpiece in your first try.

Fabulla It's no carven image that stands in need of art.

Eutrapelus True, but it's a model of one. However accounted for, it has turned out very well. I only hope the figures you weave on tapestries may turn out as well.

Fabulla But you, on the other hand, paint better than you produce.

Eutrapelus So Nature has decreed, to be fair with everybody. How careful Nature is that nothing be lost! She has exhibited two persons in one: nose and eyes recall the father, brow and chin the mother. Can you commit so dear a pledge as this to another's keeping? Women who could bear to do that seem to me doubly cruel, since they do it not merely at a risk to the child whom they banish but even to themselves; because their milk, tainted by their refusal to nurse, often causes dangerous diseases. Thus it turns out that while they pay strict attention to the beauty of one body, they're careless about the life of two; and while on guard against premature old age, they expose themselves to premature death.– What have you named the boy?

Fabulla Cornelius.

Eutrapelus That was his paternal grandfather's name. May he resemble that worthiest of men in his conduct, too!

Fabulla We'll do our best. But look here, Eutrapelus, I'll beg one favour of you.

Eutrapelus Nay, consider me your slave; command, and you shall get your wish.

Fabulla Then I won't free you until you complete the business begun for me.

Eutrapelus What's that?

Fabulla First, that you advise me about the care of the child's health; then, when he's stronger, about the elements of his moral and spiritual growth.

Eutrapelus I'll be glad to do that in so far as I know how, but in our next chat. Just now I'm off to plead with your husband and parents.

Fabulla I hope and pray your plea will please!

NOTES

1 The etymology of the names suggests that Eutrapelus is clever at rebuttals and Fabulla is a skilled conversationalist.
2 The name Polygamus is telltale. In classical Latin *polygamus* (a Greek loanword) referred, not to polygamy, but to remarriage.
3 Christian II of Denmark (1481–1559) was overthrown in a revolt in 1523.
4 Charles V, German emperor and king of Spain, had defeated the French king at Pavia (1525) and was keeping him prisoner in Madrid.
5 See note 4.
6 Ferdinand, Charles' brother, looked after the affairs of Germany while the imperial court was in Spain (1521–9). During this period the Lutheran question came to a head. The Protestant princes formed the League of Schmalkalden and threatened military action.
7 The papal bull condemning Luther (1520) referred to him as 'a boar laying waste the vineyard of the Lord.'
8 References to the doctrinal points raised by the reformers, who questioned the sacramental nature of confession and ordination, as well as the nature of the Eucharist, i.e., whether bread and wine changed into Christ's body and blood (transubstantiation) and whether the celebration of the Eucharist was an act of remembrance or a renewal of Christ's sacrifice.
9 Cf 1 Cor. 11:3–7.
10 A delicacy, cf Horace, *Satires*, 2.3.245.
11 Horace, *Epistles*, 1.2.69–70
12 Cf Plautus, *Miles Gloriosus*, 321–2.
13 As in Lucian's *Dream*, in which Pythagoras is reincarnated as a rooster. Erasmus translated this dialogue from the Greek in 1506.
14 A reference to Apuleius' romance, *The Golden Ass*
15 On the qualities ascribed to coriander in antiquity cf Pliny, *Natural History*, 20.216–18.
16 Hellebore was thought to cure madness.

17 Elsewhere attributed to Jerome and Aulus Gellius; Erasmus was evidently not sure about the source.

18 Cf Seneca, *Epistles*, 92.13.

19 Cf ibid, 65.17; Cicero, *Tusculan Questions*, 1.10; Aristotle, *On the Soul*, 407B–408A.

20 Plato, *Phaedrus*, 248C

21 Ps. 54:7

22 *On the Soul*, 412A

23 Ibid

24 Cf Pliny, *Natural History* 24.2.

25 Erasmus employs the proverbial expression *crassa Minerva*, i.e., using a simplistic argument.

26 In early medicine 'vapours' referred to exhalations within the stomach, which were considered harmful.

27 A spurious etymological explanation, deriving *meter* (mother) from *me terein* (not take care of)

29 1 Tim. 2:15

5. The Well-Read Matron:
The Abbot and the Learned Lady

This dialogue was first printed in the 1524 edition of the *Colloquies* (for the publication history see above 25). It contains the familiar Erasmian criticism of monasticism. The abbot depicted here has only worldly interests. He has neither the vocation nor the training necessary to provide the spiritual leadership and the pastoral responsibilities his position entails. Erasmus pays tribute here to the learned women of his age, although one suspects that the heroine, Magdalia, is introduced for shock value rather than as an exemplary character.

The translation is by Craig Thompson.

ANTRONIUS, MAGDALIA[1]

Antronius What furnishings do I see here?
Magdalia Elegant, aren't they?
Antronius How elegant I don't know, but certainly unbecoming both to a young miss and a married woman.
Magdalia Why?
Antronius Because the whole place is full of books.
Magdalia Are you so old, an abbot as well as a courtier, and have never seen books in court ladies' houses?
Antronius Yes, but those were in French. Here I see Greek and Latin ones.[2]
Magdalia Are French books the only ones that teach wisdom?
Antronius But it's fitting for court ladies to have something with which to beguile their leisure.
Magdalia Are court ladies the only ones allowed to improve their minds and enjoy themselves?
Antronius You confuse growing wise with enjoying yourself. It's not feminine to be brainy. A lady's business is to have a good time.[3]
Magdalia Shouldn't everyone live well?
Antronius Yes, in my opinion.
Magdalia But who can have a good time without living well?
Antronius Rather, who can enjoy himself if he *does* live well?

Magdalia So you approve of those who live basely if only they have a good time?

Antronius I believe those who have a good time are living well.

Magdalia Where does this good time come from? From externals or from within?

Antronius From externals.

Magdalia Shrewd abbot but stupid philosopher! Tell me: how do you measure good times?

Antronius By sleep, dinner parties, doing as one likes, money, honours.

Magdalia But if to these things God added wisdom, you wouldn't enjoy yourself?

Antronius What do you mean by wisdom?

Magdalia This: understanding that a man is not happy without the goods of the mind; that wealth, honours, noble birth make him neither happier nor better.

Antronius Away with that wisdom!

Magdalia What if I enjoy reading a good author more than you do hunting, drinking, or playing dice? You won't think I'm having a good time?

Antronius *I* wouldn't live like that.

Magdalia I'm not asking what *you* would enjoy most, but what *ought* to be enjoyable.

Antronius I wouldn't want my monks to spend their time on books.

Magdalia Yet my husband heartily approves of my doing so. But exactly why do you disapprove of this in your monks?

Antronius Because I find they're less tractable; they talk back by quoting from decrees and decretals, from Peter and Paul.

Magdalia So your rules conflict with those of Peter and Paul?

Antronius What *they* may enjoin I don't know, but still I don't like a monk who talks back. And I don't want any of mine to know more than I do.

Magdalia You could avoid that by endeavouring to know as much as possible.

Antronius I haven't the leisure.

Magdalia How come?

Antronius Because I've no free time.

Magdalia No free time to grow wise?

Antronius No.

Magdalia What hinders you?

Antronius Long prayers, housekeeping, hunts, horses, court functions.

Magdalia So these are more important to you than wisdom?

Antronius It's what we're used to.

Magdalia Now tell me this: if some heavenly power enabled you to turn your monks and yourself too into any animal whatever, would you change them into hogs and yourself into a horse?

Antronius Not at all.

Magdalia But by doing so you'd prevent anybody's being wiser than you.

Antronius I shouldn't much care what sort of animal the monks were, provided I myself were a human being.

Magdalia Do you think one is human if he's neither wise nor wants to be wise?

Antronius I'm wise enough – so far as I'm concerned.

Magdalia And swine are wise enough so far as *they're* concerned.

Antronius You strike me as a sophistress, so keenly do you dispute.

Magdalia I won't say how you strike me. But why do these furnishings displease you?

Antronius Because distaff and spindle are the proper equipment for women.

Magdalia Isn't it a wife's business to manage the household and rear the children?

Antronius It is.

Magdalia Do you think she can manage so big a job without wisdom?

Antronius I suppose not.

Magdalia But books teach me this wisdom.

Antronius Sixty-two monks I have in the monastery, yet you won't find a single book in my cell.

Magdalia Those monks are well provided for!

Antronius I could put up with books, but not Latin ones.

Magdalia Why not?

Antronius Because that language isn't fit for women.[4]

Magdalia I want to know why.

Antronius Because it does little to protect their chastity.

Magdalia Therefore French books, full of the most frivolous stories, do promote chastity?

Antronius There's another reason.

Magdalia Tell me plainly, whatever it is.

Antronius They're safer from priests if they don't know Latin.

Magdalia Very little danger from you in that respect, since you take such pains not to know Latin!

Antronius The public agrees with me, because it's a rare and exceptional thing for a woman to know Latin.

Magdalia Why cite the public, the worst possible authority on conduct? Why tell me of custom, the mistress of every vice? Accustom yourself to the best; then the unusual will become habitual; the unpleasant enjoyable; the apparently unseemly, seemly.

Antronius I hear you.

Magdalia Is it fitting for a German woman to learn French?

Antronius Of course.

Magdalia Why?

Antronius To talk with those who know French.

Magdalia And you think it unsuitable for me to know Latin in order to converse daily with authors so numerous, so eloquent, so learned, so wise; with counsellors so faithful?

Antronius Books ruin women's wits – which are none too plentiful anyway.

Magdalia How plentiful *yours* are, I don't know. Assuredly I prefer to spend mine, however slight, on profitable studies rather than on prayers said by rote, all-night parties, and heavy drinking.

Antronius Bookishness drives people mad.

Magdalia The company of boozers, fools, and jesters doesn't drive you mad?

Antronius Not at all. It relieves boredom.

Magdalia Then how could such delightful companions as mine drive me mad?

Antronius That's what people say.

Magdalia But the plain fact of the matter says something else. How many more we see driven mad through intemperate wining and dining, night-long bouts of drunkenness, uncontrolled passions!

Antronius I'm sure I wouldn't want a learned wife.

Magdalia But I congratulate myself on having a husband different from you. For learning endears him more to me and me to him.

Antronius Learning costs immense toil, and after all you must die.

Magdalia Tell me, my dear sir: if you had to die tomorrow, would you rather die more foolish or more wise?

Antronius If wisdom came without hard work –

Magdalia But man gets nothing in this life without hard work. And yet whatever he does win, with however much labour, must be left behind. Why should we hesitate to take pains in the most precious thing of all, the fruits of which accompany us to another life also?

Antronius I've often heard the common saying, 'A wise woman is twice foolish.'

Magdalia That's commonly said, yes, but by fools. A woman truly wise is not wise in her own conceit. On the other hand, one who thinks herself wise when she knows nothing is indeed twice foolish.

Antronius I don't know how it is, but as pack-saddles don't fit an ox, so learning doesn't fit a woman.

Magdalia But you can't deny that pack-saddles would fit an ox better than a mitre would fit an ass or a swine. What's your feeling about the Virgin Mother?

Antronius I reverence her.

Magdalia Didn't she read books?

Antronius Yes, but not these.

Magdalia What did she read, then?

Antronius The canonical hours.[5]

Magdalia According to which use?

Antronius The Benedictine.

Magdalia Very likely! What about Paula and Eustochium?[6] Didn't they read the sacred Scriptures?

Antronius But that's rare nowadays.

Magdalia So was an unlettered abbot a rare bird once upon a time! Nowadays nothing's more common. Once upon a time princes and emperors excelled as much in learning as in might. But even now this isn't so rare as you suppose. In Spain and Italy there are not a few women of the highest rank who can rival any man.[7] In England there are the More daughters,[8] in Germany the Pirckheimer and Blaurer ladies.[9] If you're not careful, the net result will be that we'll preside in the theological schools, preach in the churches, and wear your mitres.

Antronius God forbid!

Magdalia No, it will be up to *you* to forbid. But if you keep on as you've begun, geese may do the preaching sooner than put up with you tongue-tied pastors. The world's a stage that's topsy-turvy now, as you see. Everyone must play his part or – exit.

Antronius How did I run across this woman? When you come calling on us, I'll treat you more politely.
Magdalia How?
Antronius We'll dance, drink as much as we please, hunt, play games, laugh.
Magdalia For my part, I feel like laughing even now.

NOTES

1 Antronius is the name of the ass in Apuleius' story, *The Golden Ass*; Magdalia is believed to be modelled after Thomas More's daughter, Margaret Roper, whose learning Erasmus admired (see his letter to her, CWE Ep 1404).

2 French literature was synonymous with chivalrous romances; Latin was the language of scholars; Greek, a mark of humanistic learning, was a rare accomplishment in a woman.

3 The following exchange plays on the meaning of Latin *bene vivere*, to live well, in the double sense of having a good time and living a morally good life.

4 Jean Bouchet (1545) said: 'From braying mules and girls who speak Latin protect me, O Lord!' Cf Kelso 67–9.

5 An anachronism. To read the daily prayers, or canonical hours, was a medieval institution.

6 Paula and her daughter, Eustochium, were pious Roman women, associates of St Jerome.

7 It is not clear whether Erasmus was thinking of specific Italian scholars such as Isotta Nogarola, Laura Cereta, or Cassandra Fedele – none of whom is mentioned in his works; he praises Queen Isabella and her daughter Catherine of Aragon as well as Menzia de Mendoza, the wife of Henry, count of Nassau, among the learned women of Spain.

8 Cf above 10.

9 Erasmus was in correspondence with Willibald Pirckheimer, who praised his sisters Caritas and Clara for their learning. He sent Erasmus samples of their writing, which, he said, would show that they were 'women more learned than men' (CWE Ep 409:32–3). He was also in correspondence with the brothers Ambrose and Thomas Blaurer of Constance, and may have had in mind here their sister Margarete, who had received a humanistic education.

6. The Activist:
The Council of Women

This dialogue was first printed in the 1529 edition of the *Colloquies* (for the publication history see above 25). It was likely inspired by an episode in Aelius Lampridius' history of the reign of Heliogabalus (which Erasmus edited in 1518). Heliogabalus (218–222) established a women's senate over which his mother presided. It dealt with matters of deportment. Heliogabalus' institution is also mentioned in Erasmus' *The Tongue* (1525). As a literary motif the women's senate goes back to the Greek playwright Aristophanes (c445–c380 B.C.).

The translation is by Craig Thompson.

CORNELIA, MARGARET, PEROTTA, JULIA, CATHARINE

Cornelia Your full and prompt attendance at this meeting today – happy and auspicious event may it prove for this group and the entire commonwealth of women! – gives me every hope that a gracious God may direct the mind of each one of you to what concerns the general welfare and the dignity of us all. You are all aware, I believe, of how much our interests have suffered from the fact that men transact their business at daily assemblies, while we neglect our cause by sitting at distaff and loom. Hence matters have come to such a pass that we are entirely ignorant of political science; men treat us virtually as amusements and scarcely think us deserving of the name of human. If we go on like this, figure out for yourselves how it will end, for I'm afraid to utter such ominous words. Though we may neglect our social position, we should at least be concerned about our security. 'In the multitude of counsellors there is safety,' wrote the wisest of kings.[1] Bishops have their synods, congregations of monks their chapters, soldiers their assigned stations, thieves their rendezvous. And, to make the list complete, even ants have their assemblies. Of all living creatures, only we women never have intercourse –
Margaret Oftener than we should!

Cornelia – It's not yet time to interrupt. Let me finish my speech; then each one will have a chance to talk. We're not introducing a novelty; we're recalling precedent. Since, more that thirteen hundred years ago, if I'm not mistaken, that most revered emperor Heliogabalus –

Perotta 'Most revered?' How come, when we know he's the one who was thrown into a sewer and dragged along by a hook?[2]

Cornelia Interrupted again! If we approve or disapprove of a person on this basis, we shall call Christ bad because he was crucified, Domitian good because he died at home.[3] But the worst charge against Heliogabalus is that he hurled to the ground the sacred fire kept by the vestal virgins and that in his domestic chapel he kept images of Moses and Christ,[4] whom they disparagingly called 'Chrestus.' Well, this Heliogabalus decreed that as the emperor had his senate with which to deliberate about public affairs, so also his mother Augusta[5] should have a senate of her own for dealing with women's business. Either as a joke, or else to distinguish it, men called this the 'petty senate.'

This precedent, abandoned for so many centuries, our situation has long warned us to restore. And let no one be upset because the apostle Paul forbids women to speak in the assembly he calls a church. He refers to a meeting of men; this is a feminine meeting. Otherwise, if women always had to keep silence, why did nature give us, too, tongues as ready as men's and voices just as loud – though men sound hoarser and more like donkeys than we do. But we must all take care to treat this business so seriously that men won't speak of the 'petty senate' again or maybe think up some nastier name, since they're accustomed to making fun of us whenever they please. Yet if *their* parliaments were described as they deserve, they might seem worse than womanish. We see monarchs who have done nothing but make war for many a year now; theologians, priests, bishops, and people never agree together; there are as many opinions as there are men, and among these men a more than feminine fickleness. There's no peace between state and state, neighbour and neighbour. Unless I'm much mistaken, human affairs would go better if the reins were handed over to us. Perhaps feminine modesty forbids me to accuse such leading citizens of stupidity, but I dare say one's allowed to repeat what Solomon wrote in the thirteenth chapter of Proverbs: 'Only by pride cometh contention: but with the well advised is wisdom.'[6]

But I must not allow this prologue to delay you any longer. That everything may be done decently and in order, without disturbance, let us consider first who should attend the council and who should be excluded. Too large a crowd means an uproar rather than a council; and a group limited to a few smacks of dictatorship. I'm of the opinion that no virgin should be admitted, because many things will come up that are not proper for them to hear.

Julia But how could you identify the virgins? Will whoever have the reputation of virgins be regarded as such?

Cornelia No, but I think we should admit only married women.

Julia Even among married women some are virgins: the wives of eunuchs.

Cornelia But let this mark of respect be paid to marriage, that by 'women' we mean married women.

Julia In any event, if we exclude only virgins there will still be an enormous throng; it won't diminish much.

Cornelia Those married more than three times shall be excluded too.

Julia Why?

Cornelia Because they deserve retirement as *emeritae*. Likewise, I think, for those over seventy years of age. A wife should be forbidden to speak disrespectfully of her husband by name; husbands as a class may be discussed, but temperately: 'Nothing to excess.'

Catharine Why may we speak less freely of husbands here than they talk everywhere about us? My Titius, if he wants to be the life of the party, tells what he did with me the night before and what I said; and often he invents a good deal of it.

Cornelia If the truth must be told, our dignity depends on our husbands. If we slander them, what is that but dishonouring ourselves? Now though we have more than a few causes for just complaint, our position, on the whole, is stronger than theirs. In their pursuit of wealth they fly over land and sea, not without risk to their lives; if war breaks out and the trumpet calls, they stand ironclad in the battle line while we sit safe at home. If they break laws, they're judged more seriously; we're let off lightly because of our sex. In short, getting along with our husbands is largely up to us.

It remains to draw up rules about the order of seating, so as to avoid what often happens to the ambassadors of kings, princes, and popes, who wrangle in councils for three whole months before they can get down to business. Consequently I think there should be first an aristocracy in which those with four degrees of nobility shall have precedence; next, those with three; then those with two; after them, those with one; last, those with a half. And in each rank a place shall be decided by ancestry. Bastards shall have last place in their respective ranks. There shall be a second assembly of commoners. In this the women who have borne the most children shall have first place. Among equals, age shall decide. A third assembly will consist of those who have not yet had children.

Catharine What will you do with widows?

Cornelia You're right to remind me. Their place shall be in the midst of the matrons, provided they have or have had children; barren ones shall have last place.

Julia What place do you assign to the wives of priests and monks?

Cornelia We'll consider that in our next session.

Julia What about prostitutes?

Cornelia We won't let this senate be contaminated with the likes of them.

Julia What about concubines?

Cornelia There's not just a single class of these. We'll deliberate about them at our leisure. Also for the agenda is the question of how decisions should be recorded, whether by points or stones or voice votes or show of hands or division.[7]

Catharine In stones there's trickery; and likewise in points. If we walk over to the side we favour, we'll stir up a lot of dust, since we wear long dresses. Therefore the best method is to show one's preference by a voice vote.

Cornelia But it's hard to count voices. Furthermore, we must be careful we don't have clamour instead of council.

Catharine To prevent mistakes, nothing is to be done without clerks.

Cornelia All very well for counting votes, but how will you avoid the clamour?

Catharine No one may speak unless asked and in her turn. Whoever violates the rule shall be ejected from the senate. And if anyone babbles about what is transacted here, she shall be punished by three days' silence.

[Cornelia] So much for procedures. Now hear what subjects we should debate. Our first concern should be our social standing. This depends most of all on dress, a matter so much neglected that nowadays you can hardly tell a noblewoman from a commoner, a married one from an unmarried girl or widow, a housewife from a harlot. Decorum is so far gone that women of every class put on whatever airs they please. You can see women worse than commoners, and from the meanest neighbourhood, dressed up in silks, pleats, flowered patterns, stripes, fine linen, gold, silver, sables and marten furs when all the time their husbands are at home stitching shoes. Their fingers are heavy with emeralds and diamonds – they turn up their noses at pearls these days! – to say nothing of their amber and coral and gilded sandals. It used to be enough for women of modest means to use silk girdles, out of respect for their sex, and to decorate the hems of their clothing with a silk fringe. Nowadays there's a double mischief: the family budget's strained, and rank, the safeguard of dignity, is confounded. If commoners are borne in chariots and litters inlaid with ivory and covered with velvet, what's left for the rich and powerful? And if the wife of a man who's scarcely a knight wears a train fifteen ells long, what shall a duchess or countess do?

And this situation is the more intolerable because we constantly change the fashions so recklessly. Linen ribbons used to hang from 'horns' sticking out behind the head. By this adornment you could tell aristocratic women from commoners. Not satisfied with that, they took to wearing fur-lined hoods of black and white. At once the rabble followed suit. When fashion changed again, they wore black linen veils. The lower classes not only had the nerve to imitate this, but even added gilt edging and finally jewellery. Formerly the upper classes gathered their hair on top of the head, plucking the hairs from forehead and temples. This didn't please them long – everybody else was soon doing the same thing. Finally they wore their hair down across the forehead. Straightway the lower classes copied them. Only ladies used to have escorts and pages to walk before them, and one pretty fellow among them to give madame a hand when she was about to rise and support her left arm with his right when she walked. This honour was accorded only to those of good family. Nowadays, while wives far and wide follow custom, they permit anyone at all to perform this service, just as they let anyone carry their train.

Again, only noblewomen used to greet one another with a kiss; and they wouldn't allow every Tom, Dick, or Harry to kiss *them*. What's more, they wouldn't even extend their right hand to just anyone. Now fellows reeking of leather claim a kiss from a woman of the very best family. Not even in marriages is class distinction kept up. Aristocrats marry commoners, commoners aristocrats; as a result we breed a race of mongrels. No woman is so base-born that she hesitates to use all the cosmetics of fine ladies, though common women ought to be satisfied with froth of new beer or fresh juice extracted from the bark of a tree, or anything else that's cheap. Rouge, white lead, stibium,[8] and other choice shades they should leave to women of distinction. At dinner parties and in public procession these days, what disregard of rank! Often a merchant's wife thinks it beneath her to give place to one who has noble blood on both sides.

This particular situation, then, has long demanded that we legislate something definite on these subjects.[9] And they could have been settled easily among ourselves, seeing that they concern only women. But in fact we find we have to deal with men too, who exclude us from every social rank and treat us almost as washerwomen and cooks. They think *they* know best about everything. We'll yield to them when it comes to political offices and the conduct of military affairs. But who could stand their habit of always putting the wife's insignia on the left side of the scutcheon even if her nobility exceeds her husband's by three degrees? Furthermore, it's fair for the mother to have an equal voice in arranging marriages. And perhaps we'll also win the right to have our turn in holding public office; at least those offices that can be held within the city and without bearing arms.

This is a summary of the things I think it essential for us to debate. Regarding these, let each woman take thought in order that senatorial decisions may be made about every single subject; and if anything else comes to anyone's mind, she should bring it up tomorrow. For we'll meet daily until adjournment. There should be four clerks to take down whatever's said, plus two presiding officers to grant or deny permission to speak. Let this be an assembly instead of an enquiry as to who is to be appointed prosecutor.

NOTES

1 I.e., Solomon in Prov. 11:14, 24:6
2 *Historia Augusta: Heliogabalus*, 17.1–2

3 Erasmus fails to add that he was murdered in bed (A.D. 96).

4 It is not quite clear why 'Chrestos' (anointed) should be derogatory.

5 *Historia Augusta: Heliogabalus*, 2.1

6 Prov. 13:10

7 'Division' refers to the process of walking to the side one favours, thereby dividing the group according to the vote.

8 Or antimony, a white metallic substance used in powder form

9 Sumptuary laws concerning dress were in existence at the time. Cf J. Brundage 'Sumptuary Laws and Prostitution in Late Medieval Italy' in *Sex, Law and Marriage in the Middle Ages* (Aldershot, Hants 1993) XV, 343–55, covering the period 1157–1562.

WIDOWS 3

1. From *The Christian Widow*

This treatise was published in 1529. It addresses Mary of Hungary, the sister of
Emperor Charles V. Mary's husband, Louis of Hungary, to whom she had been
betrothed at the age of ten, had died in 1526 at Mohacz in a battle against the
invading Turks. The crown of Hungary passed to Mary's brother, Ferdinand;
she herself vowed not to become a pawn of Habsburg marriage politics again.
She did, however, serve the dynastic interest as regent of the Netherlands, which
she governed faithfully on Charles' behalf. It was her court preacher, Johann
Henckel, a friend and admirer of Erasmus, who invited the Dutch humanist
in 1528 to put the queen under obligation by addressing a work to her. In the
following year Erasmus dedicated to her *The Christian Widow*. Mary rewarded
him with a goblet 'made of the horn of a unicorn and gold plated' (Allen, Ep
2319:28n).

The rather sententious treatise draws heavily on biblical example and precept.
The depiction of women in the tract is for the most part cliché. Among more
progressive currents of thought is the emphasis on education ('no age, no sex,
no temperament is unsuited to Christ's teaching,' CWE 66:191) and the positive
evaluation of marriage *vis-à-vis* celibacy. Although the work is addressed to
Queen Mary personally, Erasmus hoped that it would appeal to a larger

audience and expressed an interest in seeing it translated into the vernacular: 'I would not hesitate to commission a Frenchman or a Dutchman, but it is a rarity to find someone who has the required skill in his language' (Allen, Ep 2165:41–3). In the event, Henckel translated the treatise into German, and Adriaan Wiele, secretary to the Council of Brabant, produced a French version.

The translation is by Jennifer Tolbert Roberts (cf CWE 66 200–57).

It is not my purpose here to write a treatise celebrating the dignity of widowhood; already that most honey-tongued of speakers, Ambrose, did this so ornately, so copiously, that nothing can be added.[1] Nor do I write in order to exhort you while still a young woman to devote yourself to remaining perpetually in the state of widowhood, since the apostle Paul did not dare to do such a thing, but rather preferred young widows to remarry and become matrons, fearing what they might be led into by the natural dangers inherent in youth[2] – not that widows should be denied the same qualities that are praised in virgins, but because perpetual chastity is a singular gift of God. We congratulate her to whom this gift is given, but we do not lead into a halter the person around whose neck it has not fallen naturally. Just, therefore, as virginity is revered when it is spontaneous, but is not enjoined, so the chastity of widows, while it merits the second praise after virginity, is not for that reason prescribed.

But if perpetual virginity is not demanded of anyone, since it is a rare gift and something so arduous is not to be attempted without the gravest danger, even less is it appropriate to impel youth to perpetual widowhood, as it is generally easier to abstain from pleasure entirely than to cast it aside once it has been tasted. What God wished to be decided freely by each individual, mortals should not try to legislate. Frankly speaking, however, I am not certain whether you should not perhaps make use of that liberty, which Christ (and, following the views of Christ, Paul) left to everyone, which both the demands of nature and human custom have approved – particularly since the loftiness of your station is such that even though the continence of widowhood might be more welcome to your nature, nonetheless the public interest might impel you to remarry even against your will. I know how praiseworthy the Gentiles found monogamy, how hateful polygamy; nor does it escape me that the Germans used to feel that only virgins should marry. Not without good reason has praise been heaped upon Cornelia, the mother of the Gracchi,[3] who preferred to be called the widow of Gracchus than the queen of Egypt when King Ptolemy sought to win her hand in marriage. Nor without cause is that dictum of Portia celebrated, in which she said that a modest matron need marry only once ...

But the same things are not suitable for everyone. Not only your own inclination but also the needs of the state must be taken into consideration here, and on that account I will not try to convey the great praise that Christians accord to those who profess perpetual virginity. Nor will I offer a comparison of virginity, widowhood, and marriage, a line of argument that I see has been dragged out in a most contentious manner by several authors from earliest times; for it is an invidious form of praise to exalt virginity in such a way as to disparage the status of matrimony, or to admire widowhood in such a way as to revile second marriages. How much more sense it would make to join our hands as in a harmonious dance of the three Graces, of whom each is endowed with such gifts that even if you could rank one first, you would have no idea whom to rank second. Each of these states of life has its own distinction and honour in sacred writings.

The first dignity is assigned to virginity, if it is undertaken of one's own free will and accompanied by the other virtues; the next to widowhood; and the third to marriage. You see, then, a ranking of sorts, but one that knows no competition for honours but rather is tied together by charity. For virginity is not to be preferred to marriage as gold is to bronze but rather as a precious stone is preferred to gold, and widowhood gives place to virginity only as onyx yields to a pearl, chrysoprase to emerald, crystal to diamond. If you compare gold to emerald, it is possible to doubt which you should choose; if you surround an emerald with gold, it is wondrous how beautifully each sets the other off. In this way each of the three states has some special characteristic in which it excels the others.

In married women, according to the Apostle, lies the honour of bearing children and taking charge of their religious education, in reward for which (lest it seem to you a matter of small moment) he promised eternal salvation.[4] In this regard virginity certainly gives way to marriage. Nor indeed is it of slight merit to have served the Lord in one's husband and to have won one's husband for Christ by one's pious way of life. In fact this thing seemed to the Apostle of such great moment that for this reason he did not want a Christian wife to leave a husband who was not yet a Christian, if the marriage were contracted before she was baptized.[5] Finally, virginity itself arises from marriage, and also for this reason virgins owe honour to matrons. Add, too, that marriage has been consecrated in heaven, with God himself presiding. If antiquity confers any authority, moreover, here matrimony gains ground. A virgin born from a virgin, the Lord first consecrated virginity in Mary. But, lest anyone imagine that this brings contumely on marriage, he wished to be the son of a virgin but also of a married woman, so that he should be born, if not from marriage, certainly in marriage. And if you look at the tradition of the church, you will find, to be sure, that it accords the first honour to virginity, but that marriage is venerated among the seven sacraments. Finally, though virginity is held in greater honour, by the same token marriage is the less precarious course.

Widowhood, too, has characteristics that make it in some respects preferable to either of the other two conditions, for it has continence in common with virgins but also the generation and upbringing of children (provided that one has borne them) in common with married women. As we have said, moreover, it is a greater virtue to abstain from pleasures of which one has already tasted than to reject something of which one has no experience. Then, too, it shows greater humanity to care for children orphaned of their father than when one has a husband to take to himself a large part of this concern. That a mother should raise and educate children is a natural and necessary act of piety; but that she should bring up orphans is an act of compassion more pleasing to God than any sacrifice. Widows, moreover, are responsible for the guidance both of virgins and of married girls. It is the role of widows to instruct those recently married or about to be married as to how they should conduct themselves towards their husbands, towards their children, towards the members of their household, towards their in-laws and other relatives. Theirs is also the responsibility for instructing virgins and demonstrating to them how best to act so as to preserve their character and reputation. And in this regard, plainly, both virginity and marriage must pay homage to widowhood, by whose advice and authority both are aided, for just as we kiss the bloom of chastity in virgins and admire the service performed by matrons, so we venerate the authority of widows.

From this we can see that these three ways of life do not differ in dignity but rather are three separate stages. In the same way we first cherish youth in boys as the flowering time, so to speak, of the human cycle; we honour manhood as the appropriate time for performing valuable services; and we venerate and respect old age, which can give advice to the other two stages as it has lived through them both. Everything has a beginning, a development, and consummation. Thus in the old days at Rome a vestal virgin spent the first ten years learning the arcane rites, the second ten performing them, and the third ten teaching them to others, but during these three periods she was held in the same esteem; the three stages differed only in that those who were learning had all the grace of youth, the practitioners were performing a useful office, and the teachers had pedagogical authority. Each of the three kinds of states, then, is worthy of praise of the virtues appropriate to it, and each should outdo the others in mutual respect rather than despise the others in an exchange of insults. The most frequent praise is given to virginity; but just as this state excels married women and widows in dignity, so it owes them more honour – married women in so far as they are mothers, and widows in so far as they are teachers. But amongst all the plaudits offered them, virgins must bear in mind the ominous saying of Solomon: 'The greater one's stature, the more humbly one should behave in all things.' Finally, praise in these matters hangs not so much on the group to which one belongs as it does on the holiness of one's outlook, which can be of such importance that the second or third marriages of one woman may be more acceptable to God than the virginity of another.

If weight is added to an argument by examples, let us observe that though few were celebrated for their virginity in the Old Testament, what a handsome, what a large chorus of virgins in the New Testament there is who by virtue of their love for Christ despised not merely pleasure but also life itself. These have as the captain of their squadron the mother of Christ, in whom they rightly glory. And not they alone: married women also glory in her, since she was wedded, and widows as well. There is no agreement as to whether or not Joseph predeceased his wife; but it is agreed that the most holy Virgin, if indeed she still had a husband, behaved in such a way as if she did not, going to and fro among the apostles and attending to their needs (along with other women and widows). In the Old Testament married women have Sarah as the head of their ranks, in the New Testament, Elizabeth, mother of John the Baptist.[6] Widows too have as the captains of their squadron renowned women – Judith, for example, that illustrious female of manly strength who as a woman brought back a triumph over a foe unbeaten by men. Double was the triumph of Judith: a military victory, to be sure, which she produced for her country when it had lost hope, but also a victory for her chastity, which she preserved for herself unimpaired, for she killed a very brave man and made a mockery of a lewd one[7]...

Now it is true that in the Old Testament we see that perpetual virginity had not yet attained its proper honour, and widowhood was held in reproach, as was sterility; for in that time fertility in reproduction was a major concern. But these were the views of mortals, not of God; even in the Old Testament we see that God accorded great honour to widows, taking them under his special protection. Thus for example Exodus 22 [:22–4] says: 'If you injure a widow or orphan, they will cry out to me, and I will hear their cry, and my anger will rage, and I will smite such people with my sword, and your wives will be widows and your children orphans.' What more loving concern can there be than this? For he who is the ruler of the universe specifically names himself the patron and avenger of widows. And again Deuteronomy 24[:7] says: 'You shall not take the clothing of a widow as security for a loan,' and Job 24[:3] cites the confiscation of a widow's cow as a singular crime by which the anger of God is roused. Similarly in the twenty-second chapter of the same work sending widows away empty-handed is listed as a serious offence.

But if it is an offence to have given nothing to widows, what a crime it must it be to despoil them! Now the law does not forbid the taking of a pledge of security from a debtor; but still God wished widows to have special privileges in this regard ...

If we cross over to the New Testament, we will find that God shows there an equal concern for widows – indeed that this station in life is held there in greater honour. In Matthew 23[:14], the Lord chastised the Scribes and the Pharisees because 'they devour the homes of widows, under cover of long prayers,' by which dictum the piety of widows is implicitly commended, since they could not be deceived by such simulation unless they had applied themselves to religion with great zeal. In Mark 12[:41–4] the Lord is delighted by the spectacle of a poor widow placing two tiny coins in the treasury, and he valued this pious offering beyond all other contributions. In Luke 4[:25–6] he refreshed our memory on the subject of the widow of Zarephath; to her alone Elijah was sent, starving, so that he would be nurtured by her, giving us to understand that Elijah signified the Lord himself, and the widow signified the church. For the Lord came as if in famine to the earth, hungering and thirsting for the salvation of humankind. In the synagogue he could not satisfy his hunger, for he found no faith there; but in a poor widow who had nothing of her own, and who handed over to Christ all of the little that she had, he was restored. Nor did the significance of the case of the widow of Zarephath escape the Jews, for they led him out of the city to a mountaintop in order to throw him off it.[8] The Lord did not accede to their wickedness, however, for the time appointed by the Father had not yet come.

And so, widows, let it not be a source of sorrow that the Pharisees plotted against your limited resources, devouring your households in the guise of religion; a proud city hated and oppressed you, but you have as your patron, judge, and avenger God the Lord, whose power cannot be resisted. In chapter 7[:11–17] of the same book he could not endure the tears of a widowed woman burying the lifeless body of her only son, but rather restored the youth to life and gave him back to the mother, who had transferred the entire solace of her life to her only son when she was bereft of her husband; and in chapter 18 he set before us an example of incessant prayer – and indubitably he meant by this to indicate too that it is singularly appropriate to widows to devote themselves to constant prayer. Nor did Paul, who had drunk deeply of the spirit of Christ, dissent from the teaching of his Master, for he admonished Timothy to honour widows in so far as they were true widows; and what Paul bade Timothy, Christ bade all bishops – to give widows the honour due to them.[9] By 'honour' he meant all manner of assistance and support. Writing to the same person, Paul commanded that if any Christian man or woman has relatives who are widows he or she should be of aid to them.[10] The Apostle did not consider it sufficient to commend widows to the care of Christians under the broad rubric of 'the poor'; he undertook their care specifically and by name.

Do not despair, widows, because you appear in this world to be powerless and oppressed, for you have heard proclaimed the dignity of your state; do not weep that you are desolate, for you have consolation and security in Christ. He has care for you – he without whose providence not even a single sparrow falls upon the earth. He who alone is more powerful than all others has made himself your patron. Do not look to other mortals to avenge you, for he proclaims himself the avenger of any injury offered to you; rather simply place all joy, all glory, all consolation, all faith in him who has undertaken your singular protection, for that ultimately is safest that is in his guardianship. It is essential, therefore, that you remember your role, and you will do so if you truly deserve the name by which you are called. For when Paul ordered that honour should be accorded to widows 'who are true widows,' by this he meant that there were those who were falsely called by the name of widow, and that to these none of the things pertain that we have said about dignity of widows and their care and protection.[11] For just as there are foolish virgins, whom the heavenly Spouse, the lover of virgins, does not recognize, and false prophets, and false apostles, and false brothers[12] for whom the honour of the name they have usurped provides cause for the most serious condemnation – just so there are false widows; and if these want to boast about these things that we have enumerated, let them take care that they become true widows and that their lives correspond to their name.

The very course of my argument seems, therefore, to dictate that I describe briefly the institution of widowhood, whose pattern seems to me best to be sought in these areas on which I have already touched, if we could only examine what lies within the words of divine Scripture, which, like an extremely rich vein of precious metal, will give back the most valuable treasures the further one penetrates them. Now it is true that there has been no lack of people who have handed down various prescriptions for how widows ought to live. Although I see no need for these to be cast aside, nonetheless there is no need to adhere to them as one would adhere to the precepts of God – for the same things are not always equally suited to everyone. First of all, let us contemplate Judith, that glorious ornaments to all widows – and not only a source of glory, but a fine example as well. If we examine her name closely, we will see that it comes from 'confessing' or 'praising.' For according to the peculiarity of the Hebrew language, *confession* has a double meaning; both the proclamation of our own sins and the praise of God.[13] He who recognizes his own faults will confess. Each kind of confession is most welcome to God, not for his sake but for ours. Because he is merciful, he delights in the confession of sins, that he may pardon them. Because he is kind, he rejoices in praises, so that he may lavish his bounty more richly upon mankind; for to confess his own injustice and proclaim the mercy of God is the singular justice of man. Although this is common to all Christians, moreover, nonetheless it is singularly fitting for widows, who are not worthy of the care God has bestowed on them unless they acknowledge their helplessness. Again, if they do not give thanks to the bounty of God for what they have received, even that will be taken away from them. Paul the Apostle summed this all up when he depicted a widow as virtuous if she will place her hope in God.[14] She who has placed all her hope in God has nothing but mourning in this world and expects no other solace than from God.

By the same token, clearly the widow who lives in merriment has not placed her faith in God; for she is seeking solace from those things that are displeasing to God. Likewise she who prepares herself for a new husband has not yet placed her entire hope in God but rather looks to her new mate for solace. She who piles up wealth and seeks for earthly glories is not a true Judith, nor does she give her allegiance to God but rather to those things that she prefers to God. She who, trusting in her youth, lives as she pleases is no Judith.

Widows should not simply mourn their husbands, for this is mourning of a limited kind. It is condoned by human weakness and does not merit praise. The woman who mourns the death of her husband immoderately – what is she doing but aiming at another marriage, failing to give the slightest thought to how lucky the change is that has come over her husband, who has traded his mortality for immortality? Nor does such a woman give thanks to God, who took her husband away because it was good either for him or for her – or perhaps for both. For he calls people to eternal felicity in various ways, and he alone knows what is best for each.

Whence therefore flow widows' tears? They are lamenting their own faults – or if they lack them (as no one does), they lament the faults of others. They weep for the weariness of this, their exile. They weep out of their longing for the heavenly Spouse, with whom they desire to be coupled in complete and eternal union. Those who mourn in this way will hear along with the apostles that 'women who mourn are blessed, for they will receive solace.'[15] She will deservedly be called Judith who takes responsibility herself for anything bad that happens but ascribes anything good to God and trusts in the Lord in both good times and bad, believing 'that he is good and his mercy is forever.[16] Sometimes he is more propitious and merciful to those who have suffered sadness than to those who have enjoyed happiness. Judith, moreover, was the daughter of Merari, a name that means bitterness in Hebrew;[17] the first step in turning in God is penitence, which carries with it mourning and bitterness. And penitence engenders the confession of one's own injustice. But, as Paul said, 'this sadness, since it accords with the will of God, brings forth certain salvation.[18]

The devil generally snares people to their destruction by baiting them with delicious pleasures; God, on the other hand, by salubrious pain inveigles people into eternal life. The one ensnares, the other heals. The former by petty pleasures that pass quickly decoys people to everlasting torture, the latter through a bitterness that is brief leads them to joys that are eternal. Add to this that nobody becomes a widow except by the death of her husband. Thus every Judith is a daughter of Merari, bitterness. And it happens not infrequently that this appropriate bitterness delivers a widow unto Christ; for in him, if one loves him with one's whole heart, there is more pleasure than in hundreds of marriages, however happy. Meanwhile, everybody knows what a risky business marriage is. It is the proper pursuit of all widows, moreover, to abjure all the pleasures of this world and seek all their solace from God. Like any difficult undertaking, this one brings bitterness at first, but in the fullness of time, if God is propitious, it will lead to great joy of spirit.

'Judith,' the Scripture says, 'was rich not from goods that she sought but from goods that she inherited.'[19] Why should abundance of possessions bring praise to a widow when wealth is accustomed to corrupt even people of sensible dispositions and lead them into decadence and lewdness? But for this our Judith, the wealth that was left to her was nothing but the means of succouring the poor. She possessed things as if she did not possess them; she possessed things rather for others than for herself. She came from an illustrious family, but she covered her body with a rough garment of goat's wool. She had a large household, but she prayed alone in her attic with just a few attendants. She was exceptionally beautiful, but she concealed this beauty from men and served her Spouse with her inner beauty.

Pay heed to this, you widows who use the uncomfortable, narrow straits in which your household finds itself as an excuse for living a soft life, you whom not even poverty can teach modesty. Behold the noble Judith, at the peak of her youth and beauty, a wealthy woman; for three years and six months she had lived as a widow, right up until the day when she conceived in her mind that most beautiful deed. Do you suppose it was hard for a woman of her social status, her wealth, and her beauty to find a husband? There is no doubt but that she was sought after by many. Why then did she choose to remain a widow? Was it because she preferred to live as a widow in her own way rather than subject herself to a husband? For we see that some of those faced with this choice find a second marriage distasteful. But this was most definitely not the case here. Why then? She had not read Paul, but she had drunk the same spirit as Paul. The fact is that she knew that in marriage there was an element of servitude. Though this, she knew, was not so powerful as necessarily to distract from religion, nonetheless she knew too that it often happened that the woman who marries a husband is compelled in order to keep her husband happy to think constantly about those things that are of this world, whereas virgins and widows, since they are free from the jurisdiction of a man, have nothing to distract them from the Lord but can, if they wish, cling to him single-mindedly. Often an unchaste husband will undermine the chastity of his wife; a husband who is jealous of his property will impede her generosity towards the poor; the man given to other interests will get in the way of her prayers. This sort of thing can be excused on the grounds of wifely obedience, I admit, and indeed this kind of behaviour has been prescribed for wives; but still and all a wife lacks that most fortunate of liberties, the liberty of attending on the Lord beyond any distraction. St Paul perceived this when he said: 'to secure your undivided devotion to the Lord.'[20] Only those women who have dedicated their entire selves to God can understand what this means. And since this is a product of the Spirit, it may happen to anyone anywhere if only he who alone has the power to do so will bless them with the proper disposition.

Since, moreover, according to the precepts of the Apostle a wife owes deference even to a bad husband[21] – stopping short of those things that constitute serious offences – a wife cannot along with Mary sit forever at the feet of Jesus, so that she might be nourished by the honeyed words of his conversation. But our Judith, the lady of her own home, had freely constructed a secret cubicle in which she could be all alone and speak with the Lord, praying in secret, in keeping with evangelical doctrine, and expecting her reward not from other people but from him who sees what is secret. She had a large household, but nonetheless she showed that the truly devout may find solitude even in the midst of a crowd. What others may do in their own rooms, they alone know: but there Judith prayed. The bedroom of a widow should be nothing but a place of prayer, and a kind of temple that knows no guilt but is consecrated to modesty, thanksgiving, holy thoughts, and pious prayers. She had prepared this chamber in the attic, that is to say, in the upper part of the house: for it was fitting that the body of someone whose mind daily contemplated flight into the heavens should also be far from the earth. For the Holy Spirit was sent to those who were praying and fasting in the upper room. And Peter praying in his attic saw a vision sent down from heaven.[22] Anna, the widow in the gospel, almost overcome by age, persevered in the temple,[23] but a very young widow is nowhere safer than in a secret chamber. For this reason Judith wrapped a coarse woolen garment about her loins, fasting all the days of her life, except for sabbaths, new moons, and other holy days, on which days fasting was forbidden among the Jews; because she fasted, she was filled with holy sentiments; if from time to time she ate a little, it was for purposes of religion, not for purposes of nourishment. If this example does not carry enough force today to persuade us to fast daily, surely it should serve to embarrass certain widows who never miss a social occasion, who waste the whole day first in breakfast, then dinner, then tea, of course, and supper, and even more food late in the evening – the while imagining that their modesty is beyond reproach, and that they are proper widows.

Now let us join together in considering Judith's companions, for these offer a key to understanding the character and values of the lady of the house. She spent a great deal of time in a secret chamber with her female attendants and was their teacher in holiness; her home was nothing but a school of piety. You would not have found youths there with their hair all curled by the iron, reeking of perfume, with lewd eyes and wanton tongues, nor the sort of young girls who would be likely to excite these youths by the way they look at them, the way they act, the way they move: this wealthy home did not resound with dances, silly games, and elaborate banquets. No mention is made of children – wherefore the woman's zeal of modesty is all the more remarkable, as among the Jews sterility was held in lower esteem even than widowhood.

She had as both serving-maids and disciples young girls whose efforts Judith did not waste by looking in the mirror, by fixing her hair, by making up her face, or by having them sprinkle her with perfume or fan her; rather they spent all their time either in prayers or in reading sacred books or in serious conversations or working with their hands or doing charitable deeds for the poor. She wore the clothing of a widow, which she laid aside only for a brief time, and that not for her own pleasure but rather for the sake of serving her country: only then finally did she step into a fancy dress. And even this she put on not to capture the eyes of the nobility but to slay an enemy who threatened the greatest danger both to the holy state and to divine religion. The fact that Judith did this, consequently, must not be cited as an example to be followed (unless, of course, by divine inspiration and for a cause equally compelling). Much more blameworthy are they who abandon the trappings of widowhood for the sake of a wedding or some feast. It was for this motive that Judith put on a fine dress: for the sake of saving her country, so that it was not so much a dress as a snare and a trap. For the enemy who was to be deceived was a formidable one, and it was appropriate for that huge monster who seemed to put himself on a par with God himself to fall by the hand of a woman – appropriate that he who was accustomed to lay snares for the modesty of others should be taken by the genius of a woman. Judith put on this dress, then, in order to undertake a deed more beautiful by far than any other. For the protection of her integrity, however, she wore another sort of dress.

Is there then a kind of clothing that becomes a married woman but not a widow? Most certainly there is. For although a modest and simple style is also becoming to married women and is, according to the saying of St Peter, an expression of the faith that they profess, since the true beauty of a Christian woman is buried deep within her inner self, nonetheless a reasonably elegant outfit can be justified on the grounds that married women are dressing up to be admired by their husbands; but no such justification can be found for widows. In married women simplicity in dress is praised; widows are not so much to be praised for practising it as vilified if they violate it.

Someone will ask: 'What has clothing to do with anything?' Clothing is the external manifestation of an individual. From the way a person

dresses his body, his true nature can be inferred: for the body is the
clothing of the spirit within. The manner of a person's dress reveals
the extent to which he castigates the flesh; and if simplicity of dress is
not absolutely essential to the chastity of a widow, it certainly helps to
ward off the eyes of young men to whose view clothing often sets off
the body beneath it so that they desire what they should not. And so
it can happen that someone's reputation may suffer even if in fact her
chastity has remained secure, and although a widow's chastity may be
safe, someone else's may be in danger.

Now someone may ask: What sort of clothing becomes a widow? I
will not describe here the colour or the cut. Indeed this would not be
possible, since different countries at different times have taken opposite
views in the matter of shades and style, hold some in high esteem and
look down on others; some things are hopelessly inappropriate in one
place and quite proper in others. Among some peoples a white dress
is used in times of mourning, among others in times of celebration
– of triumph, for example. Today in Spain there is no colour more
precious or held in higher honour than black; a white dress that one
might have expected to be used for a wedding or a victory celebration
now is looked down upon, except when used in the sacred liturgy. Once
vermilion was the most glorious among the different kinds of purple;
now nothing is more disdained. What dress then shall we give to our
widow? One becoming her time and place, which neither clamours
for attention by its affected shabbiness, nor by its newfangled style
makes a spectacle of the woman who wears it, nor by its elegance and
cost casts doubt upon the modesty of its wearer; which covers those
parts of the body upon which men cannot gaze without danger to
chastity; simple, that is to say, and conspicuous for neither its high
nor its low price. Account must be taken of the individual's rank and
status, certainly as far as price is concerned. What will become a royal
widow, for example, might not become a commoner. In general, no
clothing adorns a widow more appropriately than clothing that shows
no adornment but is worn only for practical and modest purposes –
practical, because it wards off the harm that might come from the cold,
and modest, because it covers those parts that provoke the lust inherent
in men.

Someone at this juncture may be thinking to himself: 'Why don't
you preach this sermon to those who have committed themselves to

perpetual chastity? What do these things have to do with those who are destined to be married?' The fact is, just as a virgin who is raised for a chaste and honourable marriage is not to be brought up differently from the way in which she would be raised if she had declared her intention of remaining perpetually celibate – in fact perhaps she should be raised with more care, lest she attract any sinister gossip before her marriage – so a widow who is preserving herself for a second marriage should not omit while she is living as a widow any of the behaviour that brings honour to widows. For who would not detest the sort of people who raise their daughters not as parents bringing them up for a chaste marriage but as a panderer brings girls up for financial gain? The woman who was not a proper virgin will not be a proper wife either. How will a woman behave with modesty towards her husband if she has learned shameless behaviour from her parents? Marriage among Christians, as Paul has recommended, should be 'honourable, and the marriage bed undefiled,'[25] full of modesty and very similar in fact to virginity. No dowry recommends a woman more than chastity and modesty.

Between a widow who will remarry and a woman who has taken a vow of perpetual chastity there is no difference save the period of time involved; their lives differ only in their rationale, not in their nature. Adorned by her strength of character, a widow who is horrified by the very thought of remarrying will find a worthy husband more quickly than one who seeks adornment in her clothing. She brings a great enough dowry who carries with her a trousseau of modesty, chastity, and decorous behaviour. If she has declared her intention of living in perpetual celibacy, why is she provoking men's glances? Or for whom is she cultivating herself when she has chosen Christ for her spouse?

Now let us also consider the dining habits of this wealthy widow Judith. She brought along with her one attendant on whom she imposed the burden of a wine-skin, a little bottle of oil, some barley, cakes of dried fruit, some bread, and some cheese – you can tell from this what were the rustic delights of that day. Probably too she led an even more frugal existence at home. With this sustenance she fasted daily. Let those step forward who deny that they are able to endure the fast of a single day unless they have started out in the morning with six different kinds of fish. Judith daily broke the whole day's fast with barley and some vegetables.

As I have said, moreover, there is a place for decorous behaviour even in the middle of revelry, if one is for some reason absolutely compelled to a partake in some such event. We read how that most illustrious woman Elizabeth the landgrave of Hesse concealed her fasting in the middle of a banquet by a clever ruse – the enjoyment on her face, the pleasantness of her speech, the gracious way she attended to things.[26] By all this she deceived her fellow banqueters so that nobody perceived that she was not eating. Now here you have an example not only of restraint but also of religion. She took care that she would never be compelled to touch anything of which divine law forbade the eating. Thus her conduct stands as a reproach to us in our own rebelliousness – we who eat all the more eagerly those foods that the authority of the church forbids us to eat on certain days precisely because they are forbidden. Just as those who judiciously change their eating habits for sound reasons are to be excused, by the same token nobody who is truly religious can countenance that sort of insolence.

Well then, widows, you have had set before you the life of Judith; now listen to her reputation of equally untarnished glory. For though it behoves both virgins and married women to guard their reputations, even more must this be of concern to widows, for this achievement is all the more beautiful on account of its special difficulty – indeed, by it they will be in good repute with God and mortals on every occasion. A good name is a more valuable possession than costly perfumes. This is the honour, this the singular adornment of the female sex. And in fact the Scriptures are not silent regarding this blessing, adding that Judith possessed an illustrious reputation in all quarters – not because she dined in splendour, but 'because she greatly feared the Lord,'[27] and these words represent the highest compliment the Scriptures can pay to piety.

It is wonderful to have a good name among all good people, but it is by far the most wonderful thing of all to have a name on which the wicked are unable to cast the slightest aspersion. 'There was no one,' the Scriptures say, 'who would say a harsh word about her.'[28] And what in this life, might I add, is really safe from the tongues of scurrilous people? An outstanding and unerring probity in one's life scarcely wins for one the kind of reputation that St Paul nonetheless required of a bishop – that he should have a good reputation not only among Christians but also among pagans and Jews.[29] Nor was he silent on this topic in discussing the good qualities of widows, saying: 'having a reputation for good works.'[30] A good name is a great treasure – but more fragile than any glass, since nothing is more easily damaged or less easily repaired.

But what means serve to preserve a good name? Why, the very same ones by which goodness itself is preserved. To tell the truth, nothing is more useful in building a solid reputation than being precisely that which you would have others think you are. The principal virtue of a widow is propriety in all aspects of life. This propriety is to be found not only in her style of life, her appearance, and her bearing, but even in her retinue. Who, having a mistress like Judith, would have dared to drink too much or to behave lasciviously or to gamble under her roof? There are voices everywhere, especially where evil is concerned: countenance, eyes, gait, the bearing of the head and other movements, laughter, one's male and female attendants, children, and companions – all proclaim the character of the lady of the house. A widow must therefore always and everywhere lead her life in such a manner than no part of it is open to the reproaches of gossips, and her integrity in all aspects of life must be so great that even the wicked should fear to speak ill of her. And it is not enough either to have abstained from all evil; rather, according to the teaching of Paul, she must even beware of 'any appearance of evil.'[31]

But rumour, you may object, is a shameless and evil thing and does not always spare even the innocent. I concede this; but the rumour that arises out of thin air soon vanishes of its own accord, and its very falseness serves only to make one's innocence more strikingly apparent in everyone's eyes. When, on the other hand, the rumour is grounded in reality, it grows constantly and 'acquires strength in its course,' as Virgil says.[32] Women whose behaviour is immodest, whose speech is improper, who spend a good part of the day on powders, rouges, mascara, cards, gaming, feasting, dancing, who take delight in the constant company of well-groomed youths, who have badly brought-up children, who have a household full of rogues – these people have no right to take umbrage at gossip. And if it is impossible to see to it that nobody speaks ill of us, at least we should take care that nobody should do so with good reason. To have an unblemished reputation, moreover, is the singular glory of the female sex. Many people spoke ill of Christ; nobody dared speak a harsh word about his

Virgin Mother. For the Lord himself protected her from the suspicion of disgrace by the formality of matrimony and by the false impression that Joseph was the baby's father.

Let a widow, then, who desires an unblemished reputation place before her eyes the example of the widow Judith and follow along in her footsteps. Why should I enumerate here the rest of this widow's virtues? Think of her patriotism, the authority she exercised among the elders and with the head of state himself. When she had summoned them to come to her, she restored their hope when they had given up, taught them when they were ignorant, fortified them with wise counsel when they were faltering. Finally, she alone, one single woman, effected by her piety a victory of which a huge army had despaired.

She brought back from the enemy camp the most splendid of trophies, but she ascribed the whole triumph to God and to her people; she herself, once this most beautiful deed was accomplished, returned to her simple garment of sackcloth. Here you may recognize the greatest bravery coupled with the greatest modesty, and the greatest wisdom with the greatest piety. It is in the nature of outstanding virtue to command reverence and respect from everybody. Judith was a woman, a widow; she ruled over no territory and held no public office. Nonetheless the elders of the people did not hesitate to go to her for advice: ... What ultimately was holier than her advice? She invited penitence for what they had done; she showed that the mercy of the Lord was waiting for them; she taught that allegiance had to be transferred to him and that the calamities that had befallen them were to be ascribed to their own sins, and that they should not hasten to seek vengeance but rather take refuge in the mercy of the Lord. Who today would tolerate a woman's reproofs or advice? But the king and the elders not only tolerated Judith, they thanked her. For thus history has it: Uzziah and the priests said to her: 'All that you have said is true, and there is no fault to be found in your speeches. Now, therefore, pray for us, since you are a holy and God-fearing woman.'[33] But she in no way accepted as her due the praise for such an admirable deed. She ordered the elders to awake by their prayers the mercy of the Lord, so that he might look propitiously on the plans she had conceived, and to exhort the people to pray. Thus she prepared everybody to place their hope for the whole enterprise not in their own strength but in the goodness of the Almighty. Once the deed was done she assumed the role of a general, ordering the people to crush the enemy and scatter them.[34]

Finally, when she had won such an illustrious victory, she did not seek to have statues set up for her or to have triumphs celebrated; rather, she herself with the virgins and matrons sang a triumphal song to the Lord, who had given victory to his people. Nonetheless, whatever wealth or booty there was from the plundered home of Holofernes the people bestowed on Judith to honour her. But since this outstanding and heroic woman proclaimed that she looked down on wealth as much as on earthly glory, she consecrated as a dedicated offering whatever wealth she received. She herself returned to her home neither prouder nor wealthier. With what a proud parade of words have eloquent men celebrated the virtues of certain commanders who, from their splendid victories, brought nothing but glory back to their own homes! But the person who wins praise and acclaim among mortals has carried away a huge reward. For about such people the Lord has also said: 'They have received their reward.'[35] How much more magnificent is what that triumphant woman accomplished, who, content simply with the knowledge of the good she had done, was indifferent to wealth and glory alike! Observe, too, that she did not think of remarrying even though she lived to the age of 105. And so that you may see what praise she merited both for her clemency and for her frugality, note that she freed the only attendant that she had.

She wished her burial to be as her life had been: for there are those whose desire for recognition not even death extinguishes. Did not a woman who had served the state so well deserve some conspicuous monument? But Judith was buried in the tomb of her husband Manasses. She had embraced him alone with a chaste love, and death did not put an end to this bond between them: she knew that the better part of her husband yet lived and that at some time in the future they would be restored to the very same life they had once shared together.

Nor, I think, did the name of her husband altogether lack mystical significance. Manasses means 'necessity' or 'destined to oblivion.'[36] When Judith first married, she was yielding to necessity: the authority of her parents dictated it, the conventions of her people suggested it, the desire for offspring, which could not be realized without a husband, compelled it. (I say this because the ardour of youth is what moves some women to take husbands.) Finally, the woman who marries comes into the jurisdiction of her husband and thus submits herself to a necessity from which nothing can liberate her save her husband's death. This, therefore, is what it means that he was called 'necessity.'

But how is it fitting that he should be called 'given over to oblivion' in whose house she lived always and in whose tomb she wished to be buried? 'Although we learnt to know Christ in the flesh,' the Apostle said, 'still now we do not know him.'[37] He who does not know him whom he knew before indeed has forgotten him in some way. In this way Judith, who had first been joined to her husband in the flesh did not, when he died soon afterwards, cling to the memory of their carnal connection but rather loved him in a spiritual sense all the more ardently, and even when he was dead kept the same faith with him that she had promised him when he was alive.

What a very different picture is presented by women who are never able to forget their dead husbands, who at the slightest provocation renew their mourning, bursting into tears and lamenting all over again. But more shameless still are those whom neither a second nor even a third husband can shake off the memory of the first. When they feel slighted in any way, they reproach their new husbands with the character of their dead spouse, and the same man upon whom they looked down while he was alive they praise now that he is dead – not so that they may take pleasure in recalling his virtues but in order to harass their current mate. 'How much more attentive *he* was,' they exclaim, 'how much handsomer! When he was alive, how much more freedom and admiration I had – and how much more money!'

Those women cultivate the memory of their husbands best who forget the things of the flesh. She remembers her husband sufficiently who refuses to marry another and keeps her plighted troth to him as if he were not dead but simply away. She has forgotten her husband in a very fortunate way who, having married once for the sake of her parents, for nature, for offspring, perseveres in a life of chastity and who, once she has returned to her own guardianship, forgets the earlier pleasures she has known and dedicates herself entirely to delights of the spirit. This sort of forgetting is worthy of Christian widows. For there are some women who forget their husbands before they have buried them; others perish in their own tears ...

Come now, let us now move on to that poor humble widow, praised by the words of the Lord because with her small gift she surpassed the magnificent donations of all the wealthy; let us too admire with the Lord the piety of this humble woman, not so much an object of praise as an example to imitate.[38] And look too how many things this brief little tale has to teach us. First, it commends kindness to the poor – not to just anyone, but to those through whom the temple of the Lord is built. For the temple of the Lord is the church. Whatever is brought for the sake of piety is sent to the treasury of the temple of the Lord – not simply what is given for building the physical temple, though even this is sometimes given in the proper spirit, but what the temple in Jerusalem signified is much more pertinent. Paul to be sure praises kindness towards all, but particularly towards 'those who are of the household of faith.'[39] Among these there exist differences. The first fruits of kindness are owed to those who are joined to us by nature, such as children, grandchildren, and other relatives. And even here one should be more generous to those who have made a place in their lives for piety than to those who indulge the flesh. Something should be given to the wicked – but because they are human and so that they may live, not so that they may run riot. Nor do we run any risk if from time to time we should err in our judgment about who deserves our generosity; if the person who receives our kindness should dissipate his legacy, nonetheless the charity with which it was given remains intact, for whatever is given out of love of Christ is given to the temple.

What more does this widow have to teach us? That it is of no consequence how much you give but of very great consequence in what spirit you do so; mortals assess the worth of a gift by its price, God by the inclination of the giver. There is no excuse, widows, for pleading the poverty of your household; for this woman had nothing in the world besides two little coins, and all this she cast into the treasury. What, did she not fear that she would go hungry? For many people excuse themselves on this pretext nowadays, even wealthy people, saying: 'I will not give, lest there not be enough for me and my family.' And who is there so wealthy that he can never be found in narrow straits? According to this line of reasoning nobody will ever give anything to anyone. I know several such people for whom any old excuse suffices as grounds for not giving: 'I am building a house, I cannot be generous to the poor. My wife is pregnant. This year's crop was bad. I lost a whole shipment in a wreck at sea.' Some even seek to ground their avarice in prophecy: 'The astrologers say that scarcity is around the corner. I will not waste what I have saved.' If friends ask for anything, they say that one should not give to friends, as that sort of thing undermines the purity of a friendship. If they are relatives, they say that charity should not be given to members of one's own family. If something is sought in the name of indulgences, they say that they will not contribute to the self-indulgence of the Romans. If they are asked for something to repair the temple, they say they do not want to support the luxury of the priests. If they are asked to give to the monasteries, they say that no money is worse spent than money given to those lazy people whose stomachs are never satisfied. If public beggars approach them, they deny that those are the very paupers whom the divine Scripture commends to our care. Oh, no; they claim that those people are sordid and wicked and often even criminals.

By looking at things in this way, we learn never to give anything to anyone. How can anyone give as long as the slightest excuse serves to blunt the impulse to liberality? How much better would we spend our time inventing excuses for always giving! 'I will give more freely since he is related to me by blood; giving to him is a way of spending money on myself.' 'He is a good man, merely reduced to poverty' or 'He is a boy who gives promise of better things' or 'He was doubtless reduced to poverty on account of his goodness.' And, finally, 'I will give because he is a Christian, and in him I will revive my Lord.' If he is not even a Christian, then 'I will aid him in his hour of need nonetheless, if for no other reason than that he is a human being, and it may be that some day he will come to his senses.' Failing to help when one can is a form of murder. Nor does it show Christian clemency to kill a Turk for no other reason but that he is a Turk. The woman of Zarephath, reduced to a condition in which she was in danger of starving, did not shirk to share with Elijah what she had – something that she never would have done had she not trusted in the words of the prophet.[40] If we have faith, we will not excuse ourselves on the grounds of our poverty but rather will rush to alleviate the pressing need of someone close to us, trusting in the promises of God. And just what is it that he promised? An abundance of all things, and a beneficence that accrues great interest. It is likely that this widow of the gospel had with the labour of her own hands acquired what she contributed to the treasury, and it may be that she had forbidden herself to eat on that day so that she would not lack something to give to the poor. She was not anxious about the morrow, knowing the beneficence of God, which feeds even the tiny sparrows and clothes the lilies of the field and will not fail those who place their hopes in it.

And for those who have nothing material to give, there is another form of charity no less pleasing to God, which is of great help to those who receive and in no way diminishes those who give. Tending to the aged and the sick, giving useful advice to young girls, offering consolation to those who are suffering, rousing the indolent from their sloth – the person who does these things is performing a service more valuable than if he were to distribute food or money. Blessed are those widows who behave in such a way as to excel in both these kinds of munificence. And yet no gift that is given in the proper spirit, that is to say, freely and eagerly, and with Christ in mind, can be so small or insignificant that it does not attain the greatest value in the eyes of God. There is no office, moreover, that is so humble that its beauty does not shine in the eyes of God if it is performed when it is needed and in the manner required. What can be humbler than treating the ulcerous sores of the poor, wiping vomit and pus from the mouth, warming with one's hand the stomach of a sick person? But no jewels, no roses, no perfumes shine more beautifully in God's eyes or smell sweeter in his nostrils.

That noble virgin Eustochium, born at Rome under gold-panelled ceilings, raised in luxury, considered these her greatest pleasures.[41] Why? Because in thinking about it she said to herself: 'Whatever of these things I do, I do not for mortals but for Christ; it is the members of Christ's body that I am treating. If he were present, suffering in this way, would it be right to turn away in distaste? But he has declared that whatever service is offered to his members is offered to him.'[42] The same piety marked Elizabeth, the landgrave of Hesse, who on account of her love for Christ classed as a delight things that are physically repugnant.[43] The person who thinks in this way with both her head and her heart will not be disgusted by any service that is owing to the poor. These humble acts by which the stains are purged from our souls are good. Nor can that good office go for naught to which Christ has attached himself as a guarantor. We are made particularly sluggish and hesitant in works of charity by the fact that we take little stock of the sort of people on whom we bestow these works. We calculate the worth of various individuals and compute what return will come to us from them. In fact, however, mere mortals should not be the issue in our minds; whatever is expended is spent on God, and we should give thought to His deserts, to what rewards He will give back to us.

From this woman there is also a third lesson to be learned, O widows. The piety of this poor woman brought her more shame than praise, for only the rich were admired for their contributions; but in fact all people had as their observer Jesus, and she alone deserved the plaudits of him who alone saw into people's hearts. Do not be discouraged, widows, if nobody among mortals recognizes your beneficence, if nobody gives you his approval; even if many people scoff at you, be content in this one admirer, for it is enough if he sees and approves. You will have done for him whatever benefits you confer on the poor for love of him alone, and no deposit is more secure than that which is hidden away in the bosom of a poor person, even if the individual who is aided by some good work of yours does not know whence it comes. The less you hope for recognition from people, the richer the reward that will come to you from God ...

There are some who build temples with shining marble. There are some who build monasteries at magnificent expense: inside and out on each column or window are sculpted or painted the insignia of the rich man at whose expense the building was erected. A college is named after him; he himself lies huge on a monument portraying him as he usually was when he went out to war. Who would not admire such unrestrained generosity? But I am afraid that Christ may not esteem this sort of gift very highly if it has been bestowed not for the sake of piety but so that the donor might in this way commend his name to posterity. Even in the most abundant munificence, however, one may be 'a poor widow' provided that one's gift derives its value not from its monetary worth but from the spirit in which it is given. If some especially wealthy person contributes a huge amount of money for the support of the poor, thinking to himself: 'I am contributing nothing of my own; even that which I keep for myself belongs to the poor; I deserve no thanks. I do well if I avoid vengeance of the Lord, and would that it were possible to bestow even this in such a way that its value comes to the members of Christ's body; I seek no thanks from mortal men'; this indeed is a poor widow, a person who barely contributes two tiny coins – tiny, but pleasing to the Lord. I would love to linger longer in the contemplation of this poor blessed woman – for who would not want this solemn procession to advance as slowly as possible? But this book must be completed ...

None of what I have said so far is derived from secular sources; I have extracted it all from divine writings. The promised consolation will not fail you, nor is there any danger that you will fall into error if you set forth from here on the road that I have pointed out so clearly to you. And so I will make a fitting end to this volume if we consider together briefly what the blessed Paul wrote about the condition of widows. For we are shaping the Christian widow, and he speaks of Christian widows, although times have changed so that not everything applies in exactly the same way today.

In the gospel, women are praised who had followed the Lord from Galilee, ministering to him from their own resources. They are praised who, after the Holy Spirit was sent from heaven, offered the same ministrations to the apostles that they had offered to Christ. Nowadays it would be considered unladylike for widows to follow preachers of the word up hill and down dale, since there are people all over to provide for the needs of teachers quite sufficiently, and they have thus been provided for by other means. That ancient purity and strength of the spirit, moreover, has waned, so that it is not safe for preachers to lead women around with them, since there will be suspicion of sin even where it is unwarranted. Add too the fact that in ancient times those who believed in the word of God were in general few, and poor, and humble in the sight of men, but the hatred of the name of God's word was enormous, nor did it seem fitting for those who had given their allegiance to Christ to seek alms from those who hated the name of Christ; those therefore who were in charge of the church took to themselves the care of widows and children. To this purpose those of somewhat loftier station contributed – some giving all they had, others a portion that was in accordance with their means, thus tempering their generosity in such a way that on the one hand others should not lack what necessity dictated but on the other they themselves would not be forced to become burdens to the church.

Hence it is that Paul wrote to Timothy, 'I wish moreover for younger widows to marry, and bear children, and become matrons, and give no occasion for an enemy to speak ill of them. For some have already strayed after Satan.' And a little earlier he had said, 'Strictly avoid, moreover, younger widows.'[44] The Apostle might appear to some to have meant that it is not fitting for a bishop to converse with younger widows and that such women should not be allowed to remain perpetually celibate once they have lost their husbands. Nor was there any lack of people who allowed only a single marriage even to men; some took away from Christianity the right to marry altogether. Since the teachings of these people have been condemned by the church, however, let us not suspect St Paul of teaching such things, especially since he would in that case be convicted of contradicting himself. For when in writing to the Corinthians he exhorts virgins to perpetual chastity, he does not require it of them, since he invites those attached to each other to that very matrimony, provided that their vow be made at the right time, with their full consent. When he was certainly writing to widows, he made his mind sufficiently clear: 'To the unmarried and widows I say that it is well for them to remain single as I do.'[45]

He does not, then, deter younger widows from resolutions of chastity, but he was apprehensive lest the church be weighed down and debilitated by the ministry of such women.[46] He is concerned here with widows who are taken into the ministry of the church and nourished by its resources because either the poverty of their station or the cruelty of their blood relations or their relatives by marriage has deprived them of the means to live. If younger widows were admitted to this ministry, a double danger would hang over the church – first, that its slender resources would not suffice for the nurture of all, and second, that the tender age of these women, which is rather inclined to self-indulgence, might in the case of their lapsing into sin bring shame upon the church; and even in the absence of such a lapse, their very youth might nonetheless offer to the pagans and ill-disposed Jews cause for detraction. There was also the danger, moreover, that certain widows would be drawn to the ministry of the church less by piety than by the prospect of food and others kinds of support. Consequently he prescribed 'that no widow under sixty years should be admitted,' on the grounds that this age is less dangerous and less subject to suspicion.[47]

Nor did the Apostle find age a sufficient recommendation. Rather he demanded the testimony of a widow's whole life: 'that she should have been the wife of one man,' for though remarriage is allowed to those who do not dedicate themselves to chastity, still it carries with it the appearance of incontinence; 'that she should have a reputation for good works; that she should have raised her children for a life of piety and chastity; that she should have demonstrated Christian hospitality; that she should have washed the feet of the saints; and that she should have ministered to the afflicted' – in the name of Christ, and even at her own peril; and finally 'that she should have been assiduous in good works of all kinds.'[48] For it is only fair that she who has aided the church with her own resources, while she had them, should in turn when she is helpless be relieved by the resources of the church, and that she should find shelter from that source to which she had given when it was hers to give; and she has offered solid promise of perpetual chastity who has been married only once and has placed the education of her children above the self-indulgent pleasure of a new marriage. It is altogether probable that she who does not desire another husband once she has had children married in the first place out of desire for children, not for pleasure. Nor does any suspicion of arrogance fall upon the woman who did not find it burdensome to wash the feet of the saints; and it is not likely that she would depart from the Christian faith whose piety the savagery of tyrants could not have dissuaded from giving aid to other Christians, or that she would simulate charity who never failed in her duty, for hypocrisy cannot be sustained so unfailingly. Finally, it must surely be the case that a woman about whose integrity all testimony agrees is indeed virtuous. Indeed, all widows should meet these criteria. Age, of course, which nobody can increase or diminish in herself, is an exception; but all these other qualifications are specifically and expressly demanded from the widow who is to be admitted into the tutelage and ministry of the church.

But what is meant by the words: 'Strictly avoid younger widows'?[49] Clearly that younger widows should not be received into the class of those who are to be supported by the resources of the church. Not even those who are needy, and are recommended by all the aforementioned virtues? No. Why? Because there is a way of life that is more fitting for them. Their youth and beauty will easily find for them husbands at whose expense they may live and for whom they may bring forth children. In raising these up they will offer a great service unto God, nor in the mean time will a strain be placed on the resources of the church, nor will the reputation either of the woman or of the church be in danger. And it was not rashly that Paul arrived at this caution; rather experience taught him what a great danger was involved here. 'For when younger women,' received into the charity of the church, 'begin to lust against Christ,' whom they had chosen as a spouse for themselves, and end up by 'wanting to marry' with great injury to this spouse, and to the shame of the church, and 'with damnation' of their souls, 'since they have abandoned their original resolution,' this itself is no slight danger;[50] but to this is added another, namely, that freed from the jurisdiction of husbands, and corrupted by leisure, they will make a habit of going about to other people's homes, not only doing these people no good but indeed even making nuisances of themselves with their chatter and their prying, saying things that would disturb the peace of good Christian people. For those who suffer from the vice of curiosity suffer from garrulousness, and nobody who comes running to you to inform you of the doings of others will be silent among others where your own doings are concerned.

For all these evils marriage is the remedy. The authority of a husband will bring the natural levity occasioned by his wife's youth and sex under control; then too the responsibilities of a family give little space to idleness. And just as all widows should excel according to their means in all those things that Paul requires in a virtuous widow, so all widows must shun those things that he lists as base. The church must not, however, receive all women simply because they are of mature age and virtuous, but only those who have neither the hope of finding a husband, because of their age, nor a relative who might support them. To this he added: 'If any Christian man or woman has widows in the family, he or she must attend to their needs so that the church shall not be burdened, and in this case it shall suffice that they be true widows.'[51] The Apostle, then, neither prescribed monogamy to an older woman nor discouraged continence in very young widows, provided that their resolution be spontaneous and that their households have sufficient resources to sustain them. He makes quite clear, moreover, that the natural dangers inherent in tender age and beauty stand in the way of their easily being received into vows of chastity. For though the virtue of continence is illustrious, still it is far safer, albeit less glorious, to marry. Accordingly, even in marriage he advocates an interruption of normal marital relations so that the partners may have leisure for prayer – but only by mutual consent and with the good faith that each partner owes the other; and after a time they should return to regular relations, lest the natural incontinence of the flesh lead Satan to tempt them. In sum, though it may be more glorious to profess perpetual chastity, this chastity is distinctly more secure if it is offered with free will and if nothing in the meantime is omitted that pertains to the protection of one's virtue.

Now someone may ask at this juncture, what age is suitable for a vow of chastity? I am not unaware that the ancient authorities declared that any age that is fit for marriage vows is also fit for this sort of vow. Nowadays indeed people often do not even wait for puberty. But if age and the examples of many who fell away from their holy vows deterred Paul from accepting younger widows, how much more cautious must we be today, when unhappy examples abound, both of women who departed from their vows and of women who did not – for some keep these vows in such a way that it would have been far better for them not to have. Perhaps it would be the best and safest thing for mere mortals to abstain entirely from vows binding in perpetuity that are merely human inventions: nobody should be compelled to take any vow.

Along the same lines, it is unwise to tie an indissoluble knot before the thirtieth year – particularly for those of the female sex, which is by nature more unstable unless it is anchored by a grace that is singular and granted to very few. Nonetheless, all Christians should see to it that from their very first years both boys and girls should be brought up with an eye to chastity, modesty, and piety. In this way virtue will come naturally and snares be cast for none. I confine myself here to addressing those men and women who have thus far preserved their liberty. Those who are already bound I think should do nothing rashly or against the authority of their elders. This will ensure both a reputation that is more secure and a conscience that is more at rest. At the same time, care must be taken lest anyone seek out such liberty in order to indulge the flesh.

It is moreover the obligation of a widow while she is celibate to live as if she had taken a vow of perpetual chastity. It is emphatically the case that absolutely nobody is compelled to take such a vow – and that no one should be received into such a vow rashly. Let a widow be allowed to make use of the free will that the Lord has granted unto her; let the rewards of celibacy be pointed out – but by the same token let the burden and the danger be pointed out as well. Just as St Paul quite openly proclaimed a widow's freedom to marry again, provided it be in the Lord, at the same time, however, he pointed out the disadvantages that accompany this liberty, for he said: 'Those who marry will have affliction in their flesh.'[52]

Now as a general rule serial polygamy has a bad reputation, exposed as it has been to the scathing and scurrilous remarks of humankind; but it is no crime in the sight of God. There are three considerations, therefore, which argue against a new marriage for widows by whom children have been brought up: reputation, age, and piety. All good omens favour the weddings of virgins, but not so those of widows. Now rumour and the gossipy chatter of the rabble should not be so important to a woman that she prefers to burn than to marry. Disapproving gossip, however, tends to pursue a woman who is rather more advanced in years (particularly if she has arrived at that point at which there is no longer any hope of progeny.) The auspices are hardly good that attend on a marriage prompted by incontinence, a practice not without blame, though it may be no crime. (The church, it should be noticed, does not even in these cases forbid the remedy of marriage, taking the view that it is motivated here not by lust but by the desire for companionship in old age.)

For the rest, there are two kinds of piety – towards God and towards one's children, whence it extends to any neighbour whatsoever. The first sort of piety consists in faith and charity. It is practised and nurtured by prayer, thanksgiving, and meditation upon heavenly things. These activities call for sobriety, fasts, purity of life, vigilance, and the study of the philosophy of the gospel. That philosophy is acquired through listening frequently to sermons and by conversing with people outstanding for both piety and learning. If from time to time there should be a dearth of these (which would be natural, since such people are so rare that they are often in short supply), the mind should be fed on reading of the Scriptures. In these it is appropriate for a widow to verse herself with a pious curiosity accompanied by the reverence due to divine revelation, seeing to it that you overlook nothing and that you make sure to accommodate your inclinations to the law of Scripture rather than interpreting Scripture according to your inclination. Do not indulge in any audacious pronouncements on the meaning of the text, and abstain from questing vaingloriously after useless points of detail. Those things are most particularly to be learnt that excite in us faith and charity; that correct our lives; and that inspire, nurture, and bring to very perfection the desire for life in heaven.

Now although all portions of Scripture contribute to these ends, still some parts are more suited to some readers than to others. Some parts, for example, are helpful for princes, or priests, or married people, and are not particularly appropriate for widows. There are also some cruxes that are more safely left to those who are learned and trained in scholarly methods. Nor will it be without profit to pore over the works of devout men, plucking wherever one can whatever snatch of wisdom conduces to progress in piety. Among these one must make careful choices both of authors and of subject-matter. For some were meant to be read by few, such as Hilary; some have tempered their style to the level of fairly simple people, such as Cyprian, Ambrose, Jerome, and Augustine; some, like Thomas and Scotus, simply teach and do not affect people's emotions, whereas some do both, such as John Chrysostom and Basil.[53] One must beware only of those who by wicked teachings vitiate the sincerity of one's faith, for certain things are better left unknown than studied at peril. But just how one should pray, I myself have shown in another work,[54] and before me, indeed, celebrated Doctors of the church wrote very fully on this topic; there is no need, therefore, to go into this again here.

Nor should any heed be paid to those who think women should be excluded from the very source of solace and advantage for Christians, unless we [regard as mad] ... the most admired Doctors of the church, who in the volumes that bear their names both praised and encouraged the study of sacred Scripture by women. The only thing you need guard against is the danger of being overwhelmed by that apostolic reproach: 'always learning, and never arriving at the genuine knowledge of the truth.'[55] Here it will behove the widow to graft the prudence of the serpent onto the simplicity of the dove, so that she may be discerning in choosing those to whom she pays heed and in accordance with whose counsels she organizes her life. For it is the singular mark of the female sex to rejoice in accepting the authority of some male.

There have been, moreover, many people in ancient times, and large numbers today, who in accordance with the words of Christ 'devour the homes of widows, under cover of long prayers,' and who in keeping with the teaching of St Paul 'enter the homes of women weighed down with sins, who allow themselves to be led according to various desires, and lead them captive,'[56] and those whom the grandeur of their station allows to advance those whom they favour to positions of respect and honour are in particularly great danger in this regard. To whom indeed would not such rich booty teach hypocrisy and fawning? Take care lest you be deceived by the false image of piety. This can be prevented if you first use perfect judgment in choosing what to read and then keep your mind's eye clearly focused so that you will not be tricked by illusory holiness. For Satan is a versatile craftsman, from time to time 'transforming himself into the angel of light,' nor is he anywhere more noxious than when he deceives the unwary in the guise of religion.[57]

It is necessary therefore to apply to the choice of teachers a mind that is pure and sincere, in order to avoid what the same Apostle wrote – that when we have ears that itch after evil we take to ourselves teachers who delight rather than instruct.[58] For the things that give health are often bitter. In making these choices, accordingly, do not look to a sorrowful expression, a wildness of the eyebrows, or cloaks or phylacteries and the other illusions with which the Pharisees are accustomed to lay snares for widows whom they wish to devour; rather, look within, before you commit yourself to someone. For sometimes those who are in reality greedy wolves come clothed in the skins of sheep – people whom Paul described along the same lines when he said 'having the appearance of piety but denying the actual truth.'[59] Once such people have been received into your home, moreover, they insinuate themselves into its inner recesses, nor is anything so hidden that they do not sniff it out, so that they still pose a threat even if one manages by chance or luck to detect their deceit. Thus it happens that, having accepted them before they proved themselves, you cannot shut them out once they have proved wanting.

Let a widow banish this sort of person far from her home if she wishes her own modesty and that of her sons and her daughters and her maids to be secure and if she does not wish her resources to be eaten away. It is by far the safest thing to admit none of these people at all as a regular visitor to your home, for even if you find one of them who is pure of mind, nonetheless you have someone who can be corrupted by familiarity. And to see to it that this does not happen, he will not come alone, but rather will come accompanied now by one person, now by another. Who can guarantee the integrity of another? As Paul says, moreover: 'What is done by these in secret it is shameful even to recount.'[60] Nor will it be difficult to detect the true colours of such people, if only you put your mind to it. When the opportunity has arisen for them to drink rather more deeply than they should, that which has been lurking in their breasts comes out into the light. But if they should be victorious and so successful that their hostess welcomes them even though she has fully recognized how nefarious they are, then a woman has admitted into her home not a spiritual mentor but a tyrant.

I do not mean by this to suggest that we should think ill of everyone whose garb suggests holiness. Piety can of course lie concealed beneath clothing of any sort. I only wish you take care lest you are ensnared by such deceit and, when you believe you have taken a lamb into your home, discover that you have in fact gotten a wolf, or a fox, or an ape, or a boar, or some other such beast. And it is not sufficient for the home of a widow simply to lack all sin: it must lack the slightest suspicion of sin as well. Even to repeat the sorts of things that are said in some cases would be embarrassing. It is particularly important, moreover, for every widow to see to it that she does not confer as a solitary woman with a solitary man, without some sober matron as a witness. Nor is it proper to abuse the privacy of constant confession with endless recourse for purposes different from those for which it was established. We are walking a path laced with snares, and scarcely any precautions are sufficient. Safer, therefore, familiarity with books. For the things they have to say are holier; when you want them, there they are; and they relieve the tedium of solitude with a pleasure that is most salutary. Now leisure and solitude are teachers of many bad things, particularly to women; and so it is fortunate that the Christian widow need give no place to leisure and need never be alone. For how can it be that someone who is given to such holy, sublime, and pure studies should be able to endure wandering to and fro to other people's houses or to waste away the day with silly talk? For Mary, whose leisure Martha envied, knew no real leisure; rather she was occupied differently, when she sat at the feet of the Lord.[61]

Coming now to the other side of piety, indeed there will be no leisure if we give due and frequent attention to Martha's complaint against Mary. Nor does anything prevent both sisters from being combined in one woman, and this reproach is most welcome to Christ. God indeed is to be loved alone, and for himself, and above all, whereas mortals are to be loved because of him, or in him. Because of him we love even our enemies, and in him we love them. Now among all these relationships, that of parents and children holds pride of place. What leisure, therefore, can there be for a widow who has sons and daughters at home and a household that is dependent upon her care? What can be more consuming labour than forming the character and temperament of children in the first stages of life? The widow who leaves her young children at home and is constantly dining out, constantly runs here and there to weddings, to performances of one kind or another, to dances, and is constantly moving from one place to the next – this sort of woman is no mother to her children but rather a stepmother. On the other hand, the widow who under the pretext of religion neglects the care of her children and devotes herself instead to those who pass themselves off in apostolic roles, defrauding her own heirs while supporting the luxury of others with her own resources, stands far away from true piety. They boast that they are giving to God what in fact is spent on themselves. Admittedly, whatever is given for the love of God is spent on God; but in the sacred writings those are scolded who do well to give but give to an unworthy cause.[62] It is not uncommon that what they give is given to the indolent, or to those who are strong and capable of earning sustenance with their hands – were leisure not sweeter than labour: what is being given is going to those who already live in abundance and who will use what more they get as grounds for spending still more. To see to it that nothing of the kind happens, therefore, the first demand of piety is care for one's children; for God is in them, and what is spent on them for love of God, God will allow to be added to this account.

If by chance anyone is inclined to become angry with me for daring to teach these things, let him hear Paul speaking even more strictly and be angry with him sooner than with me; for this he wrote to his beloved Timothy: 'If any widow has children or grandchildren, let her learn first to govern her own household, and to render the aid that is owing to parents. For this is pleasing in the sight of God.'[63] Do you hear the Apostle? 'Let her learn first,' he says, and adds: 'for this is pleasing in the sight of God.' When he says 'first,' he is indicating the order in which things are ranked. When he adds 'in the sight of God,' he bids the decrees of mortals to give way before divine commands. And where are those Pharisees who teach that a son should answer back to a destitute father or mother: 'The gift you would have from me is given to God'?[64] To these very authorities should be said: 'What is owing to one's parents to support them is deposited in the treasury of the temple, and the precept of God is violated because of a merely human tradition.' And is this not the very thing that the Apostle indicated when he added: 'For this is pleasing in the sight of God'? At all times and in all places it is agreeable to God to come to the aid of one's parents and one's children, for nature dictates this and God has taken care to prescribe it ...

Now if a widow who neglects her children and dissipates her resources in the guise of religious zeal is condemned by Paul, what place shall we assign to those who squander their resources basely on their own pleasures – in some cases even reducing their neglected children to poverty by giving what is owing to them to their adulterous lovers instead? But that solicitousness that widows owe to their children and other relations extends not only to physical nurture but, much more important, to their entire upbringing. To be sure, the care of the body is a necessity; but it is far crueller to let one's children grow up devoid of all natural feeling for religion than it is to allow them to perish of hunger. If there are no children, their place can be filled by nephews and nieces and then all the other gradations of physical and spiritual relationships. In the third place, all who are members of Christ are our brothers and sisters. Paula,[65] that most illustrious Christian, did not retire to Bethlehem until she had brought her children up to that age and that station of life that does not demand parental care. Having first satisfied nature, she set aside what was left for relieving the needs of the poor, and though she had few children of her own, she gathered together a huge number of daughters in the spirit, for whose physical needs she provided and whom she instructed in the teaching of the Lord, so that she was in all ways the mother of all. Nor indeed did she support them in idleness, for this is not to support but rather to corrupt. And this example it behoves all widows to imitate in such a way that they do not support either their female relations or any poor people whatsoever in idleness, provided they have the capacity to work; but they should see to it that each should work with her hands, and they should not only minister to their want with money but also add to this the admonition and exhortation to live devoutly; for often this class of people is in greater need of spiritual than of bodily aid.

Do you see now the high level of activity that is demanded of a Christian widow? Such a widow the Lord will doubtless 'bless with a singular blessing, and will satisfy her poor with bread.'[66] The widow therefore who deserves the highest praise is the one who refrains from remarrying for this reason: so that she may be utterly unencumbered in the eager practice of piety and may enjoy Christ her heavenly Spouse without distraction. I do not deny that this is indeed an arduous task, but a large part of this enterprise lies in goodwill – which is a gift of the Lord, to be sure, but certainly given to those who seek it, to those who live in modesty and prayer. For the common crowd remembers all too well the saying of Paul: 'It is better to marry than to burn.'[67] But many of those who burn do so of their own free will, do so because they themselves supply the very tinder and kindling for the fire. For the rest, though the spontaneous love of perpetual chastity is best, still it is safer to feel one's way towards this commitment cautiously and not to bind oneself completely in one sweeping vow. It is a good idea to reserve judgment on first impulses; the strength of an individual's resolve must be explored over a long period of time and in a variety of ways. This is the first aspect of piety, about which I spoke.

The widow next deserving of praise is she whom concern for her children dissuades from a second marriage. For it is proper that a widow should appropriate to herself the care her husband would have bestowed on their children and in their upbringing be both father and mother. But the woman who introduces a stepfather into her children's lives can barely be half the mother she once was to the children she had by her previous husband; for she is no longer her own mistress, and besides, she may be afraid of offending her new husband if she favours her children by her first marriage. For just as it is rare for a stepmother not to hate her husband's children, similarly it is not common for stepfathers to love their stepchildren from the bottom of their hearts. And so it happens that those who before were orphaned of one parent are now orphaned of both, having received in place of a mother, a stepmother, and in place of a father, an enemy. Even if none of these things should happen, moreover, still it is against human nature for love that is pulled in many directions to remain as strong as before, just as the force of a river is lessened if it is diverted into several different streams. The woman who has resolved to remain a widow eternally loves her children with a double love – once because they are her children and once more because she sees her husband surviving, as it were, in them. But the woman who remarries immediately transfers to her new mate a great part of her attention – and then, if there are new children, what is left of her attention is diverted to them.

Finally, even if a woman in this situation should remain ardent in her love for her children, she does not have the time or opportunity to manifest this love in her actions. The celibacy of which I speak will be the more praised if the widow in question aims thereby not so much to assure her children riches and high position but to bring them up in a way conducive to holiness and lives of integrity. Just as the first praise therefore must go to a young bereaved widow who because of zeal for piety towards God fails to remarry, so the woman who has retained no children as pledges from her dead husband has a greater excuse for remarrying, for the wish for progeny obviates the suspicion that it is her own desire that has overtaken her.

To the third order of widows belong those who, conscious of their own weakness, by remarrying flee hell-fire lest they perish in Sodom, fleeing with Lot into the city of Zoar,[68] a city great and not great – great with respect to the number of its inhabitants, but not great with respect to outstanding virtue. These women merit no praise, but they are entitled to kind consideration. To these, however, it is not denied to counterbalance their human weakness with good deeds, so that in this they are equal to the first kind of widow, or even to virgins. But as for the others, who abstain from marriage neither out of love of piety nor out of concern for their children, but only in order to live at greater liberty under their own jurisdiction and do whatever they like – these are so far from deserving praise for their self-restraint that indeed they deserve no tolerance nor do they escape the taint of criminality. For this is a way not of embracing continence but rather of loosing the reins of concupiscence.

I return now to you, Mary, renowned for your royal descent, conspicuous for your pious zeal, a woman with whose station in life these precepts may not seem to correspond in all particulars. Although this treatise is dedicated to you alone, however, it is nonetheless written as if it were not for a single individual; rather these counsels are inscribed with your name so that the lesson of your precept and example will flow to many people. To be sure you have, as I understand, no children; but there is no lack of nieces and nephews, young ladies of your household, and matrons whom your authority may refine in the discipline of piety. Indeed, the more exalted the station in which God has placed you, the more widely your good works will extend, the more people the light of your piety will inflame to purity in their lives. Whatever the masses catch sight of in their rulers they will imitate eagerly. Men will be ashamed not to do what they see can be done by a woman, and women of lesser nobility will be ashamed not to do what they see done by a girl who is a daughter, sister, and niece of so many kings and emperors.

Finally this sort of widowhood arises not from one's external situation but rather from within. For God appears to seek a special closeness with women whose husbands he has taken away. He desires that every human be joined closely with him; but souls that are not 'widowed' and 'desolate' of all worldly connections will not find their consolation in the world to come. She is not desolate who possesses something in this world to which she may affix the anchor of her hope, which she dearly loves, which if some chance should snatch it away from her she will lament that she is wretched without it. The soul that trusts in riches, in honour, in noble descent, in temporal power, in the pleasures of this world – she is no widow, but rather has a husband whom she would like to live forever. Similarly the soul that places its hope in famous parents, in children, in bodily strength, or in youth is no widow, and indeed God often propitiously takes these comforts away from us so that he may draw to himself those who have been wrenched away from the love of these things: he is jealous, and wants to be loved alone and with people's whole hearts. Thus it is that women who have been joined to husbands cannot have hope in the Lord unless they become widows.[69] But she who has not placed her hope in the Lord will not reign alongside the Lord. For without hope 'it is impossible to please God.'[70]

If you ask how it can be that the same person is at the same time both widow and wife, I will explain this easily. The woman who loves her mortal husband in such a way that because of her love for him she neglects those things that pertain to piety – this woman has but one spouse, and that a mortal one, whom she nonetheless loves as if he were immortal. And as long as she enjoys this spouse, she is no widow, nor is she worthy of Christ as a spouse. But the widow who, according to the teaching of Paul, has a husband in such a way as if she did not, and stations the garrison of her happiness not in a man who is mortal and perchance a sinner but rather in God, to whom she is joined in her mind by a faith even more holy – this sort of woman is desolate and a widow even while she is married.

Nor indeed does that celestial Spouse vitiate a marriage as if by adultery when he is received into that conjugal relationship; rather he renders that very corporeal alliance holier and more auspicious. Indeed those into whose relationship he has not been received are joined together more in fornication than in marriage. Nor does Paul mean that only widows must 'hope in the Lord,' as if virgins and matrons were exempted; all must hope in him, but such hope is impossible unless one is in spirit a 'widow,' that is, possesses what he has in this world in such a manner as if he did not possess it. For whatever the stage of this world displays is flimsy and ephemeral, and however great and everlasting it seems, in the contemplation of the eternal scheme of things it is ordinary and evanescent. These things the Scriptures set before us in the name of widows, because the female sex is almost entirely accustomed to depend on the protection of some man until by the spirit of Christ it is constituted a 'new creation.'[71] Nor do my words seek to encourage any Christian woman to love her spouse less or be less obedient to her husband. On the contrary, she will love him all the more and all the more truly if she loves him in the Lord, and she will obey him all the more devoutly if she recognizes that the submission she offers to her husband she is offering not to a mortal but to God.

The sacred Scripture moreover seeks not only to teach by the example of a widowed woman 'all who wish to live devoutly in Christ Jesus,'[72] calling their faith back from secular things to eternal ones; it wishes also to console women bereft of beloved husbands. At the side of the woman tearing her hair and crying out in true female fashion: 'Oh, I am desolate! Why should I go on living?' is the Scripture in the role of a comforter saying: 'You are not alone. I am here who can be more powerful than hundreds of husbands; there is no reason for you to hand yourself over into the power of some man henceforth. You may keep yourself entirely for me alone, and the more you adhere to that which contains all good things, the less desolate you will be. And to that end, I have snatched your husband away, so that there should be nothing to keep us from the sweetest of embraces.' A widow embraces this celestial Spouse and kisses him with all her heart as often as she prays, glorifying him and giving thanks; she speaks with him as often as she reads the sacred text and receives its word into her inmost being. From such things mortal marriage does not distract totally, but as a general rule it either interrupts this deeper familiarity with God or at least puts a damper on it – though not every widow is thus joined with the Lord, but only she who is a true widow. For thus St Paul wrote: 'She who is truly desolate and a widow hopes in God and persists in supplications and prayers by night and by day.'[73] I do not know how 'by night and by day' can apply to those who are married except as it refers to those who by mutual consent have cut themselves off from the normal marital relations. Just therefore as nothing forbids one from living like a widow while married, so nothing prohibits anyone in any style of life from living like a Christian.

For whoever is reborn in the baptismal font renounces this world and all its pomp and pleasures. But just as it is the disposition of our soul that separates us from the things of this world, and not physical distance, so our contempt for pomp and pleasures set us apart from them. And it often happens indeed that those who live in the middle of nowhere and are hard pressed by poverty are richer and more refined than others whom either high station or noble birth or some other necessity holds fast in self-indulgence. For a person must be inwardly laden with money and luxuries if he cannot cease loving them even when necessity has deprived him of them in fact. Temperance, on the other hand, is all the more illustrious in the person who is not corrupted by the presence of abundance but rather resembles the fishes of the sea, which are more delicate than those of the rivers and bear no trace of the ocean salt. And so a widow, though she be renowned, though she be wealthy, though she live in a great palace, is desolate; and she fixes her hope in the Lord and persists in prayers and supplications by day and by night if she has transferred her faith from temporal things to God; if looking around her she finds no true refuge, no true joy, except in the Lord; if, as often as the opportunity is offered, she rejoices in speaking with the Lord, rejoices in hearing the words of the Lord; if, in short, she places all her deeds and thoughts and desires in the context of her relationship with God ...

But I do not direct these remarks to you, illustrious young woman; I know that your suffering is so mitigated by your piety that it neither deserves nor needs to be criticized, and I do not doubt either that you are accustomed to apply either these very remedies or even still stronger medicines to others who indulge their grief beyond what is proper. Truly your mind is so fortified by your strong faith that it is able to stand firm, protected by that faith, in the face of whatever misfortunes chance may bring. Indeed, your own fortunes have been so happy that if we were to add up the account of sadness and joy we should find many more reasons to congratulate you than to console you; and of all good things in your life – and there are many – nowhere are you more fortunate than in the praise you receive for your piety. Other things are either outside us, or not in our power, or purely temporal. But what you possess no adversity can snatch away, and it will remain with you perpetually in the life that lies ahead of you.

Go forth, then, illustrious woman, to uphold the standard of piety for all widows and all high-born ladies and, following in the footsteps of women who have been highly praised, be at once the teacher of the court of princes and an example of evangelical integrity.

NOTES

1 Entitled *On Widows* (PL 16:147–76).
2 Cf 1 Tim. 5:14.
3 Cornelia was the daughter of the Roman general Scipio Africanus. After the death of her husband in 154 B.C., she refused the hand of the Egyptian king Ptolemy VII. Erasmus lists another half dozen classical examples of widows who remained loyal to their dead husbands.
4 Cf 1 Tim. 5:14.
5 Cf 1 Cor. 7:13.
6 Sarah was the wife of Abraham, cf Gen. 11:29–30; for Elizabeth cf Luke 1:5–25.
7 Cf Jth 13. Erasmus continues with a long list of exemplary women praised in the Bible or in the writings of the Fathers.
8 Cf Luke 4:29.
9 Cf 1 Tim. 5:3.
10 Cf 1 Tim. 5:16.
11 1 Tim. 5:3
12 Cf Matt. 24:11.
13 The etymology comes from Jerome's *Interpretation of Hebrew Words*.
14 Cf 1 Tim. 5:5.
15 Cf Matt. 5:4.
16 Ps. 106:1
17 According to Jerome's *Interpretation of Hebrew Words*
18 1 Cor. 7:10

19 Cf Jth 8:7.

20 1 Cor. 7:35

21 Cf Col. 3:18; Eph. 5:22–4.

22 Cf Acts 10:9–15.

23 Cf Luke 2:36–8.

24 Cf 1 Pet. 3:1–6.

25 Heb. 13:4

26 St Elizabeth of Hungary

27 Jth 8:8

28 Ibid

29 Cf 1 Tim. 3:2–7.

30 1 Tim. 5:10

31 1 Thess. 5:22

32 A reference to Dido, the passionate queen of Carthage, who broke her vow
    of fidelity to her dead husband by her union with Aeneas: rumour of Dido's
    liaison with Aeneas travels through North Africa, according to Virgil, *Aeneid*,
    4:175.

33 Jth 8:28–9

34 Cf Jth 14.

35 Matt. 6:2, 5, 16

36 According to Jerome's *Interpretation of Hebrew Words*

37 2 Cor. 5:16

38 Cf Mark 12:41–4; Luke 21:1–4. PL 16:255–7.

39 Gal. 6:10

40 Cf 1 Kings 17:8–16.

41 Eustochium (c 370–418), daughter of Paula. Both were pious Roman women,
    associates of St Jerome.

42 Cf Matt. 25:31–45.

43 See *Golden Legend*, II, 678.

44 1 Tim. 5:11, 14–15

45 1 Cor. 7:8

46 Cf 1 Tim. 5:9–16.

47 1 Tim. 5:9

48 1 Tim. 5:9–10

49 1 Tim. 5:11

50 1 Tim. 5:11–12

51 1 Tim. 5:16

52 1 Cor. 7:28

53 Church Fathers, except for Thomas Aquinas and Duns Scotus, who are medieval theologians

54 *Modus orandi Deum* (*How to pray to God*)

55 2 Tim. 3:7

56 Matt. 23:14; Mark 12:40; Luke 20:47; 2 Tim. 3:6

57 2 Cor. 11:14

58 Cf 2 Tim. 4:3.

59 2 Tim. 3:5

60 Eph. 5:12

61 Cf Luke 10:38–42.

62 Cf Prov. 11:24.

63 1 Tim. 5:4

64 Cf Matt. 15:6.

65 See above n41.

66 Ps. 132:15

67 1 Cor. 7:9

68 Cf Gen. 19.

69 Cf 1 Tim. 5:5.

70 Heb. 11:6. Erasmus substitutes 'hope' for 'faith.'

71 2 Cor. 5:17, Gal. 6:15

72 2 Tim. 3:12

73 1 Tim. 5:5

2. Berta Heyen:
An Obituary for a Christian Widow

This funeral oration for a benefactress was written by Erasmus around 1489. The name 'Heyen' is frequent among the magistrates of the city of Gouda in the fifteenth and sixteenth centuries. Berta Heyen was the widow of Baert Jan Heyenzoon. She lived in comfortable circumstances and used her wealth for charitable purposes. The oration is addressed to her two surviving daughters, Augustinian nuns resident in Gouda. The composition remained in manuscript and was published only posthumously in Erasmus' *Opera omnia* (Leiden 1701).

The translation is by Brad Inwood (cf CWE 29 18–28).

It has been a long time, my dearest daughters and sisters, since I decided to send you some pages with which you could soothe the grief inflicted upon you by the death of your mother. But whenever I take pen in hand in order to set down on paper the praises of our Berta, believe me, I immediately break out in tears, my fingers turn numb, my joints stiffen, my spirit swoons, and I am so overcome by sorrow that I cannot even give a bit of serious reflection to your mother's virtues, let alone write about them … She is gone, she, my guardian, my benefactress, my refuge in times of need. She took me in as an orphan, supported me in my poverty, helped me when I was in need, consoled me time and time again in my despair, encouraged me when I was faint-hearted and sometimes (although I am ashamed to mention it) aided me with her advice when the situation called for it. She embraced me with the same love, and equal love, as she gave to her own children. She was as fond of me as though she had given birth to me herself. Indeed, she was not related by blood, but no one could be closer spiritual kin. Why shouldn't I have loved her as I would a mother, since she cherished me like a son? She was as much like a mother to me as I could have wished, with the sole exception of the actual blood relationship, which I definitely think is the least important aspect of motherhood. Other than that, she fulfilled every single duty of motherhood with a truly remarkable devotion to me … Although, therefore, I who wish to console you am myself in need of consolation, and I who am endeavouring to be a physician to you do myself need the attentions of a physician, nevertheless, since I have good reason to feel that the death of your mother has inflicted a more painful wound on your hearts (for you were linked to her by a double bond, both physical and spiritual), I decided to use this short speech to portray for you your mother's virtues, as a consolation, such as it might be.

In this I am following the custom of the Ancients, according to which sons used to give mournful speeches for their parents' funerals at an assembly in the forum.[1] These speeches were designed to induce grief in the hearts of the listeners and to make the ancestral virtues familiar to everyone. Even the famous Jerome used just this literary genre to console Heliodorus for the death of Nepotianus and Eustochium for the demise of her mother, Paula.[2] Following this example only as far as the general line of the speech, but not with an equal rhetorical power, I thought it right to set down in literary form the divine virtues of our Berta, both to console you and for the edification of all who might read this work. When you read this commendation of your mother, you will not only forgo grief for the loss of her, but will, rather, rejoice that such a one has been sent on ahead. And the others, when they admire these most outstanding feminine virtues, will for time eternal praise her to the skies in immortal commendations ...

Cicero's instructions on the art of rhetoric advise us to trace far back the virtues and reputation of someone's ancestors, when we wish to eulogize him, and to note the outstanding deeds of his grandfathers and more distant forebears.[3] This was so that he would be considered worthy of more illustrious praise from everyone, since we could show not only that he had not declined from his ancestral virtues, but that he had surpassed the very reputation of his forefathers. But judging someone by another person's merits is foreign to Christian practice. Just as it is unfair for children to pay the penalties incurred by their parents' sins, so we think it unjust for them to gain glory from their parents' efforts. 'For the soul which has sinned shall itself die.'[4]

To avoid, then, adorning our Berta with borrowed plumage (like the crow in Aesop) I pass over the reputation and good character of her ancestors; I will not mention the abundant material wealth and the other advantages bestowed on her by good fortune. This alone I set down as praiseworthy, that she despised all these advantages and, in her mind, embraced only virtue. For although she was abundantly wealthy, enjoyed the bloom of youth and the flower of beauty, had a generous supply of the other luxuries conducive to baneful pleasure, and could have safely passed her time in leisure, dressing too fashionably, dining too luxuriously, and sleeping in excessive comfort, she preferred only to follow in the footsteps of a bride of Christ and chose the rough rigours of the Christian life before the blazing vanity of the world. She did not, as girls usually do at that age, concentrate on adorning her wardrobe or dedicate herself to learning about cosmetics; she did not divert herself with the empty pleasures of dances; she did not, in fact, devote herself to any girlish pastimes. Rather, she overcame the bloom of her playful youth with a kind of premature spiritual gravity found in old age; she subordinated the flesh to the spirit, obeyed her parents' commands, attended church often, and devoted all of her spare time to prayer.

Perhaps some will be puzzled why she did not instead reject the world completely and dedicate herself to the monastic life. I do not deny that this would definitely be the safer course, but I think it is much nobler to live innocent of all vice amid numerous temptations to wickedness and to lead the peaceful life that only virtue can provide amid the great storms and billows of the secular world.

And what better description could I pick for the world today than a sea – tossed by constant tempests, beset by dangers beyond number? How rare it is to see a person who can sail this sea and save his ship, who can make it to the desired port safe and sound, with no loss suffered. There are a thousand ways to die on this sea, a thousand dangerous trials and, as Virgil says, 'On all sides a great fear and everywhere the faces of death.'[5] But our Berta gave no thought to the times she lived in; she conquered dangers of every kind with an admirable strength of spirit. She was not frightened by the terrifying sound of Scylla's barking dogs; the bottomless Charybdis of greed did not suck her under; the jagged Syrtes of ambition did not smash her onto the thundering rocks; and finally, she sailed past the Sirens with her ears stopped against their deadly songs.[6] Moreover, I can well believe that it was the divine will that our Berta, who would have preferred to sit at the feet of our Lord like Mary, should have to be troubled like Martha and disturbed by so many trials[7] – in order to increase the fame of her virtue, which was tested by the constant attacks of evil, and also so that she could be a source of aid not just to herself, but to as many people as possible, and especially to the poor, which someone of her social standing could readily do.

Thus, when she had overcome the temptations that come with the bloom of adolescence (I pass over her girlhood for the sake of brevity) and had reached a marriageable age, she was joined to her husband in the bond of wedlock at her parents' command, although she had always had a remarkably strong desire for celibacy. Her husband himself was as outstandingly virtuous as he was wealthy, and above all diligent in his concern for domestic affairs – a worthy husband indeed for such a saintly wife. Furthermore, since she was aware that the marital tie was designed not for physical pleasure but for the production of children, she spared no time for the enticements of Venus, she paid no attention to luxuries, and she did not, as most women do, begin to treat her belly like a god. But she pondered in her troubled heart the message of the Apostle: 'As for the rest, those who have wives should live as though they have them not, etc.'[8] She curbed her fleshly desires with incredible strictness. Whenever she had the opportunity, she withdrew herself from the troubles of this worldly life in order to devote herself more calmly to reading and prayer. Finally, this most blessed woman was so keenly desirous of chastity that it almost seemed as though she lived as a maiden, a wife in name only.

However, one must not think she ignored the Apostle's commands: 'Women, be obedient to your husbands,'[9] and also: 'Let women fear their husbands.'[10] She was so accommodating to him in all matters that you would have believed she was a servant, not a spouse, and she was so modest that you would have thought her a sister, not a wife. They competed with each other by turns in the duties of kindness and modesty, this most saintly of wives and her husband, who was correspondingly happy to have such a wife. What could be more chaste than this relationship? What more pure than this marriage – indeed, what could be more pleasant? Their marriage provided no grounds for that poetic criticism: 'The marriage bed is always filled with quarrels and mutual strife. / Where a bride lies, there is little sleeping.'[11] In their marriage there were no noisy quarrels at night, no screaming wrangles in the daytime – not even the slightest disagreement troubled it. Such a mutual and certainly such a modest love had bound them one to the other that her desires were always his and his were always hers.

I need not refer to the assiduity she showed in the conduct of domestic affairs, to the strictness with which she brought up her children, or to the generosity with which she supported the needy. For if she happened to see some student poor in material goods but rich in learning and good character, she would immediately bring him to her home and set him among her own brood of children, both to relieve his want and to mould her sons' characters and behaviour by his example. And when he had been prepared for the priesthood or some ecclesiastical order, or at least for the religious life, she took the greatest care to see that he achieved his goal just as he wished and as soon as possible.

One thing, however, did cause her considerable trouble in these activities: she could not do exactly as she wished in bringing their noble spiritual efforts to fruition; her generosity suffered from a lack of freedom. She felt she was constrained by the restrictions binding her to her husband; she clearly felt that the marriage bond was holding her back in accordance with the word of the Apostle: 'A woman is bound to her husband as long as her husband is alive.'[12] Therefore, she still had to live in part in an uncongenial manner, since she was not yet independent.

But after her spouse had died and she was free of a husband's authority, she immediately devoted herself with unlimited zeal to every virtuous pursuit, as though she were at last able, after long, misguided delays, to begin a holy life. She vigorously rejected a second marriage, although from all sides a great crowd of suitors, of no humble station I assure you, pressed their intentions on her. This was the answer she used to make to friends and relatives who urged a remarriage: 'Until now, the claims of wedlock have forced me to serve my Lord with only half my efforts. From now on, for all that remains of my life, please allow me to live entirely for the Lord; I belong wholly to him, who has given me everything. Why dissuade me, to no avail, from what I have for a long time greatly desired?'

And this noble woman's words were matched by great deeds. She immediately scorned all worldly pomp and completely rejected beautiful clothing. So great was her modesty of speech, so great her love of frugality, that you would have thought she was not a widow, but a nun (although these virtues were not so much changes in her former way of life as they were complements to it). She was almost constantly at prayer, regular at church, and very seldom in the market-place.

Moreover, she was more eager to work at emptying her purse than other rich people usually are to see their purses stuffed. It is amazing how generously and assiduously she bestowed for the use of the poor all of her wealth, which was quite exceptionally large. What pauper was not dressed in clothing she gave? What poor man ever asked for alms in vain? Who asked a favour of her that he did not receive – or even, to whom did she not offer it unasked, if she happened to see a man burdened by want? The whole crowd of paupers filled her ears with laments as though she were their mother. She was possessed by a concern for them equal to that for her own children. And so that none of you should criticize her unfairly for doing good deeds only with the wealth she had in such abundance, she used to sew clothes for the poor every day by the labour of her own hands so that she would have ready something to give to each one when the opportunity arose.

But why do I go on describing all of her deeds in detail in this speech? They are innumerable and difficult to recall, and also all of Gouda, even today, testifies in admiration to her very great benefactions to the poor, and the entire city cries aloud about her overflowing and profoundly compassionate heart. Nonetheless, this one point can, I think, hardly be passed over in silence: that on the day before Good Friday each year she summoned thirteen people from the ranks of the poor and seated them at her own table; she herself set the serving of food before them, and when the guests had eaten well, she washed their feet with her own hands in an outstanding example of humility.

Moreover, she used to make frequent visits to the almshouse, generally referred to as the Hospital, which is next to the monastery of the Minorites in the city of Gouda, and which was established for the relief of the illnesses of the poor (and to which she herself had given considerable financial support). She visited each one's sickbed and ministered to each one's needs. What is more extraordinary than this woman? What more exceptional than her virtue? Although she was accustomed to delicate circumstances, she did not shrink from the stench caused by the decaying rags or avoid the dangers of foul air infected by the breath of the sick, provided she could earn the right to hear on the Last Day the voice of the Lord, saying: 'What you have done for one of the least of my people, you have done for me. I was sick and you visited me.'[13] Do you not think that she resembled a second Elizabeth?[14] She

certainly did, and if you ignore the difference in names, you will see
that they differ in no other respect.

Another point: surely one thinks this incident worth mentioning?
One day she chanced to be giving alms to a woman and criticized
her gently for some fault or other (since Berta thirsted for everyone's
salvation); the woman, demonstrating that she was as bereft of wit as
she was of material goods, took offence somewhat, turned on Berta,
and began to shower her with an endless stream of outrageous abuse.
'Hey you,' she said, 'you hire a town crier and go around the crossroads
and street-corners, boastfully scattering your alms – do you think you'll
get any reward for this? For a fact, I'll make you this prediction: these
expressions of gratitude from people, which you pursue so eagerly, will
be your payment for your good deeds, if you have in fact done any. But
what should be the reward for your hypocrisy? What garlands should
be the payment for such an appetite for glory? It's none of my affair,
but you'll find out soon enough, poor woman.' That cursed woman,
driven by the last of Tisiphone,[15] bawled out this and a great deal of
similar abuse, which was not fit to be heard by the ears of such a saintly
woman; she shouted words speakable and unspeakable together. But
Berta bore it, not just calmly but even cheerfully; later she told me about
the incident with great joy and promised to give the women a gift twice
as big, in return for her curses, as soon as she returned.

Finally, who could adequately describe in words the generosity of
her expenditures in aid of the monastery of the sacred brothers, or
the kindness she displayed to all religious people? She had an estate
outside the city walls of Gouda, which contained seven small dwellings;
she donated it for the construction of the monastery of the Brigittine
brothers. Of course they did begin to work on their house there, but
somehow or other they felt it would be more convenient to move from
there to the city. And so, when the farm was sold and the buildings had
been put up for sale, they began again to build their house near the city
walls. It can be seen there to this very day. It is a charming building
and is packed with the most saintly company of brothers and sisters,
praising the beneficence of Berta in undying memory.

We ourselves have often witnessed the kindness that she lavished
on religious men. Whenever she happened to hear that one had come
to Gouda, she would immediately welcome him hospitably; her home
was like a wayside inn for them all; her door was open to all of them,

even without invitation. As a result, they flocked to her home as though to their mother, and she took them in, each and every one, as though they were her sons – or rather, like Fathers – and then refreshed them with generous meals. She thought it would be to her great profit if she sowed her material seed and reaped our spiritual harvest, if she fed us with material food and was in turn nourished by the example of our virtue or by a word of blessing from us. The situation, however, was just the opposite (although this is shameful for us): most often we went away having learned much more from her modesty than she did from ours. For if during a meal anyone carelessly let slip even one word that suggested that someone was in disgrace, she immediately broke in on the villainous conversation with a frown and said, 'Forbear, dear Fathers, while you sit at my table, forbear to cast abuse at someone who is not present, or to repeat shameful stories about anyone. This sort of talk offends my ears.' She had, indeed, protected her ears with a hedge of thorns, as it were, to avoid hearing whispered words.

I am omitting many of her virtues so that the reader will not weary of a long speech. But why not give at least one example of her extraordinary fortitude? I pass over the strength of spirit she showed in sustaining the attacks of hostile fate; I make no mention of her stout endurance of the misfortunes befalling her children. I myself was an eyewitness of the event I report, so no one should suspect me of fabricating empty fictions.

She had a daughter, one who stood out among all others for her beauty; her name was Margareta, and she was her mother's only dearest darling. She was married to her husband in a ceremony of the most fitting dignity, with a very large crowd in attendance. And oh! how suddenly her mother's joy disappeared! How unreliable is the lot of human life! The newlyweds had not yet enjoyed six weeks together, when suddenly the girl contracted a very grave disease and took to her bed. In a few days the disease began to get worse, and the usual human symptoms began to suggest that death was near. We were summoned to her; we hurried, even ran. All who were present – a very large number of both men and women – wept most bitterly. No one could hold back the tears. Even a man with a heart of stone could not watch dry-eyed as such a virtuous, beautiful girl was so suddenly snatched from human life, in the flower of her youth and in the early days of her marriage. Only her mother, in Virgil's words 'holding her eyes steady and straining to hide the pain in her heart'[16] was able to resist bursting into tears. For a short time we indulged in silent weeping, when suddenly her daughter, the mother's only joy, passed out of this life.

Then suddenly everyone's grief, restrained until now, burst forth, and the tears turned into vocal lament. The wailing of her husband, the moaning of the household, the outcries of the women at her side – they were all extraordinary; the entire house re-echoed with the mournful turmoil.

But the mother was still dry-eyed and absented herself from the grieving throng for a while. My thought was that she was going off to find solitude because of her deep anguish, since there is nothing more congenial to grief or more welcome to misfortune. I watched her and noted what she would do next; but she retired to her couch, propped herself up on her elbows and pondered reflectively on I know not what, her eyes glazed. I thought that she had been overwhelmed by her inner grief (for I will admit to my error) and was considering some bitter savage act, the way madmen often do. I believed that she was only hiding the distress she felt at so great a misfortune; I did not think she could completely conquer the pain, and I applied to her the lines of Virgil: '... and sick with a terrible sadness / She feigned hope on her face and hid deep in her heart the grief'; and these: '... and so, when she was overwhelmed by grief and infected by madness / and concealed her plan behind her expression, showing hope on a peaceful brow, / I become worried and went to soothe the mother's grieving heart / and to divert her sad woe with words.'[17]

When she realized my purpose, she stared at me more sharply than usual and said: 'Father, do you come to console me, as though what happened to me today were an injustice or a proper reason for chagrin? How could I be so shameless as to resent the fact that the Lord has taken away my daughter, except perhaps through ingratitude, forgetting that he also gave her to me? Has not he who granted her to me himself taken her back? And what reason do I have for a legitimate complaint? I have better grounds to be vexed at my own failings, for in my opinion they were the reason that she was snatched away from me by an early death. The fault was mine and she paid the penalty. For indeed, I was perhaps too proud of her at her wedding.'

What could be more amazing than this fortitude in a woman? Do you not think that this woman's words exactly echo those of the most blessed Job, after the loss of his wealth and the deaths of his children? 'The Lord gave; the Lord has taken away. As it pleased the Lord so was it done. Blessed be the name of the Lord.' What worthy precedent for this fortitude can I cite? Surely the histories in Latin do not refer to any of the Ancients who is worthy of being compared to her virtue. Mention is occasionally made of Pericles,[18] a man outstanding among the Ancients, who donned a garland and spoke in an assembly despite the loss of his two children ...

These are notable precedents, but in my opinion they are hardly comparably to the virtue of our Berta. For it is one thing to ignore the feelings of family love in order to win glory (or, to be more precise, to conceal one's inner distress behind an insincere expression), but it is altogether different to overcome the love she felt for her daughter by means of her exclusive love for Christ and, moreover, even to give thanks for what happened.

Furthermore, the frailty of the weaker sex is an addition to the full measure of her glory. For who would not deem these characteristics, which we consider worthy of admiration in men accustomed to warfare from the very cradle (as they say) or in philosophers with their universal knowledge, even more glorious in a woman? Who will be able to find a woman who has such courage? Such a woman has definitely been found – unless perhaps we think she should be termed a maiden rather than a woman.[19] Certainly, there is nothing else womanly about her, if you ignore the one difference – that of gender. Why should I not with justice call her a maiden, since she scorned death itself, which terrifies all mortals, with a manly spirit? When she suffered with a grave illness and was worn down day by day by the horrendous pain of the disease, she endured it with such strength of spirit that she did not ask for much attention, not even from the doctors. Yet she did not refuse it either, for fear she would seem to be testing God. She had put all her trust in the Lord; she was totally dependent on his will; she entrusted herself completely to him. She knew that without God even the doctors' efforts were useless.

One day when I went to visit her and asked with concern about the state of her health, she admitted to me that she was tormented by an unbearable pain. But while I was trying somehow or other to urge on her the virtue of fortitude, I got this answer from her: 'I am aware of all that, most honoured Father; I know, I know that my present sufferings are not worthy of comparison with the glory to come which will be revealed in us. I know, I tell you, what prizes will be awarded to us by our judge, if we fight bravely to the end. But although the spirit is willing, so also is the flesh weak. Just let him who set me the trial give me the strength to endure; no, he *will* give me the strength. For God will not allow us to be tried beyond our strength, but with the trial he will bring it about that we shall be able to bear it.'

Then, when the agonies of approaching death had already set in, she forgot about family concerns and was content to take no thought for any of her children; she remembered only the poor, and amid the last breaths of her failing spirit, she repeatedly whispered these words into the ears of the people at her bedside: 'Do as you will about the rest, only remember the needy!' and she repeated this time and again. At the last, she lifted her eyes to heaven, folded her hands, and, free of bodily chains, on the feast of St Bridget[20] (for whom, as I said before, she felt an astounding love) she passed to Jerusalem, the mother of all freedom, borne along by troops of angels. Her body, which had been a dwelling not unworthy of her most saintly soul, was interred in a solemn funeral accompanied by great lamentation from all.

It is hard to describe the grief and tears of the entire city as it marched in her funeral procession. No one's grief, though, seemed more bitter than that of the poor who were once her wards. For when according to the custom of solemn funerals the final alms were distributed, the poor suddenly broke out in such a storm of wailing that it would be hard to describe, difficult to believe, and pitiful to hear. What plaints were not uttered then? What cry of grief did not ring out? What kind of complaint, what laments were not heard? They all competed in crying aloud that they had each lost not just a guardian, but a very mother – no, someone dearer than a mother. Voices broken by sobs were heard, from old women on one hand and from children on another: 'Alas! Who is there to feed us in the future? Who to clothe us against the winter winds? Whose ears shall hear our cries in the future? Who shall be a second Berta to us?'

They at least have a reasonable cause for tears. We, however, dear daughters, ought not to grieve so much as to feel triumphant joy. For we have not lost a mother (and such a mother!) so much as we have sent her on ahead. How long will we go on indulging our tears and wasting away in useless grief? Berta triumphs among the starry thrones in the gleaming ranks of heaven's residents, wreathed in sparkling garlands ...

So let us rejoice for Berta's own joy, triumph for your mother's triumph, O dearest daughters. Let us dry up our tears, cease our weeping, and put an end to grief. Let us try instead to follow her, with the same determined effort that she used in preceding us. And we will accomplish the task if we too cling to the path of virtue that she has trodden, if we have a zeal for fortitude equal to hers, if we have the same abundance of deep compassion and hold with equal firmness to justice and faith.

And may he who makes blessed your mother with his presence for everlasting time, grant us these gifts according to her merits. Amen.

NOTES

1 See Jerome, *Letters*, 60.1.
2 Jerome, *Letters*, 60 and 108. Paula and Eustochium were pious Roman women, associates of St Jerome.
3 A reference to pseudo-Cicero *Rhetorica ad Herennium*, 3.13
4 Ezek. 18:4
5 Virgil, *Aeneid*, 2.369
6 These were dangers encountered by Ulysses in the Homeric epic *The Odyssey*.
7 Mary stands for quiet obedience; her sister Martha represents active service. Cf Luke 10:38–42.
8 1 Cor. 7:29
9 Col. 3:18
10 Cf Eph. 5:33.
11 Juvenal, *Satires*, 6.168–9.
12 1 Cor. 7:39
13 Cf Matt. 25:34–40.
14 St Elizabeth of Hungary (1207–31). After her husband's death she did charitable work as a Franciscan tertiary.
15 One of the Furies
16 Virgil, *Aeneid*, 4.331
17 A pastiche from *Aeneid*, 1.208–9 and 4.394
18 Erasmus gives a number of examples of steadfastness drawn from Greek and Roman history.
19 The Latin word is *virgo*, but it should perhaps be corrected to *virago*.
20 See above 236.

Chronology of Erasmus' Life

For the publication dates of works included in this volume see headnotes to individual texts.

1466?–92   Erasmus is born, the illegitimate son of a priest. He attends the school of the Brethren of the Common Life. After his parents' premature death he is left in the care of guardians, who persuade him to enter the Augustinian monastery at Steyn.

1492–9   He is ordained a priest, becomes secretary to the bishop of Cambrai, and is sent to Paris to study theology. He tutors young noblemen for a living.

1499–1500   He accompanies his pupil and later benefactor Lord Mountjoy to England. There he makes the acquaintance of John Colet and Thomas More.

1501–9   He returns to the Continent and publishes *Adages*, an anthology of classical proverbs. He journeys to Italy and obtains a doctorate at Turin. He stays for a year with Aldo Manuzio, the famous Venetian printer.

1509–14   He publishes the satirical *Praise of Folly*. He teaches at Cambridge University.

1515–21   He becomes councillor to Prince Charles (later Charles V), dedicating to him *The Education of a Christian Prince*. He moves to Louvain and is co-opted into the faculty of theology at the university. He publishes his *magnum opus*, the bilingual edition of the New Testament, and becomes embroiled in theological controversies.

1522–8   He moves to Basel, where he maintains close connections with the printer Johann Froben. He publishes editions and translations of classical and patristic writings, paraphrases on the New Testament, textbooks of style, and educational treatises. He begins a polemic with Luther over the concept of free will. His controversies with Catholic theologians continue. His works are investigated by the Spanish Inquisition and the faculty of theology at Paris.

1529–35   After Basel turns Protestant, he moves to Catholic Freiburg.
          The theologians of Paris condemn passages in his writings
          as blasphemous and heretical.
1536   He returns to Basel and dies there in August.
1559   After his death his works are placed on the Index of
          Prohibited Books.

Further Reading

Davis, Natalie Zemon, and Arlette Farge. *A History of Women in the West*, vol 3: *Renaissance and Enlightenment Paradoxes* (Cambridge, MA 1993)

Goody, Jack. *The Development of the Family and Marriage in Europe* (Cambridge 1983)

Jordan, Constance. *Renaissance Feminism: Literary Texts and Political Modes* (Ithaca 1990)

Kelly, Joan. 'Did Women Have a Renaissance?' *Becoming Visible: Women in European History*, ed. Renate Bridenthal and Claudia Koonz (Boston 1987) 137–64

Kelso, Ruth. *Doctrine for the Lady of the Renaissance* (Chicago 1978)

King, Margaret. *Women of the Renaissance* (Chicago 1991)

Kuehn, Thomas. *Law, Family, and Women: Toward a Legal Anthropology of Renaissance Italy* (Chicago 1991)

Labalme, Patricia, ed. *Beyond Their Sex: Learned Women of the European Past* (New York 1980)

McCutcheon, Elizabeth. 'Erasmus' Representations of Women and Their Discourses' *Erasmus of Rotterdam Yearbook* 12 (1992) 64–86

Maclean, Ian. *The Renaissance Notion of Women* (Cambridge 1987)

O'Donnell, Anne. 'Contemporary Women in the Letters of Erasmus' *Erasmus of Rotterdam Yearbook* 9 (1989) 34–72

Rose, Mary Beth, ed. *Women in the Middle Ages and the Renaissance* (Syracuse 1986)

Rummel, Erika. 'A Human Affair: Erasmus and Rabelais as Marriage Counsellors' *Canadian Catholic Review* 9:5 (1991) 177–9

Schneider, Elisabeth. *Das Bild der Frau im Werk des Erasmus von Rotterdam* (Basel 1955)

Sowards, Kelley. 'Erasmus and the Education of Women' *Sixteenth Century Journal* 8 (1982) 77–89

Wiesner, Merry. *Women and Gender in Early Modern Europe* (Cambridge 1993)

Index